John Frederick Brennan

Erin Mor

The Story of Irish Republicanism

John Frederick Brennan

Erin Mor
The Story of Irish Republicanism

ISBN/EAN: 9783743328884

Manufactured in Europe, USA, Canada, Australia, Japa

Cover: Foto ©ninafisch / pixelio.de

Manufactured and distributed by brebook publishing software (www.brebook.com)

John Frederick Brennan

Erin Mor

CONTENTS.

	PAGE
CHAPTER I—FAMINE	1
CHAPTER II—SOME STRUGGLES FOR EXISTENCE	9
CHAPTER III—TRUE CAUSES OF IRISH FAMINE	14
CHAPTER IV—THE LAND OF PROMISE	25
CHAPTER V—DEVOY BECOMES A POLITICAL LEADER	32
CHAPTER VI—KNOWNOTHINGISM	38
CHAPTER VII—WAR	43
CHAPTER VIII—PROSPERITY AND PIETY	49
CHAPTER IX—EARLY STRUGGLES	54
CHAPTER X—A BASE CONSPIRACY	61
CHAPTER XI—REVENGE AND A RUINED MAN	67
CHAPTER XII—AN IRISH-AMERICAN LAWYER	71
CHAPTER XIII—RULE BRITANNIA	77
CHAPTER XIV—IN FENIAN TIMES	82
CHAPTER XV—AN EPISCOPALIAN FRIEND	88
CHAPTER XVI—ESCAPE OF ANDY DILLON	95
CHAPTER XVII—ARRANGING FOR DEPARTURE	101
CHAPTER XVIII—THE EXILES OF ERIN	106
CHAPTER XIX—GETTING ACCLIMATED	114
CHAPTER XX—HOW DEMOCRATS ARE MADE	119
CHAPTER XXI—"GREATER IRELAND"	124
CHAPTER XXII—STILL CHASING HIS "ERIN MOR"	129
CHAPTER XXIII—IRISH INCONSISTENCY	135
CHAPTER XXIV—PETTY POLITICAL REVENGE	141
CHAPTER XXV—THE BELFAST OF AMERICA	147
CHAPTER XXVI—DEATH OF NANCY MCHUGH	156
CHAPTER XXVII—GLORIA IN EXCELSIS DEO!	160
CHAPTER XXVIII—AN IRISH EVICTION	166
CHAPTER XXIX—TRAGIC DEATH OF DEVOY	171
CHAPTER XXX—VOYAGE AROUND CAPE HORN	175
CHAPTER XXXI—THE DEMOCRATIC "ROUND-UP"	180
CHAPTER XXXII—A SMALL POLITICIAN'S REVENGE	184
CHAPTER XXXIII—AMONG THE CALIFORNIA INDIANS	192
CHAPTER XXXIV—"BLESSED ARE THE MERCIFUL"	197
CHAPTER XXXV—TEN YEARS OF SOLITUDE	202
CHAPTER XXXVI—ATTEMPTED CONQUEST OF AMERICA	208
CHAPTER XXXVII—DAY DAWNS ON "ERIN MOR"	213
CHAPTER XXXVIII—ENGLISH CIVILIZATION SOCIETY	219
CHAPTER XXXIX—"GREATER IRELAND" IN COUNCIL	226
CHAPTER XL—AFTER FIFTEEN YEARS	232
CHAPTER XLI—GROVER CLEVELAND AND THE IRISH	239
CHAPTER XLII—"ERIN MOR'S" AGE OF REASON	244
CHAPTER XLIII—A RESURRECTION	253
CHAPTER XLIV—WEDDING BELLS	258
CHAPTER XLV—SOME PERSONAL HISTORY	264
CHAPTER XLVI—CONCLUSION	270

INTRODUCTION.

THE writer of the following pages candidly believes that while foreign rule has been the crowning and all-comprehending curse of Ireland, and while landlordism has been among its most potent ills, yet *British free-trade*, identical with the *tariff reform* which the Democratic party now seeks to inflict upon the United States, was the underlying, if not the immediate, cause of the terrible famine of 1846–47. Ireland, one year with another, produces sufficient food to fatten more than double its present population; yet among the working people there poverty is perpetual and famine periodical. Since the destruction of Ireland's manufacturing industries under the operations of free-trade, agriculture is the only important industry of the people; and a country devoted to agriculture alone is a country already doomed, while a nation whose industries are healthily diversified is proof against famine and decay.

It is not difficult to understand why England favors free-trade with America; nor is it to be wondered at that among a people of great intelligence and of many minds like the Americans, England should find many devoted believers in her plausible theories; but it is a mystery of the mysteries why Irishmen, of all other citizens in America, should be relied on to vote in

American elections precisely as England would have them vote; and that when Grover Cleveland or *Harper's Weekly* sounds the drum-beat of England calling for soldiers to fight her battles at the American ballot-box, those who most cheerfully respond to the roll-call should be the sons and kindred of Irish exiles, driven from their island home by that same free-trade policy; why those whose own factories have been destroyed by English free-trade should be so anxious to vote upon themselves and their fellow-citizens the same calamity in America, or desirous to vote themselves into the conditions from which they fled when they left their own green land with tears in their eyes and curses on their lips.

In seventy years preceding 1890 three and a half millions of Irish landed in the United States (and this does not include the children of Irish parents who came from Britain and British North America). If we take into account those who were in the colonies and those who came prior to 1820, it is safe to say that Ireland contributed to the United States not less than four and a quarter millions of people; and that their descendants are no fewer than thirteen millions, which, with the parent stock now living, would swell the Irish element in this country to something like fifteen millions. Let us say that one-third of this element has forgotten the parent lake to which this life blood ought to be traced. Let us say that the Irish element in the United States is ten millions. They cast in Congressional and Presidential elections two million votes. Their sway is absolute in many American cities; they are powerful in the New England and Middle States. When England drove them out they did not seek homes in Georgia, Alabama, South Carolina or Kentucky. They settled in New York, New Jersey, Pennsylvania and New England, where Northern enterprise and Northern capital built factories and inaugurated public improvements, and gave them labor for their hands and bread for their families. Acting under the natural law that men decide to live where they find least resistance to living, two-thirds of all the Irish emigrants that ever came to the United States settled in that region bounded on the south by the Ohio River, and on the west by a line drawn north and south through the western limit of Pittsburgh, Pa. And yet it is strange, and to the American mind incomprehensible, that the tremendous political power of this vast mass of men has been wielded almost solidly, until within the present decade, in co-operation with the slave oligarchy of the South and exactly in accordance with the wishes and the interests of England, and in opposition to the interests and desires of the Northern people by whom these Irish exiles were employed and among whom they and their children made their homes. At last the lines are broken, and thousands of self-respecting Irish-Americans refuse longer to be dragged at the chariot wheels of England in American politics under the lash of the old slave oligarchy and their allies in the cities of the North.

America and England cannot both be foremost among the manufacturing and commercial nations of the world. One of them must go under. *England or America—which?* The decision is in the hands of Greater Ireland. If free-trade is to succeed in this country, it can succeed only by a practically solid "*Irish vote.*" We venture the belief that this vote can never be solidified for the Democratic party on a free-trade platform. The schoolmaster has been tampering with the Irishman on both sides of the Atlantic, and the labors of the educator have not been in vain. In the following pages we have endeavored to trace the growth and progress of American principles in the Irish mind. The pictures have perhaps been crudely drawn. Some people may say that they have been too strongly drawn, especially the pictures of famine in Ireland. But they represent *facts*, attested by history and within the memory of living men. It is not the writer's purpose to invoke a new Ireland in America. Quite the contrary. It will be a blessed day when the great rivers of immigration shall be merged and mingled in the ocean of American nationality. But so long as one great political party in this country lays claim to a solid "Irish vote," regardless of the issues to be determined, and seeks to perpetuate that claim, so long will self-respecting Irish-Americans resent that claim as odious and insulting, and insist that they are not the pariahs of American political society, but a race of liberty-loving men not less American than other Americans, and who insist upon voting for the best interests of America in accordance with their own material welfare, their judgments and their consciences.

CHAPTER I.

FAMINE.

IT was late in the summer of the year 1847, in the dawn of the morning, at a certain Irish town in the valley of the River Shannon. The morning air was laden with the odor of the newly-mown hay in the surrounding fields; the dew was dripping from the trees; the grain was ripening into golden loveliness; the drowsy cattle, rising from their night of rest, were commencing to browse upon the verdant hills; but the potato fields that had bloomed in luxuriance only a month before, were blackened and putrefying masses of dead vegetation.

John Dillon, the butcher, a stalwart, manly-looking, dark-haired man of six-and-twenty, walked forth from his cabin, coatless and hatless, and entering a paddock, led forth an ass, a creature of the female kind, young and well-conditioned. This animal he killed and dressed before the people appeared in the street; and at the time which, to those who had food, was the breakfast hour, John Dillon was distributing gratis, to his famished neighbors, cutlets and steaks from the carcass. There was no public announcement as to the character of the meat, and the unfortunate people were in no condition to make embarrassing inquiries. After setting aside some of the choicest cuts for the neighbors who were convalescing from the typhus fever at the improvised hospital at the old ruins of the woolen mill, and a fore-quarter for his own family, he distributed the remainder to all of his neighbors who were not too proud to accept of his generous offering. It might seem foolish to think of pride among people who were slowly starving to death; but there were still left traces of pride among a people who, before that famine, were proud as they were virtuous and gay— the proudest people in Europe. His guests were not all of the human species. Gaunt and hungry dogs gathered from the neighboring streets, and even from the surrounding country, attracted by the scent of blood, and animated by the instinctive expectation of animal food. The butcher divided the heart, the lungs and liver, and other odds and ends, among the dogs.

A wretched looking man, named Barney Devoy, disputed with a hungry cur for an attractive looking piece of liver, and to signalize his triumph, when he had secured the prize, he gave the brute a kick; and then remarked apologetically:

"This is the first meal of meat my family has had since Easter." The butcher kindly but firmly reprimanded the kicker.

"Barney," said he, "don't kick the poor brute. He is one of us, one of God's creatures, a victim of the calamity that has befallen our country."

And on that blessed summer morning the incense of cutlets, fries and fricassees went up to heaven with the thankfulness of those who feasted on the body of the ass.

John Dillon hastily cooked some juicy steaks, and placing them in a warm iron pot, hastened to the old factory building. He carried a bucket full of pure spring water from the great well in the public square, and entered the building intent upon feeding those who were able to eat. In a remote corner of the ruined building, a young peasant named Patsy Kenny, and his wife, lay side by side. They had passed through the heated period of the fever, and on the preceding night were in the condition of the disease vulgarly called "the cool." The butcher approached them with the feast. He sprinkled their faces with the cold water, and the young husband responded with a feeble moan, but the woman made no sign. Her partially opened eye-lids revealed the ghastly whitish indications of death. Her soul had passed into eternity during the night, but the husband knew it not. Through the long hours of the night the festering remains of the dead peasant woman had lain upon its pallet of straw, beside the emaciated living body of a husband, whom hunger and disease had rendered insensible, and too feeble to realize that the wife was dead.

He gave drink and meat to Kenny, and hastily returned to his residence and brought with him a clean sheet, in which he tenderly wrapped the slender form of Kitty Kenny.

The corpse was placed in the hospital coffin; a grave was hastily dug, and the mortal remains were dropped coffinless into earth.

The public coffin of the period was a hinged contrivance, in which persons were borne for interment. The bottom was fastened by a clasp to one side, with hinges on the other side. This coffin with its corpse was carried to the grave, the bottom unclasped, opened upon its hinges, ashes returned to ashes, and dust to dust, and the coffin was returned to the hospital for future use. There was no funeral, and rarely ceremony. While Dillon and three other men were burying the remains of Kitty Kenny, a poor peasant entered the graveyard with the body of his child wrapped in a piece of sack-cloth, dug the little grave with a spade in his own hands, and returned the infant clay to mother earth. At the same time a cart, provided by the public authorities, returned from its daily round of collecting the dead who had perished by the road-side; and these horrible spectacles excited little notice or comment, because such scenes were of daily and hourly occurrence in many parts of the western and southern counties of Ireland, all the way from Donegal in the Northern province, to Western Cork in the South, and all through the counties on the coast of Connaught in the West.

John Dillon knelt upon the grave of Kitty Kenny and prayed—implored Almighty God to soften the hearts of Ireland's oppressors, or preserve sufficient numbers of the race to become the administrators of God's vengeance upon them. He then washed his hands at the horse-pond below the public spring, and returned to the old factory building to render such relief as he could to the fever-stricken patients.

The typhus fever, which usually followed extreme hunger, was highly infectious; and hunger begets cowardice and fear. As he approached the old ruin he saw Barney Devoy walk up near the door of the building with a little can full of milk, and after placing the milk at the threshold, hastily beat a retreat. Another man came near the door, and fixing a loaf upon the point of a long pole, placed the bread inside the building and retired. It remained for some fearless person, and sometimes for the convalescing patients, to distribute the food and drink among the sick.

The hospital was now crowded with the fever-stricken and the famishing; and it was no uncommon sight to see applicants for admission lying in the sun upon the sidewalks, until death had made some vacancies.

John Dillon's heart seemed to sink within his breast as he saw these poor creatures, their faces upturned to the sun, their blackened teeth obtruding through their fever-parched lips. But nature has its special as well as its general claims. His own family was on the verge of starvation, and this fact had been painfully impressed upon him before he decided to kill the ass, the only domestic creature that he owned. He had decreed the death upon the preceding night. Three days previously he had expended his last shilling for food, and the day preceding that upon which the donkey had been slaughtered, he had entered his cabin to witness a scene which impelled him to certain determinations. His wife was in tears, and his infant child was hungry.

"Mary, *macree*," said he to his wife, "it seems as if we had reached the end of our rope. I have traveled all over town, and found no friend. Amid the horrors of famine there is little friendship. Our neighbors are dying all around us. There's Paddy Kenny, one of the decentest men in the parish, dying of typhus, and Tom Byrne, the free'st-hearted craythur that ever lived, gone to his grave in a charity coffin, dumped into the earth as dogs are buried."

"God's will be done," replied the wife. "But surely, *acushla*, you could borrow a few shillings to save the child from starving, until Heaven somehow comes to our relief."

"Maybe I could," he replied; "but I hadn't the heart to try. To beg and to receive is hard enough, but to beg and be refused is more than flesh and blood can bear. I saw men just as good as I am beseech a shilling's worth of yellow meal on credit, and I saw them refused. I myself can suffer hunger. I can, if it comes to that, get food by force; but, Mary, darlin', it would brake my heart to beg and be refused."

The conversation between husband and wife was abruptly terminated by a voice from an adjoining chamber, from the sleeping apartment of the Dillon mansion. It was the voice of little Andy, their infant boy; not the boisterous, robust outcry of a baby suddenly awakened from a healthy sleep, but the agonized wail of a hungry child; a voice that bespoke human suffering more eloquently than the frenzied periods of a labor agitator. The father entered the bed-room. The sunlight of an Irish summer afternoon fell softly upon the emaciated face of the child, revealing the ravages that two days fasting had made.

"There, now, Andy, *acushla machree*, be aisy. What can daddy do for the boy?"

"Meat, meat!" cried the famishing child. "Mary," inquired the father, "is there nothing in the house?"

"Not as much as you could put in your eye," responded Mrs. Dillon. "Not a morsel has crossed the lips of the child since night before last. I have often heard," she added, "of people out at sea livin' on a drop of blood. Perhaps a drop of mine would save the child until Heaven comes to our relief;" and she bared the wasted arm, requesting the father to open a vein and draw some blood for the child.

"No, no, wife," he said, "you must not think of doing that. This land of ours has plenty of food. A hundred firkins of butter were sold in the market yesterday; and the Longford road is black with carts carrying provisions for shipment to the English market. There are fat cattle and sheep in the valleys all around us. I don't care to sware, Mary; but by that God to whom we have prayed in vain for mercy, while there is life in this heart of mine, and yet some strength in this arm, my infant boy will not die of hunger."

During the conversation, as if by special dispensation of Providence, the suffering child had fallen asleep. The father moved the infant to the inner side of the bed, lay down beside him, and wept as only strong men weep. And the summer sun had set behind the hill of Knockadoo ere John Diilon was awakened from his slumbers by the renewed clamor of the child for " Meat, papa, meat."

" Yes, meat, Andy," he said to the child, as if he were addressing a full-grown man. " Yes, meat, *ma bouchal*, I'll give you meat."

And seizing an axe, he rushed from his cabin, out of the town, in the direction of the broad demesne of Lord Mount Packenham.

CHAPTER II.

SOME STRUGGLES FOR EXISTENCE.

THE long gray twilight of an Irish summer evening was darkening into the blackness of a moonless night, as John Dillon arrived at the corner of Lord Packenham's demesne. There was an apple orchard surrounded by a twelve-foot wall, and he could dimly see the ripening fruit hanging on its branches above the wall; but he could hear the deep-mouthed voice of the bull-dog inside, aroused, no doubt, by his approach.

A little further on there was a broad field of turnips; but he could see the form of the game-keeper, shot-gun in hand, guarding the field against anticipated raids from the famishing people of the town.

He retreated beyond the possible range of the game-keeper's gaze, and entered a field on the opposite side of the public road; and hearing the heavy fall of marching men behind him, he hid in a deep ditch behind a hawthorn hedge, and he saw the police night patrol, six constables and a sergeant, march past him in the direction of Carrick.

All animated nature, save the armed agents of English law in Ireland and the civil protectors of private property, had apparently gone to rest. He passed through the field, close to the recumbent forms of great fat bullocks, without disturbing them. He aroused a covey of partridges from their nest in the rank after-grass, and he saw sheep and lambs lying peacefully upon the gentle elevations in the fields. He selected his meat, and delivering a blow unnecessarily violent with his meat axe, a fat lamb lay dead at his feet. Half an hour later he appeared at his cabin; the door opened responsive to his knock, and he dropped his dead lamb upon the floor.

"John, *agra*," said Mrs. Dillon, "what does this mane? Is it stalin' you have been? Sure you wouldn't bring disgrace to our good name, and the black stain of sin upon your soul by stalin' a lamb?"

"Mary," said the husband, "This manes meat. It manes that my poor starving child will sleep tonight with his body full of the best our country affords. The voice of nature within me, which is the prompting of God, told me to get that meat; and there it is. Don't preach to me now. Bar the door. Blind the window wid a blanket, stir the fire, put on some turf, down wid the iron pot, and don't talk religion to me till the child is fed."

And these directions of the father complied with, he hastily skinned the lamb. But the voice of little Andy rose impatiently in protest against waiting for the pot to boil; so, using the tongs for a grid-iron, he broiled a tender chop, which the infant ravenously devoured.

"Come on now wid yer peelers and yer sheriffs," he said; "I have done a father's duty to-night."

He next piled the pelt, the entrails, the kidney fat, and the blood of the lamb upon the hearth, and surrounding them with turf coals provided for their destination. The carcass of the lamb was by himself and his wife so fairly reduced as to render identification impossible. Then solemnly the couple knelt and slowly told their beads, begged forgiveness for their sins, and petitioned for their daily bread; and soundly slept as if the command "Thou shalt not steal," delivered on the Mount to Moses amid the thunders of Sinai, was never intended for the victims of a law-created famine.

Next morning a lamb was missing from the demesne of Lord Mount Packenham; but if foot-prints had been made by the vulgar brogans of the thief, the recording angel must have obliterated them; and if the thief himself had not confessed, the question of who stole that lamb might remain a mystery to the present day.

It was early on the morning succeeding the night upon which the lamb was stolen, as the reader will remember, that the death and distribution of the ass and the other events related in the first chapter occurred.

Late in the afternoon of the same day a party of ten policemen, headed by a sub-inspector, made diligent search of every house in the street where John Dillon resided for traces of the stolen lamb. They found no trace at Dillon's; because he had fed the fragments to the children of his neighbors, and had carefully consumed the bones in the fire. But they did make a discovery at the hovel of Barney Devoy. They found some white hairs resembling lamb's wool upon the right sleeve of his coat; and they found a piece of liver upon a plate in his cabin. He was promptly arrested and conducted before the stipendiary magistrate, whose court was in almost continuous session at the time.

Lord Packenham's shepherd testified as to the lamb having been stolen. Sub-inspector Thornhill produced some white hairs from an envelope in which he had treasured them, and unrolling a red handkerchief he displayed the piece of liver which he had captured at Devoy's. One Archibald Macready, the veterinary surgeon of Lord Mount Packenham, testified that the white hairs were lamb's wool, and the liver was the liver of a lamb.

Devoy requested the privilege of making a statement, but the peelers laughed derisively, and the magistrate shook his head.

"The statement," said the magistrate, "you can reserve for the Assize Court. The finding of this court, on preliminary hearing, is that a felony has been committed, and that there is reasonable ground for believing that Barney Devoy committed the crime; and it is ordered that the prisoner be committed to the county jail to await the action of the Assize Court; and that he be admitted to bail in the sum of one hundred pounds."

There was a commotion at the door of the Petty Sessions Court; and the mass of people who thronged the room divided into two bodies, clearing a passage way for a coatless, blood-bespattered man who had entered the door; and even the policemen moved aside and gave him right-of-way as he approached the bench. It was John Dillon.

"Your Worship," he said, addressing the magistrate, "Barney Devoy is an innocent man—as innocent as your Worship is as to stealing that lamb."

The magistrate looked at him in mingled doubt and astonishment. He knew John Dillon well, and though the butcher had a reputation of being handy in a fight, and though there were strong and reasonable doubts as to his loyalty to the British Crown, he was regarded as the soul of honor in business affairs, and his word in the purchase of a sheep, or of an ox, in the prosperous times that had passed, was regarded as good as his bond.

Mr. Curran, the stipendiary magistrate, dispatched a mounted policeman for Lord Mount Packenham; the court ordered a recess, and the crowd awaited patiently the arrival of his lordship.

When Lord Mount Packenham arrived, the inquiry proceeded. John Dillon was sworn and took the witness stand. Mr. Curran conducted the examination.

"You say, Dillon, that Devoy is innocent. How do you know?"

"I know, because another party did it; and so Barney must be innocent."

Lord Mount Packenham here became sufficiently interested to ask a question.

"Dillon," he said, "if Devoy is innocent, as you say, and another party stole the lamb, you can end the prisoner's difficulty and serve the ends of justice by stating who that party was."

"My lord," said the witness, "it was I, myself, John Dillon, who stole the lamb."

Here a murmur of pity and pain rose from the

audience who packed the body of the court room. Mr. Curran ordered silence, and the Sub-inspector of Police called "Silence!" in authoritative tones.

"Dillon," said Mr. Curran, "if Devoy is innocent, how do you account for the lamb's wool upon his coat-sleeve, and the lamb's liver in his dwelling?"

"Who said that there was lamb's wool upon his coat, and who found the liver, and where are the liver and the wool?" inquired the witness.

The liver and wool were produced, and Dillon examined them.

"Who," he repeated, "said that these things came from the body of a lamb?"

"Mr. Archibald Macready, the veterinary surgeon, so testified," said the magistrate.

"Then," continued the witness, "there are a brace of donkeys in the case. Your veterinary surgeon is an ass; and the hair and liver came from a baste of the same species. The lamb's wool there is ass's hair, and the liver is the liver of an ass."

Lord Packenham obtained a microscope and some wool, and compared the hair introduced in evidence with real wool. The examination satisfied him that Dillon spoke the truth. The examination of Dillon, and of other witnesses, revealed the story as to the slaughter of the ass, the scenes at the hospital and the grave-yard, the hunger of little Andy, and the stealing of the lamb.

Their worships retired for a moment for consultation, and on their return to the court room made an order that Barney Devoy be discharged.

John Dillon turned to leave, but Sub-inspector

Thornhill laid a hand upon his shoulder, and a group of sub-constables formed a cordon around him.

A murmur of dissent arose in the body of the court room, and a voice spoke from the bench: It was the voice of Lord Mount Packenham addressed to the Sub-inspector.

"Mr. Thornhill, let Dillon depart."

And as the butcher and the lord walked out into the street, the voices of the crowd broke forth into cheers.

O faithful, generous Irish hearts! How little your rulers appreciate the nobler side of your nature! Hearts that are seemingly cold and callous, kindled into generous enthusiasm by a single touch of that human nature which "makes the whole world kin;" and tongues that are parched by thirst, and lips that have grown enfeebled by famine, overcome the enfeeblement of deprivation and utter soul-felt cheers responsive to justice and generosity.

CHAPTER III.

TRUE CAUSES OF IRISH FAMINE—THE PLUNDERED NATION AND ITS RUINED INDUSTRIES.

JOHN DILLON bade his weeping wife and infant boy farewell upon the morning succeeding the events in the magistrate's court.

"Mary," he said, "it is hard to lave you, but for me to remain here means certain death. The town is now a plague-spot, and will soon be a wilderness. There is no sort of employment. I cannot beg, and I will not steal. I must earn bread somewhere for Andy and you."

He kissed the wife and child again and again, and his still vigorous frame trembled with emotions that were but partially revealed in words. He handed to her a silver coin, the half-crown received for the donkey's hide, took up his bundle containing a little clean linen, and stepped from the threshold of the cabin in which he had enjoyed his happiest years—the cabin wherein his child was born.

He halted in front of the old woolen mill before turning the corner into the public square. Here he turned round to take a last look upon his cabin, and as he did so he saw his wife still standing on the stone door-step holding little Andy forward in her arms. He waved his blackthorn in a united farewell and a signal of hope, and to terminate the agony of the wife, he rapidly walked around the corner and into the public square. Here he took a lingering farewell look at the old woolen mill. To him it was something more than a ruin or an object of historic interest. Five-and-thirty years before his father was proprietor of that woolen mill. It was erected by his grandfather in the last quarter of the eighteenth century, and before he was born it had given employment to four hundred hands in the manufacture of friezes, flannels, tweeds and blankets; it had paid wages to the amount of twenty thousand pounds a year, and its annual product of manufactured goods was more than fifty thousand pounds. It was now the central ruin of the ruins, amid the squalid cabins of the poor, amid broken hearts and famishing human beings, sheltering the living skeletons of the fever patients; a ghastly monument to the memory of national industry; a painful reminder of the happy and prosperous days of protective tariffs and bounties under native government.

A crowd of neighbors, old and young, escorted him out of town, and loud were the wailings and bitter the tears when the time for parting came.

The party halted at the cross-roads, where the highway that led to Carrick turned at right angles from the great stone wall that enclosed Lord Mount Packenham's demesne. The spot was shaded by ancestral beeches and elms; and here at this cross-road, under the generous shade, full fifty times, in the happy days of his boyhood, before the famine came, he had led the dance to the music of blind Ned Murtagh's bagpipes. Here the crowd would assemble even on Sunday afternoons, contrary to the wishes of Father Joe, and beat the road to the tune of Irish jigs and reels, with hearts as light as if those blissful days were never to be succeeded by days and nights of suffering and of sorrow. Here it was he bade his friends farewell, and during the afternoon of the same day he crossed the Shannon River and entered the town of Carrick.

There was music in the street—the shrill sweet strains of the fife corps, with kettledrum accompaniment. At the head of the band marched a sergeant of the British army, a gallant looking, soldierly man, with a white cockade in his cap, and silken streamers of red, white and blue depending on the side of his head, under the cockade. In his right hand he held perpendicularly a sabre, and on the point of the sabre there was a purse, which, according to the announcement of the sergeant, contained ten British sovereigns. The recruiting party halted near the market place, and the sergeant delivered his message to the assembled crowd.

" 'Ere you are, my 'arties — 'ere's your h'opportunity. Ten pounds bounty; thirteen pence a day; plenty of fine, fat beef, and the life of a gentleman."

John Dillon stood upon the curbstone, and the sergeant and himself, both soldierly men, viewed each other in mutual admiration. Not a word was uttered between them, until Dillon stepped into the street and extended his arm with up-turned, open palm. The sergeant raised his hand and deposited the "Saxon shilling" in the hand of the new recruit. John Dillon passed the medical examination, transmitted the ten pounds bounty to his wife, and three days later donned the scarlet coat of the English infantry at the depot in Athlone. After learning the facings and manual of arms, he joined his regiment in Dublin—the First Battalion of the Eighty-seventh Foot, the historic *faugh-an-beallaghs*.

* * *

"Order reigned in Warsaw." Ten thousand soldiers garrisoned the city of Dublin, and thirty thousand additional bayonets preserved the peace of Ireland. The flagstones of the ancient capital fairly trembled beneath the tread of infantry, cavalry, artillery, and engineers. The ordinary barrack accommodation was utterly insufficient, and many of the great buildings formerly used as factories, now vacant under the operation of England's free-trade policy, were utilized temporarily as military quarters. The great houses occupied by wealthy manufacturers, by merchants and aristocrats, in the days of Ireland's national and industrial independence under Grattan's Parliament, were now converted into sleeping apartments for England's soldiery. The deserted halls of manufacture and trade in the "liberties," and the once famous "Linen Hall," were occupied by detachments. The old Aldborough House, once the home and haunts of Irish aristocratic mirth, gaiety and beauty, become the temporary quarters of the military. The Bank of Ireland, formerly the old Parliament House, had cannon mounted upon the entablatures of its stately ionic colonnades, and the spacious and splendid custom house where Ireland, in Grattan's time, and down to 1820, had collected her protective duties upon English and other foreign merchandise, having passed out of use for revenue purposes (the export and import trade of Ireland being now exclusively with England), was conveniently utilized as barracks and an arsenal. The streets of Dublin were the scenes of daily military parades. Squadrons of hussars, lancers and dragoons galloped through the principal thoroughfares of the city; infantry practiced platoon firing in the squares; great cannons were constantly moving over the pavements, and the light artillery gave the populace daily exhibitions of how dexterously they could load and fire.

Ireland had produced, in the year 1847, agricultural products of the value of nearly forty-five million pounds sterling (two hundred and twenty-five million dollars)—sufficient to feed more than twice her population; yet in that same year five hundred thousand human beings had perished of famine and typhus fever in a land that was teeming with food.

Indian meal came into Dublin Bay in clipper ships from America, but for every cargo of the meal that entered the harbor of Dublin, ten cargoes of Irish produce went out; beef, and butter, and bacon, the finest that the world yields, went to England, where a people, engaged in manufactures and commerce, had money to pay for food.

It was in early spring in the year 1848 that a great meeting convened at Music Hall in Dublin, for the expressed purpose of "considering the peril of the country;" but for the actual purpose of begging concessions from the British Parliament. The parliamentary agitators and loyal sycophants intended to pass some sugar-coated resolutions and expressions of loyalty to the Crown, in the hope of securing legislative favors.

This was precisely what the English government desired. That government had but recently conferred a favor (?) upon Ireland, by the repeal of the corn-laws; so that "suffering Ireland," as Lord John Russell argued, "might have cheaper bread;" as if every well-informed Irishman did not know that the repeal of the corn-laws was the "last straw" in free-trade legislation that "broke the camel's back" in Ireland. Ireland had bread to sell, and the repeal of the import duties which cheapened the Englishman's loaf, reduced the income of the Irishman who had wheat to sell, precisely in the measure of the import duty.

An English treasury clerk named Trevelyan had been sent over to Ireland that he might write to the London press, asking Queen Victoria to issue a royal letter, imploring for Ireland alms in all the churches of England upon a certain day that had been appointed by the Archbishop of Canterbury as a day of thanksgiving to God for the abundant harvest.

Richard O'Gorman, who subsequently became an eminent lawyer and jurist in New York City, was then a very young man, a resident of Dublin, and a member of the Irish revolutionary society. The meeting called by the Lord Mayor at Music Hall was intended to be of the strictly constitutional sort; but young O'Gorman arose and put an end to the meaningless platitudes and "blundering amendments" by a resolution to this effect :

"The one great want and demand of Ireland is, that foreign legislators and foreign ministers shall no longer interfere in the management of her affairs."

And he followed his resolution with a powerful and indignant speech, concluding as follows:

"But the truth, my lord, must be told, and the truth is that Ireland starves and perishes because England has eaten us out of house and home. It is for that sole end they have laid their grasp upon Ireland, and it is for that, and that alone, they will try to keep her."

John Mitchell, editor of *The Felon*, the organ of the Irish patriots of the period, spoke upon the proposed subscription in the British churches on Thanksgiving Day. He indignantly uttered the protest of the Irish people.

"It is an impudent proposal," he said, "and ought to be rejected with scorn and contumely. To-morrow, all over broad England and Scotland and Wales the people are to offer their thanksgiving for our abundant harvest, and to fling us certain crumbs and crusts of it for charity. Keep your alms, ye canting hypocrites; button your pockets upon the Irish plunder that is in them, and let the begging-box pass on. . . . Once more we scorn, we repulse, we curse all English alms, and only wish these sentiments of ours could reach, before noon to-morrow, every sanctimonious thanksgiver in England, Scotland and Wales."

Thomas Francis Meagher, who became in after-years a famous general of the Union army in America, enlightened the meeting as to the true cause of

Irish famine. He said that the abolition of native government, followed by British free-trade, were the underlying causes of the famine. He enumerated some of the leading Irish industries that had been destroyed by free-trade. He said:

"The cotton manufacture of Dublin, which employed fourteen thousand operatives, has been destroyed; the stuff and serge manufactures, which employed fourteen hundred and ninety-one operatives, have been destroyed; the calico looms of Balbriggan have been destroyed; the flannel manufacture of Rathdrum has been destroyed; the blanket manufacture of Kilkenny has been destroyed; the camlet trade of Bandon, which produced one hundred thousand pounds a year, has been destroyed; the worsted and stuff manufactures of Waterford have been destroyed; the rateen and frieze manufactures of Carrick-on-Suir have been destroyed. One business alone thrives and flourishes, and dreads no bankruptcy; that fortunate business which the Union Act has stood by; which the absentee drain has not slackened, but has stimulated; which the drainage acts and navigation acts of the imperial senate have not deadened but invigorated; that favored, and privileged, and patronized business is the Irish coffin-maker's."

The presence of an army, and of the crowds of Irish land-owners who then resided in Dublin for peace of mind or safety's sake, somewhat relieved the appearance of squalor and distress among the unemployed; but in some of the provincial towns the general situation was simply appalling. Unemployed working people feasted upon the dead bodies of horses, asses and dogs. People wandered about listlessly, with a stupid and despairing look. Children looked like old men and women, and even the lower animals seemed to feel the general despair; merriment totally disappeared, and the generosity, the gaiety, the open-heartedness and the self-reliance which hitherto characterized the Irish peasant vanished, and have never fully returned.

Boat-loads of Irish-born people, who had lived for years in England, were hurried across the Channel to their native parishes in Ireland, to render still more hopeless the task of relieving the impoverished; while ocean vessels bore across the seas to the ends of the earth the bone and sinew of the Irish race.

CHAPTER IV.

THE LAND OF PROMISE.

ON a certain morning in spring of 1848, Barney Devoy was seen walking gaily across the public square, with a yellow-covered letter in his hand. He walked into the little white-washed, oblong building which was at that time occupied as a "soup-school." There was a vigor in his step, and an air of independence on his one-story brow such as no one had ever witnessed before. He wore a West-of-England broadcloth coat, which had, at some former period, adorned the portly figure of some English business man; and the stiff breezes of spring inflated the garment around him, so that the observer might regard it as a coat or a tent, according to his fancy. The skirt of his Prince Albert, when in repose, ran down below Barney's knees, but it was now sailing gloriously behind him in the breeze.

A cynical observer remarked that Barney's body was "as straight as the split in a peeler's poll," and that "you could sit and ride upon his coat-tail."

The soup-school was a characteristic English institution. The State having reduced the bodies of the Irish by starvation into a proper mood for repentance, the missionary spirit followed up the work of conquest and spoliation, Bible in hand, to confer upon the souls of the benighted Celts the light of religion, as by law established. Religious education was imparted to all the wretched children who came, and the unpalatable pill of the creed which they abhorred was washed down by missionary soup, furnished by those who were devouring Irish beef and mutton.

Devoy, upon entering the school, and without deigning to notice the superintendent, the Rev. Loyd Jenkins Jones, took his two little children, Mike and Francis, and led them hurriedly to the outer door. Here Mr. Jones crossed his path.

"Bernard," he said, with his sanctimonious smile, "the children 'aven't 'ad their soup this morning."

"My boys are no hands for soup, anyhow," snappishly responded Barney; "they never did care about soup."

"Mr. Devoy," said the superintendent, "somethink must 'ave 'appened to sever the pleasant relations 'eretofore h'existing."

"You're jist whistlin'," said Barney; "allow me to complimint ye on the quickness of your parception;" and opening his American letter (for such was the contents of the yellow envelope) he displayed a passage ticket for himself and wife, and his four little children, Michael, Frank, Anthony, and the baby Bridget.

"There," he said, "there's the document of deliverance—our passages and a five-pound note sent by my brother Darby from Connecticut."

Within a week Barney Devoy had chartered a pony and cart, and was on his way for Cork, en route for America. His family formed part of a great procession. Two hundred and fifteen thousand Irish emigrants found their way to America in the single year of 1847. When the famine was at its worst, and eviction swept the sufferers out of their hovels, they rushed in the direction of the seaports, some bound for America, some few for Australia, some for the continent of Europe.

The poorest and the feeblest went to England

and to Scotland, as the nearest places of refuge, but to the vast majority of the fugitives, America was the "Promised Land.". The bosom of the Atlantic was whitened with the sails of the emigrant ships that bore them over; and such was the mortality among them in transit, that their route of passage might be traced by the bones of, the fever-stricken dead at the bottom of the sea.

Not less than a million of these exiles crossed the ocean and found homes in America during the decade ending in 1856.

As our story relates to them and to their descendants, this chapter is necessarily a part of the record, as briefly stating the causes and the circumstances that influenced their coming to, and remaining in the United States.

Upon their arrival they generally settled upon the sea-board as a matter of necessity, and more than two-thirds of that great multitude found homes in the region bounded on the south by the Ohio River, and on the west by a line drawn north and south through the western extremity of Pittsburgh.

Following some blind or enlightened instinct, perhaps in obedience to the general law that men will continue to live where they find least resistance to living, they permanently settled in the great industrial centers of New England, New York, Pennsylvania and New Jersey, where Northern capital inaugurated great public improvements, and maintained great manufacturing industries.

Hundreds of thousands of their race had gone before, and other multitudes were destined to follow; but the famine exiles founded the swarming colony of Greater Ireland on the American side of the Atlantic.

They became like a great tree imbedded in the sandbar of some broad, shallow river, around whose decaying trunk and branches the drifting sands and seeds of other generations found a resting place, and from which, in time, has sprung the tremendous and incomprehensible power which the politicians conveniently designate as "the Irish vote" in America. Barney Devoy and his children were drops in the human streams that rushed from the interior to the sea.

Somewhere near the borders of Limerick and Clare, near the head-waters of the Shannon estuary, Devoy's party was augmented by a family named Sullivan, consisting of husband and wife and four small children, named James, Jerry, Margaret and Mary. Tom Sullivan, the head of the family, was by trade a stone-mason; a sturdy man, about fifty years of age. He was dressed in Irish frieze, with knee-breeches of "doe-skin," long woolen stockings and low shoes. His legs displayed the muscles of a well-fed mechanic; he carried his head erect, and looked at all he met with an eye of independence untamed by tyranny or the lordling's frown. He was not poverty-stricken. His wages, though small, had supported him, and left him a margin for the "rainy day." He greeted the Devoy family with a hearty "God save ye," and received an equally cordial response of "God save ye kindly." He soon learned that himself and Devoy were traveling toward the same destination—New Limerick, in the State of Connecticut.

The ocean voyage, from the Cove of Cork to Castle Garden, New York, was made in six-and-thirty days. There were no unusual incidents on the voyage. The five hundred and forty steerage passengers were assigned to their foul-smelling berths, around which at night they assembled in groups and recited the rosary. There were little disturbances at the cooking galleys from day to day, but nothing noteworthy. The young people danced and sang, indulged in love-making and merry-making; and only the frequent announcement of deaths aboard interfered with the routine.

Day after day the solemn tolling of the ship's bell announced a funeral, and the corpses of those who had survived the famine to die by fever were sewed into sack-cloth, and, duly weighted with shot or heavy irons, were thrown into the ocean, to make a meal for the deep-sea fishes that followed in the vessel's wake.

There was rejoicing at the first sight of the promised land, and cheers went up in gratitude to Heaven when the green coast of Jersey and the countless buildings on Manhattan Island and Long Island became visible from the mouth of New York harbor; and there were heartfelt farewells when the emigrants were scattering out of Castle Garden.

The future home of the Sullivans and the Devoys was only a two-hours journey by omnibus and rail from Castle Garden.

Near the border line of the states of New York and Connecticut there grew and flourished a pretty manufacturing village, in which a great many of the Irish exiles found a home. They built a church, from whose spire could be seen the vessels sailing up and down Long Island Sound. Between the village and the sea were many a pretty grove and garden, and the waters of the sound stole up at high tide between the hills, as if the ocean's finger tips loved to twine themselves in the summer verdure of New England valleys. The Irish settlers named the village New Limerick; and though mapmakers and geographers would have it otherwise, New Limerick it was, and rather than differ with the early settlers over the trifling matter of a name, New Limerick let it be.

Manufacturing there was still in its infancy, though

already there were pioneer ventures in the making of cotton goods, cutlery and blankets. The Irish men found profitable employment in connection with quarries, buildings and public roads, and in the conversion of the wild hills and valleys into the civilized habitations of the wealthy people overflowing from the great cities, while the larger boys and girls found employment in the mills and factories.

Upon a sunny hillside was erected, at public expense, a tasteful and commodious building for public school purposes.

"Do you be tellin' me," said Tom Sullivan (to the father of another family), "do you mane to say, that the great big brick school upon the hill is for our boys and girls, as well as for the children of the Yankee?"

"That's what the selectman says," replied the party interrogated.

"Be-gorra, then," said Tom Sullivan, "if that be so my little Jimmy will be among the first wans to warm the benches. By manes of an education," he added, "my poor boy, when he becomes a man, may be able to avoid the black slavery and the poverty of his countrymen."

The school was completed, and Tom Sullivan was as good as his word. On the opening day he led little Jimmy to the great building and saw his hopeful take a seat side by side with the son of the village banker, and with the son of the Yankee millionaire by whom the elder Sullivan was employed.

"You can talk as you plaise," old Tom would remark, "but America is a wonderful country. We have mate every day, there is bread *galore* and fruits and vegetables and oysters; and I heard Mr. Cheney, of the factory, remark wan day, that some day my little Jim may be a mimber of the Connecticut Parlement."

Little Jim had a head and a heart in thorough sympathy with his father's passionate desire to see the children educated, and within a year from the date of his admission to the school, he could read the Boston *Pilot* for his father and the neighbors.

Sullivan would say: "My Jimmy is the boy can give ye chapther and verse. When I come to me supper of an evening, and the bigger boys and girls come home from the factory, and shed their workin' clothes, and put on their clane linens for the evenin', then Bridget sets the table wid the nice white cloth, and the glassware and the pitcher of water, and while I'm aitin' me beautiful quarther section of beefstake, and me half an acre of apple pie, wid the bread and fruit, and other fine things—as fine a dinner as iver a landlord had at home—its little Jim will take the evenin' paper, and read about the California gold mines, and the doin' of Congress, and the blessed memories of the ould art." And the father would glorify God, that if the Creator had seen fit to drive them from a lovely land, He had more than compensated them by happy homes in free America.

CHAPTER V.

DEVOY BECOMES A POLITICAL LEADER.

"OH, man, it's in Mullingar you'd see the stir-about. If you broke a spoon, the divil a a word they'd say, but hand you another."

This sentence was the keynote of Mr. Barney Devoy's argument whenever a discussion on the subject of free-trade led him to compare the superior advantages of living in Ireland with the privations of American laborers.

"Oh, man, it's in Ireland you'd see the English broadcloth. It's there you'd get a coat big enough to cover a bull for two pound ten." And he would rush into a closet, and without any indication or suggestion of shame or mortification, would exhibit the cast-off English coat which had been given him in charity by the Rev. Loyd Jenkins Jones, the English superintendent of the soup-school.

Tom Sullivan, who was thoroughly satisfied with life in America, and deeply grateful to the American people, would venture on these occasions to say a good word for America, and to remind Mr. Devoy of the sufferings at home under free-trade and famine.

"Famine? famine? famine? where was the famine? Sure, there never was a famine in Ireland. It's full and plenty they had at home, lashins and lavins galore, wid the finest English broadcloth and Scotch tweeds to wear."

And the crowd of Barney's political supporters would rise indignantly to protest against any suggestion of hard times in Ireland. None of them had ever before heard of famine, and if party necessity demanded it, they stood ready to prove that the country roads were paved with four-pound loaves, and that three millions of the race had emigrated just for a change of air and relief from a diet of roast beef, turkeys and terrapin.

"Barney," inquired an American gentleman, "have you any lobsters in Ireland?"

"Yes, sir," responded Mr. Devoy; "the rivers and bog-holes are red wid 'em."

"Yes; but, Barney, you know that the lobsters inhabit the sea."

"Yes, sir, they go down from the rivers and bog-holes to the say. What's to hinder 'em?"

"Oh, nothing; but you know the lobster when raw is not red; it becomes red when boiled."

"Certainly. There are boilin' springs in the Irish waters, and the lobsters get red in passin' through the springs."

Mr. Devoy, with a look of triumph, would then compliment the crowd as "the finest pisintry that the sun of God looks down upon," and would lead them up for "the wettin' of their whistles" at the James Buchanan Exchange.

There was an Irish blacksmith, named Peter McIntyre, commonly called "Peter the Pagan," who, on these occasions, took Sullivan's view of the case. He was an educated man, thoroughly conversant with American and Irish history; and whenever he told them the truth as to the destruction of Irish industries by British law and policy, he raised around him a storm of indignation.

Meanwhile, Barney Devoy became prosperous in the liquor business. He was the recognized leader in his ward, and was reputed to have "a big pull" with the Democratic powers of New Limerick. And so the irritating discussions were continued day after day and night after night. Old Barney was forever boasting of the superior advantages of life in Ireland. Whenever Tom Sullivan eulogized the New

England pies, old Barney cut him short with—

"Ah, man, it's in Ireland you would see the pies."

"Oh, yes," Tom would respond, "oh, yes, in the bakers' windows."

"So near, and yet so far," added little Jim.

"Yes, *ma bouchal*," Tom Sullivan added; "our people can fly in the face of God as much as they plaise; they can put on their foolish pride; but there is no country like this. They can talk of things at home to their hearts' content, but God never gave to the world a country like America."

Old Devoy had attended a meeting addressed by one of the college professors from New Haven. A society of English manufacturers had offered a prize for the best essay on "Free-trade," and this professor had arisen to the occasion.

The subject of the discourse was "Cheapness." The professor dilated on the cheapness of things in Europe—"potatoes only four pence a stone."

"And devilish hard to get the four pence," said Sullivan.

"And the cheapness of the beautiful Irish apples," said Devoy.

"Oh!—an' its apples are so chape," said Sullivan. "They have beautiful apples in Ireland, but Barney, *avic*, how much of them did you and I get? I lived in sightin' distance o' wan of the finest orchards in Limerick, but it was enclosed by a twelve-foot wall, and guarded by a game-keeper and a bull-dog. I saw the trees bloom in spring-time; I have stood beside the wall—on the outside—in the autumn, till I was wet wid the dripping of the dew from the branches, and tantalized by the odor of the fruit, but the winter came—and the divil an apple. What's the good of your chapeness if there's no labor for yer hands, and no money to buy the apples?"

"And the fine tastin' oysters," said Devoy.

"Yes, in the oyster-man's cart," responded Sullivan, "lovely oysters for a shillin' a dozen. The divil a sowl I ever saw aitin' oysthers in Ireland but the landlord, the parson, the pr'est, and the peelers; and when the famine came, Father O'Grady quit aitin' oysthers and wid the oysther-money bought meal for the poor. Here, in New Limerick, its the commonest thing in the world, of a Saturday night, to see the boys take the cailins into the oyster parlors, and fill them wid oysters, and the craythurs are like a Connemara stockin'—the more you stuff them, the more they stretch."

And Devoy sympathized with the Yale professor in the desire for greater cheapness in English broadcloths.

"Arrah, Barney, jewel," responded Sullivan, "aren't ye tired of English broadcloth? And when did you take to wearin' broadcloth? When did the common people, at home, wear broadcloth? *Mawrone, avic*, some of them wore the hand-me-downs, the cast-off clothing of the English, and that's the only broadcloth you or yours ever wore in the ould art."

And so life ran in New Limerick. Gradually the laboring people built cosy little cottages around the factories; their c ildren went to school; there was now and then heard a snarl from some of the poor native Americans, but the educated and the wealthy, the pious and the refined of the American people sympathized with and assisted them. Their children, male and female, wore clothing after the manner and form of the wealthiest Americans; until soon, at the theaters and other places of amusement, in the political meetings, and places of assembly generally, it was only by the physiognomy, or the color of their countenances, that one was enabled to distinguish between the children of the Irish exiles· and those of the wealthiest Americans.

But the old serpent found its way into this new paradise. Two factions sprang into existence—the Sullivans and the Devoys. Tom Sullivan had two sons, Jim and Jerry; and Barney had three sons. The oldest, F. X. (Francis Xavier), was an ecclesiastical student; the next one, Albert Michael, had opened a money-lending office, where it was said that he kept "a brick-bat to grind the face of the poor;" and the youngest son, Tony, assisted his father in dispensing liquid nourishment at the James Buchanan Exchange. Tom Sullivan and his two boys lived by their manual labor. They were not factionists, but of that "homely plodding cast who labored hard to make up by assiduity all that they wanted in wit." Their crime, in the eyes of Mr. Devoy, was that they appreciated the advantages of their American home and fraternized with the Yankees. It was whispered around that the Sullivans were slandering the Irish; that old Tom had declared that he "had lived forty years in Ireland, and never tasted a pie;" that his son Jim was seen in the company of Methodists, and was a probable candidate for holy orders in that denomination. It was further hinted that old Sullivan was on friendly terms with Cheney, the mill-man; and that on last election day he had permitted Mr. Cheney to put a stratch upon the Democratic ticket which Mr. Devoy had handed to him all straight and undefiled.

The Devoys were influential, and the Sullivans instinctively avoided a conflict with them; and if there was a Sullivan faction, it came into existence without their sanction, and purely out of sympathy with a worthy old Irishman and his two estimable boys. The Devoys were aggressive, and combined all the elements of power in politics.

Old Barney had a tongue like an adder; Francis Xavier, being intended for the church, contributed sanctity, and commanded deference; while the father engendered fear. Albert Michael was at once a petty banker and a pawnbroker; while young Tony wielded his far-reaching influence through the liquid nourishment at the James Buchanan Exchange. For any man to seek a Democratic nomination without the consent and approval of the Devoys were futile as the effort of the camel to pass through the eye of the needle. If he would succeed, he must first make Barney his financial agent, and obtain a loan, from Albert Michael, and with the blessing of Francis Xavier upon his undertaking, go down to young Tony and invest the borrowed money. The Sullivans timidly abstained from active participation in politics; so their sin was not so much a thing of commission as a failure to acknowledge the sway of the Devoys, and thereby place themselves in harmony with the party.

Old Sullivan would shake his head in genuine solicitude for the future of the colony. "Bad luck to yer politics," he said, "and a shame upon yer gratitude. Ye came among these Yankees. They built factories, and opened all kinds of improvements; they gave ye labor for yer hands, money in yer pockets, and bread for yer families; and just as soon as ye get the wrinkles out of yer hides, and the look of hunger out of yer faces, ye turn upon them wid yer politics, and run counther to their interests and their wishes. Ye ask me if I'm a Dimicrat. Yes, I'm a Dimicrat, av coorse; but if dimocracy manes war wid the wealth and dacency of New Limerick, I may scratch me ticket. If Mr. Cheney or Mr. Devoy is to boss this town, give me the dacent Yankee every time."

One of the things that Tom Sullivan could not understand was the meaning of the curse, the nature of the original sin, that prompted many of the exiles into hostility to the Yankees among whom they had made their home.

CHAPTER VI.

KNOWNOTHINGISM.

THE new brick church building of St. Loyola occupied a sightly position in the center of New Limerick.

A gambler named Billy Percival, from the city of Baltimore, established a keno room, with saloon attachment, across the street from the sacred edifice. So the young men who attended mass on Sundays were not compelled to go much out of their way when they sought a little amusement. Mr. Percival's mind was richly stored with the literature and vocabulary of Baltimore politics, and he was accustomed to edify the minds of the Irish-American youth with all the funny compliments paid to the nigger and the Yankee in the bar-rooms of Baltimore. In recognition of his pronounced Democracy, he secured the support and fidelity of his customers, and in brief time he became the proprietor of a powerful pull with the "Irish vote." They rallied to his support on election day, and made him a member of the town council.

A little colony of weavers, from the Irish city of Londonderry, established a lodge of a certain loyal organization which had brought much grief and shame to the good name of Ireland. In America they called it the "A. P. A." It was observed that Mr. Percival was on intimate terms with the members of the "A. P. A.;" and was further remarked that he temporarily neglected the keno game and engaged in a mysterious activity in public affairs. It was understood that he had established some sort of secret political lodge on his own account, and he might be seen in the darkness of night engaged in earnest whisperings, warning his friends to beware of the Catholics. But when any of these men were questioned as to the subject of the conversation, or as to Mr. Percival's lodge, they merely shook their heads and said, "I know nothing." Similar proceedings were observable in various parts of the country, so that in time, for want of a better name, Mr. Percival's brethren of the secret order were generally styled "The Knownothings." In 1856 that powerful organization "showed its hand" in politics as the "Native American Party." It was especially powerful in the South. The old slave states gave its presidential candidate nearly half a million votes, and gave to him the electoral vote of the State of Maryland. Its strongholds were cities like Baltimore, Louisville and St. Louis—cities that were then, and are now, most powerfully Democratic. It was numerically strong in certain parts of New England and the Middle States; but in the new States of the West, where Republicanism was well organized, Knownothingism never made much headway. This was equally true of certain New England States. It received less than four thousand votes in the State of Maine, while Maryland gave its candidate forty-seven thousand votes, and the electoral vote of the State. It originated in the South, in the nature of a Democratic bolt. When O'Connell scornfully refused the proffered gold of the slave-holders for his Irish movement for repeal of the Union, the slave-holders became indignant, and the Irish rallying cry of "Ireland for the Irish" was paraphrased by the counter-cry of "America for the Americans."

In the North it was animated by an entirely different motive. In the industrial centers it became a question of bread and butter, of life and death. The prosperity which the United States had enjoyed during the decade ending in 1856 had disappeared. This prosperity, despite the low tariff revenue system, had been maintained by several causes, particularly the demand for American agricultural produce, created by short crops in Europe; by the Crimean War (1854-56), and by gold discoveries in California (1849), which attracted a large tide of labor from competition with the workmen in the East, and returned an immense flow of gold, aggregating hundreds of millions of dollars. These causes of national prosperity were at an end, and the flow of California gold had disappeared, had left the country, had gone to England for manufactured merchandise imported under a low tariff. American workshops and factories were shutting down; American laborers walked the streets of their native cities, and famine was impending in many hitherto prosperous industrial centers.

The New Limerick Woolen Mills, having closed their doors, advertised for fifty men to repair certain roadways and embankments; and in addition to a hundred Irishmen who rushed for the proffered fifty cents a day, four hundred skilled American workmen appeared upon the ground solicitous for employment upon any terms. Bill Percival, the gambler and Democratic wheel-horse, appeared at their head, and many of them were armed with bludgeons, and not a few with knives and pistols. At the demand of Mr. Percival, Mr. Cheney, of the mills, was compelled to hang a sign at the gate of the institution, reading

NO IRISH NEED APPLY

The Irish, without weapons, and in such inferior numbers, discreetly retired. The native American workingmen, suffering from the depression in manufacturing, were led to believe that their misfortunes were due to the foreign immigrants, especially to the swarming Irish, and while they were moved by motives purely personal, the anti-Catholic cry was raised by the Southern gambler and the little colony of Londonderry weavers.

During the afternoon of the same day there were mysterious movements among Percival's followers, and a rallying at the keno room. It was rumored that an attempt would be made that night to burn the new Catholic church, and this rumor was apparently verified when an excited crowd, armed with various weapons, appeared just after night-fall in the vicinity of the church. The Irish, with shot-guns, bludgeons and implements of their labor, rallied to the support of Father Ventura.

"My brethren," he said, "do not be solicitous for me. Take your places at the church;" and they entered the church, removing the sacred vessels and vestments, and barricading the door and windows. Percival had started a report that Father Ventura had recently imported some instrument of torture, intending to establish the work of the Spanish Inquisition in America. The object of the mob was to capture the instrument of torture. Percival led the way. Father Ventura appeared at the door of his residence in response to the calls of the mob. Mr. Percival demanded the instrument of torture.

"Since you have seen it so lately, and marked it so particularly, you can certainly identify it," said the priest. "Walk in, Mr. Percival."

The political leader entered the parsonage, and in a moment re-appeared, dragging with him a framework of iron.

"Why, Percival, you fool," said one of his companions, "that is an iron bedstead."

At this discovery the crowd broke forth in cheers.

"*Iron-ical* cheers," said Father Ventura.

This happy incident put the natives in good humor, so they abandoned the purpose of burning the church.

At the next municipal election Mr. Barney Devoy was pitted against Mr. Percival as candidate for alderman in the first ward ; and the native American candidate won by a narrow majority. There was a torchlight procession to celebrate the victory, and again the rumor spread that the followers of Percival, aided by the Londonderry weavers, would fire the church of St. Loyola ; and again the Irish rallied to its defense, but they were happily disappointed. No effort was made to destroy the church, but by way of diversion, the victorious party did, on their return march, set fire to the frame shanty erected by Barney Devoy near the town meeting-house, and operated by him as a tavern.

They also enjoyed themselves by unmercifully pounding old Tom Sullivan, the most respectable and well-meaning Irishman in New Limerick. Mr. Devoy was wrathful. He never forgot nor forgave that defeat ; and though his Knownothing victors came chiefly from the Democratic party, and were re-absorbed into that party in 1861, old Barney insisted forever afterwards that the Knownothings and Republicans were identical.

He delighted to pose as a religious martyr.

" Baiten," he would say in a tone of resignation, "on account of me religion;" and he would gently draw an Irish-American youth into an alley or a hallway, and enlighten him on Republican hostility to his " religion."

The effort which sought to identify Knownothingism with the party of Lincoln and of Logan, of Grant and of Blaine, has done duty among the credulous Irish long enough. As a matter of fact, there is no more truth in it than in the similarly malignant assumption that the Israelites crucified the Savior. Knownothingism in the South was political. In the North it was begotten of industrial depression. It bore some bitter fruit; but "let the dead past bury its dead."

A time was at hand when the Irish emigrants were to be afforded an opportunity to prove their devotion to America; when all minor differences at the North were swallowed in the terrible calamity of disunion threatening the Nation; and when the cry for help was sounded throughout the land, New Limerick was not unfaithful to America.

CHAPTER VII

WAR.

IT was early summer in New England, in the year 1861. The rugged hills were clothed in emerald green; the small birds twittered among the tender leaves of the tall trees; the breezes of health were blowing inland from Long Island Sound; cattle were browsing in lazy peacefulness in the valleys; children played as their ancestors played; but in the minds and faces of men and women there were excitement and unrest. Groups of men were seen talking vigorously and with serious faces on the street corners. At sundown a drum-and-fife corps played along the main street of New Limerick. A crowd of boys took up the rear, and throngs of men and women followed upon the sidewalks. The band entered the town "meeting-house," and the multitude followed.

Rev. Edward Morley, a young Methodist minister, called the meeting to order, and on his motion Mr. Cheney was called to preside.

Mr. Cheney said that he would be very brief. It

was no time for speech-making. Traitor hands had desecrated the Nation's flag. It was a time for action. In face of the national danger it was fitting that all loyal men should put aside every consideration of party and race, and rally to the defence of a government which, whatever be its faults, was the best government the world ever saw.

"I, myself," he added, "am too old for active service. I can only do a man's duty as a citizen in upholding the arm of the government, but I have an only son, Charley. He is in the hall."

In the body of the hall rose a young man and a grey-haired woman — Charley Cheney and his mother.

The audience cheered, and when silence was restored the mother spoke:

"Charley is my boy—my only boy—dear to my heart as the apple of the eye, but in the course of events it is God's will that his country calls him to defend its integrity. He desires to go, and though great the sacrifice, he goes with a mother's blessing and consent."

The audience renewed its cheers as Charley, responding to his father's call, took his stand beside the platform.

"And now, my countrymen," said Mr. Cheney, "are there any other volunteers?"

"I have two sons," said old man Sullivan, "and" —but his remarks were interrupted with cheers— "and," he continued, "I have talked wid the boys. They were very little when they came to Connecticut. Jim is now a man, and Jerry is a good stout boy. They say they will fight for America, and God forbid that I should hinder them. They are just as dear to me as Charley Cheney is to his parents; but let it never be said that in the hour of danger the Sullivans were false to America. What d'ye say, Jim, and what d'ye say, Jerry?"

"I say," said Jim Sullivan, "that I will bear a man's part in defence of that flag (pointing to the Stars and Stripes). It is the only flag I know. There is another flag—the harp and sunburst of my native country. I love it for my father's sake, but 'tis not my flag. It will prove to me a memory and an inspiration, but in the hour of this Nation's peril I know but one flag—the banner that in 1847 waved above the ships that brought bread to my famishing kindred, and that before that time and since gave protection and shelter to millions of my exiled race."

And Jim Sullivan strode up beside young Cheney. Little Jerry followed, and, without uttering a word, stood shoulder to shoulder with his brother Jim. Again the audience cheered. Man after man went forward, until fifty names were entered on the roll; and three days later the New Limerick company marched to the depot to join their regiment, with Charley Cheney as captain at their head, and Jim Sullivan as first lieutenant.

On the evening of the meeting at the town hall there was a counter demonstration up at Barney Devoy's. The James Buchanan Exchange, in the language of its proprietor, "like the Faynix, had risen from its ashes," and the gambler Percival, and the whole Devoy family, with numerous supporters and retainers, had assembled at the "Exchange," and were loud in their denunciation of the "Lincoln hirelings."

Jim Sullivan was, according to the general verdict, the most admirable youth in the village. He had graduated with honors from the high school, and while he worked ten hours a day at the woolen factory, he devoted every leisure hour to the study of literature and of history; and at the time the dread cry of war was sounded, the whole Sullivan family were hoarding up their savings for the purpose of enabling him to study law. He was an athlete in all the village games, and a leader in the village lyceum. He had assisted Father Ventura in the collection of a young men's library, and he was secretary of the Young Men's Catholic Association; a youth of admirable physical form, of manly countenance, merciful and brave, and modest as he was merciful.

It became the subject of gossip in the village at the time, that when the recruits were leaving on the train, and when Laura Cheney, the village belle, the wealthy manufacturer's daughter, presented to Jim a tiny silken flag, she gave to him quite as much attention as she gave to her brother Charley; and that, when she gave him the final adieu, a tear trickled down her cheek, and her delicate frame trembled with emotion. In short, it was said that Laura Cheney loved the Irish boy; and amid the excitement of the time, the assertion passed uncontradicted, though in "piping times of peace" such a rumor would startle and scandalize every Puritan in Connecticut.

Among the kindly farewell tokens given to the recruits, young Jerry Sullivan received a morocco bound, gilt-edged Douay testament from the hands of Mrs. Cheney; and Father Ventura invested him with a tiny golden cross. Little Jerry was known to all his comrades as the "kid;" for though in strength and size he was a man, in fact he was a beardless youth less than twenty years of age. On reaching the field the Sullivans, on account of certain old associations, were permitted to join a regiment which subsequently became a part of General Meagher's Irish brigade; and Charley Cheney and his boys were mustered into a regiment of Connecticut cavalry. Lieutenant-Colonel Cheney returned from the war in 1865, covered with scars and with honors. He subsequently made his home in one of the growing cities of the Missouri Valley, where he still lives, wealthy, honorable, and honored among men.

* * *

It is an oft-told tale, which is current still at Fredericksburg, Virginia. It has been sung and written in song and story—the record of a hero's death, whose name had been forgotten, but whose record shall be deathless. The battle of Fredericksburg was a Confederate victory. During the desperate struggle, the lines of the Union Army were hurled repeatedly against the impregnable heights in vain. Shattered and torn by the Confederate fire, they renewed the assault again and again, but to be shattered and repulsed. The Irish brigade of Meagher occupied a position before the heights of St. Mary. They shared the defeat of the Union Army with terribly disastrous results. Two-thirds of the command were either killed or wounded. It was noticed that on the morning of the battle, though there was neither shrub nor tree in the vicinity of their camp, every member of the brigade wore a sprig of green-of-boxwood in his cap. On the morning of the day succeeding the battle, the Confederate soldiers came down in melancholy curiosity to look over the field of the dead. The bodies of the Union dead lay like the sheaves in harvest, ripened by the Southern sun; but in advance of the foremost line of dead lay one man, a stone's throw from the Confederate cannon. He lay face downward, and the curious Confederates raised the body tenderly, upturning the dead face to the light of the sun.

He was no bearded veteran, but a beardless youth, and in his cap they found a sprig of boxwood, still unwithered, and in the pocket of his coat a Douay testament, morocco bound, finger worn, with faded edges of gilt, and around his neck a slender string to which was attached a tiny golden cross. And the story runs that they buried him where he fell, with cross and testament, and planted above the rugged mound the dead boy's sprig of boxwood. It was the body of little Jerry Sullivan. It was to this boy that Benjamin Harrison, in one of his gems of campaign oratory, at Indianapolis, referred when he declared that "the young soldier whose dead body lay in advance of all the rest before the heights of Fredericksburg, was no less an American because he wore a sprig of green in his cap."

Brave men perish, but little Jerry Sullivan's is

"One of the few immortal names
That were not born to die."

And if this chapter shall to some extent rescue that heroic name from the countless thousands of the nameless dead, the labor of the author will not be entirely in vain.

In the same disastrous battle, Jim Sullivan left an arm on the field of Fredericksburg. On his return in 1865, he was received joyfully by the whole people.

Mr. and Mrs. Cheney, and the Lieutenant-Colonel and Miss Laura, were conspicuous figures at the reception. Jim's modesty never forsook him, and when the audience clamored for a speech, he merely smiled and bowed, but the elder Cheney spoke for him.

"Captain Sullivan," he said, "the sacrifices of your aged parents, the death of your heroic brother, and your own valor, which that empty sleeve attests, will never be forgotten in New Limerick while gratitude warms the breasts of Americans. I might justly complain of the conduct of some of your recreant countrymen; but the heroism and sacrifices of Tom Sullivan and his sons can be cheerfully accepted in vicarious atonement for the sins of a good many Devoys."

CHAPTER VIII.

PROSPERITY AND PIETY.

NEW LIMERICK shared the abundant prosperity of the war period. The expenses of the government necessitated high duties on imported merchandise, and under these high tariffs old industries flourished and new ones were created and fostered. Manufactories of carpets, plated ware, furniture and clocks were established. Old worn-out farms in the suburbs were converted into town lots, and the banks of Perry Creek were fairly lined with factories.

A rolling-mill for the manufacture of steel rails was among the contemplated enterprises. A company of Massachusetts capitalists had purchased Tom Sullivan's old apple orchard as a site for the rolling-mill, and were only waiting for favorable legislation by Congress to commence the work of construction. At this time the American people were rapidly building railroads and importing the rails from England at a cost of one hundred and sixty dollars a ton. American rail manufacturers appeared before Congress and urged that a duty of twenty-eight dollars a ton be imposed on the imported rails, as a matter of protection and encouragement to the contemplated rolling-mills, promising Congress at the same time that the ultimate effect of the tariff would be a reduction in the cost of steel rails. The Congressional campaign was in progress, and it was declared, emphasized and understood by all parties that the issue was for or against protection, and that the question of a great rolling-mill at New Limerick depended on whether the district in which it was situated would return to Congress a friend or an enemy of American industry. The fight for free-trade was inaugurated at a public meeting, addressed by Counseller Murphy of New York City, and the college professor from Yale. Barney Devoy was one of the vice-presidents, and Francis Xavier Devoy was secretary.

Francis Xavier had become a fixture at New Limerick. Having completed his Latin course under a private tutor, he applied for admission at Fordham College, but the lynx-eyed president of that institution gracefully declined his patronage. The young man was accompanied to Fordham by his father. All that wealth and the tailor's art could do were employed to give them the best possible appearance. Barney was dressed in a suit of English broadcloth, patent leather shoes, plug hat and faultless linen, with a watch chain heavy enough for logging purposes; while the aspirant for theological honors wore Scotch tweed, with a fancy French vest, a forty-candle power diamond, blear eyes and a rose-colored nose.

"This boy of mine," said Barney to the college president, "has a vocation for the clargy, and I have brought him to your Reverence to give him his college coorse."

"And your name?" said the president.

"Bernard Devoy, may it plase you."

"And your residence and occupation?"

"I am a wine merchant by trade, and my home is New Limerick, Connecticut."

"Very well," said the president; "let Francis Xavier have a *va*cation for two weeks, and we will inquire as to the *vo*cation."

The result of an inquiry on the part of the college authorities was that, when Barney and the son returned to Fordham, Francis Xavier was politely but very firmly refused admission into the institution, and the youth, intended by his parents to become a shining light in the church—a bishop or a cardinal, perhaps—was extinguished like a spark from the blacksmith's anvil.

The president, in private consultation with the elder Devoy, gave him convincing proofs that the youth, in addition to the fixed habit of intemperance, had other habits fatal to the father's pious aspirations and ambitions regarding him, and so father and son returned to New Limerick. On the return journey, and for days and years that followed, in the happiest hours of the day, and through "the silent watches of the night," the closing sentence of the college president kept ringing in the ears and through the chambers of Barney's brain, though it never reached his heart. It was: "The wages of sin is death. You will not have to wait for eternity; iniquity brings its own punishment. You can pile up wealth as much as you please in your present occupation. Your children may be clothed in silks, and even educated and refined, but 'Vengeance is mine, saith the Lord,' and for the wretchedness which you create you will suffer through the ruin of some member of your own family."

It was the first time that any clergyman had ever ventured to intimate that Barney was not immaculate.

But the Devoys continued to flourish. Albert Michael was treasurer of the church. He inherited his father's money-getting propensities, and the wide waste of mouth from ear to ear. His teeth, too, were abnormally pronounced, and there was something chilling and repulsive when he opened his weak and watery eyes, and contracted the muscles of his mouth, exposing the teeth in the offensive exhibition which he intended as a smile. Albert Michael was now a private banker, who conducted his business on the principle that "the poorer the man the larger the rate of interest."

Old Sullivan, before he had sold the apple orchard, once approached him for a loan of a hundred dollars.

"What rate of interest do you charge, Mr. Devoy?"

"No interest, sir, no interest;" and he gave the offensive exhibition of a smile, took Sullivan's note for one hundred dollars, and handed him eighty-five dollars.

Little Tony Devoy had become an important character. He had "a pull" with every wretch who had been besotted in the James Buchanan Exchange, and local politicians were known to pay him as high as one hundred dollars for his labors on election day. Little Tony was practically non-partisan. He never inquired as to the politics of the scoundrel who employed him, but he always waited until five minutes before the closing of the polls to vote, and he sold his vote to the highest bidder for cash.

The pride of the Devoy family was Birdelia (Yankee for Bridget). She was a plain, sweet, modest creature, inheriting the graces of a virtuous Irish mother. She was happily innocent of the ways and means that surrounded her with every conceivable luxury. She took unkindly, at first, to the change in her name, but when she learned that it was essential to the dignity of the family, when she learned that Frank had become Francis Xavier, and Mike had become Albert Michael, she yielded to the inevitable.

The old frame building which had long done duty as the "James Buchanan Exchange," had been sold to an unpretentious Irishman for a cattle shed, and an elegant two-story brick had been erected in its stead.

The "James Buchanan Exchange" now gloried in its French plate-glass windows, and the strains of Birdelia's piano were heard through the open lattice of the second-story window.

Meanwhile old Barney and young Tony did a "land-office business" down stairs. Their temple was the shrine at which all politicians worshiped. Ugly rumors had gone forth as to drunken men having their pockets picked, and of gilded youth who had been beaten on "skin games" of cards in the "private office;" but all this was dispelled upon the assurance that Barney and his family "belonged to the church," that Francis Xavier had a vocation, and that Mrs. Devoy and Birdelia were almost heavenly in their devotion.

It was known that old Barney had a hickory club with which he used to bring defaulters to terms. If a man tried to leave without paying his bill, old Barney would grasp the hickory club and say, seizing the defaulter by the throat: "Faith, be me sowl, you won't." He would threaten to "commit suicide" upon anyone who refused to pay for the drinks, and when seriously questioned as to whether he intended to commit suicide, he assured the inquirer, "Be me sowl, I'd rather commit suicide on anybody else than on meself."

He would climb upon the wagon of a farmer or a wood-hauler, and, under the terror of his club, collect a whisky bill.

Yet he was forever pious. He would denounce in the bitterest terms the courageous Irishmen who dared to entertain an opinion in politics, or who felt an intelligent sympathy with American institutions.

He was an expert in the card game of "forty-fives." Sitting on a high chair behind the bar, he would play "forty-fives" with all comers, and so great was his passion for the game that, when his superior skill had over-awed all players for drinks and for nickels, he continued the game with little boys for buttons; until it was said that half the pantaloons in the town were gaping wide open, because the boys had cut the buttons off their fathers' pants to play with old Barney Devoy.

Meanwhile Francis Xavier was "sowing his wild oats." He had been found several times insensibly drunk on the floor of the Buchanan Exchange, and one morning, to the great scandal of his poor old mother and sister, he was found lying asleep on a public sidewalk, under the morning sun, in the embrace of a drunken showman.

CHAPTER IX.

EARLY STRUGGLES.

THE congressional election was a protectionist victory. An Irish youth named Scanlan acted as protector of the few timid Irishmen who entertained opinions and who dared to vote accordingly. Scanlan was among those who had left Ireland during the great famine. He was a poor boy, and in his distress "sought the nearest port in a storm." He went to England, and during his three-years residence there, had many a bloody encounter in defence of his nationality and his creed. When he came to Connecticut, he became "the hired man" at the seminary of Dr. Park, of Emmanuel Hall, in the vicinity of New Limerick. Under the generous guidance of Dr. Park, he became more American than the Americans. He called a public meeting at New Limerick on the night before election, and, in a brief address, he guaranteed protection to all Irishmen and others who proposed to vote the Republican ticket. On the morning of election he was approached by young Tony Devoy, who told him that there "would be hell all around the sky" if any Irishman attempted to vote the Republican ticket.

He quietly replied, "We will see," and, drawing a Republican ticket from his vest pocket, approached the polls and handed it to the judge of election.

"The name, please?"

"My name," he replied, "is Charles H. Scanlan. For ten years I've been told that I was a Democrat because I was an Irishman; to-day I am a Republican because I am an Irishman. My soul is my own. Let whomsoever will resort to the graveyard and the gutter. I vote as I please, and I please to vote the Republican ticket."

Old Barney Devoy and young Tony, with a severe looking crowd of their followers, approached him menacingly. He quietly retired from the polling place, calmly drew from his pocket a pair of revolvers, and, holding the weapons muzzle downward, addressed the crowd.

"Gentlemen," he said, "these are not concealed weapons. I expose them under the privilege that the right of the people to bear arms shall not be infringed. I believe that whatever an American citizen may lawfully do, he may do with perfect safety. Now, if any citizen wishes to vote according to his judgment and his conscience, let him approach the polls."

Jim Sullivan advanced with an open Republican ballot, and voted. American gentlemen opened wide a passage-way and smiled upon the modest looking youth with the armless sleeve.

Old Tom Sullivan came close behind his son, with a ballot in his hand. Young Tony Devoy seized him by the collar, and old Barney grasped him rudely by the arm.

"Whaat!" said old Barney; "Goin' back upon

yer blessed religion, votin' the abolishin ticket?"
And a crowd of the "heelers" surrounded him, as if
they would tear the old man to pieces. One of them
tore his ballot from his hand, and another placed a
Democratic ticket in the empty palm.

"Here's yer ticket—yer Democratic ticket."

Scanlan advanced to the center of the throng and
roared: "Stand back, gentlemen, stand back, or I'll
shoot the lining out of you!" and the crowd un-
handed old Sullivan and spread into a wide circle,
leaving Scanlan and the voter in the center; and the
old man advanced to the polling place and deposited
his Republican ballot.

Captain Jim Sullivan approached Mr. Scanlan and
thanked him for protecting, not his father, but the
right of free ballot; and there arose from the bystanders a vigorous cheer as the Sullivans, father and
son, and the protector of the ballot-box moved away
from the polls.

On the morning after election Colonel Hoggitt, a
famous Connecticut lawyer, was found upon the floor
of the James Buchanan Exchange, dead, as all the
bystanders supposed. There he remained; for the
body was too heavy for removal by ordinary hands.
He weighed three hundred pounds. He had been
in his day a famous criminal lawyer, very popular
among the Irish of Connecticut, but dissenting from
his Republican brethren on the question of saloon
control, he gradually gravitated to the Democracy.
In vindication of his newly-inspired doctrines he
became an habitue of the James Buchanan Exchange;
played seven-up with old Barney during the day, and
"took rooms" in a commodious old arm-chair in the
Exchange bar-room at night. On the night of election there was a terrible lightning storm, unaccom-
panied by rain. Young Tony Devoy, in closing the
bar-room at two o'clock in the morning, noticed that

the lightning flashes through the plate-glass windows of the Exchange illuminated the bar-room so that he could clearly see a stale tobacco-quid pasted against the wall in the remotest corner.

When young Tony opened the bar-room and saw the form of the old Colonel spread before him, his first impulse was to sweep it out, or kick it out, as he had kicked out many prostrate forms before ; but Colonel Hoggitt's body was too ponderous for broom or boot-toe, and so young Tony called a policeman. The policeman called the coroner, and that functionary, being a physician, soon discovered that Colonel Hoggitt was not dead, but merely stupefied, and the empty chloroform bottle beside him bore testimony to the medium of the stupefaction. The coroner noticed that the label had been removed by being wetted and rubbed, though traces of the paper still remained.

Inquiry proved that young Tony, on leaving the bar-room, had locked both doors, and had raised the blind upon the plate-glass window, so that the policeman in passing might easily look into the Exchange. Through the patient efforts of several physicians Colonel Hoggitt was at last restored to consciousness. He drew his soft hand, large as a ham of bacon, slowly over his ample stomach, and up to the region of his heart; then, rising from the chair, he muttered the single word: "Robbed." He had received on election day a thousand dollars in greenbacks for a piece of real estate, and to his discomfiture he discovered that wallet and greenbacks were gone.

Suspicion was at once directed to Tony Devoy, but neither Colonel Hoggitt nor the police officers would believe him guilty, though facts strongly argued his crimination; but his means, his character, and his appearance contradicted the suspicion that he was a sneak-thief.

The chief of police at last put in an appearance. Colonel Hoggitt was still resting in the chair. The chief pulled up the blind which had charitably concealed the colonel from the vulgar gaze of passers-by all morning. He noticed some figures on the window, as if a skillful hand had been doing the work of an artist on the glass with soap. He hastily pulled down the blind, and ordered the crowd out of the bar-room. He then summoned all of the members of the Devoy family—old Barney and Mrs. Devoy, Albert Michael, Birdelia and young Tony. He placed them in a group outside the window, and, asking their attention to the glass, hurriedly raised the blind.

Birdelia Devoy screamed; Mrs. Devoy fell fainting into Tony's arms; old Barney Devoy turned pale. There, plain, unmistakeable and indelible on the plate-glass window, was a photograph of Colonel Hoggitt in his chair, and in front of him the figure of young Francis Xavier Devoy, with a small bottle in one hand, held up to the Colonel's nose, and the other hand extracting the wallet from over the Colonel's heart. A flash of lightning had done the photographing—had registered the crime of Francis Xavier Devoy.

Colonel Hoggitt had been replaced in his chair after the coroner had decided not to hold an inquest upon his body, and now, during the conversation between the police officer and the Devoy family, the ponderous form moved uneasily in the chair.

"The Colonel needs a little air," said the chief, and with a stroke of his club he smashed the two-hundred-dollar plate-glass window.

The chief beckoned the family up stairs. Mrs. Devoy, overwhelmed with confusion and shame, lay down upon the sofa. Birdelia sat languidly in a rocking-chair; old Barney leant with a subdued looking aspect against the piano; while Albert

Michael, assuming an air of business, stood in the center of the parlor, facing the chief of police.

"Now, my friends," said the chief, "charity is charity, and business is business. Your son Francis has robbed Colonel Hoggitt. For the sake of Mrs. Devoy, his aged mother, and for the sake of Miss Birdelia, his charming sister; for the honor of the family; for mercy and for charity's sake, I am willing that the crime should go unpunished; but on one condition only: you must restore Colonel Hoggitt's money. I'll give you an hour to get the thousand dollars. You've got the means. Pay the Colonel his money without regard as to who committed the crime. You will thereby acquire a reputation for justice and generosity, and no questions will be asked. Fail in this, and I will have Francis Xavier in the meshes of the law before sundown. He has left the city, but I am on to him. He left in the caboose of a freight train at four o'clock this morning, for New York city, in company of Herman Levi, the drunken showman. I'm on to both of them."

Albert Michael Devoy was a man of business, and after a brief consultation with old Barney, the money was produced and laid upon the table.

"Will you hand it to the Colonel?" inquired Albert Michael.

"No, sir," responded the chief. "Your father is proprietor of the Exchange. The graceful and honorable thing will be to have the old man restore the Colonel's money upon the plain principle that he cheerfully restores the amount of the loss incurred at the hands of a robber upon the premises."

"But wouldn't this criminate the boy?" inquired Albert Michael.

"Not at all," said the chief. "The Devoy family belong to the church; are way up in business and politics; have the biggest kind of a pull with the powers that be; in short, are above suspicion."

"Yer head is level," said old Barney. "You're a business man and a gentleman," said Albert Michael.

Miss Birdelia bestowed a smile of gratitude upon the chief, as he started to leave the room, and Mrs. Devoy rewarded him with a blessing and a copious flow of grateful tears.

Old Barney descended to the bar-room, where Colonel Hoggitt was now enjoying his morning dram. Young Tony had secured a special glass for the Colonel's accommodation—a glass constructed upon the pattern of a champagne bottle whose bottom runs close up to the neck. The Colonel was addicted to filling any vessel placed before him, and young Tony always said that after filling the glass the Colonel, by an ingenious use of the fingers, "put an extension on it."

"Might I pershwade you, Colonel," said Mr. Devoy, "to take a little smile wid me this morning?"

The Colonel said he might.

"Be-gob," said young Tony in an undertone, "the Colonel is as aisily led as a child."

After expressions of mutual friendship and admiration on the part of the Colonel and the Irish leader, they drank heartily, and then Mr. Devoy proceeded to business.

"Colonel," he said, "you lost a thrifle o' change in my place of business last night. How much was it?"

"A cold thousand dollars."

"Are you sure?"

"When Hoggitt says its so—its so. Do you know anything about the money?"

"Here it is," said Devoy.

"That is a thousand dollars, sure enough," said the Colonel, "but it is not my money. Mine was all in large, new bills—fifties and hundreds—while this money is in small bills, greasy and finger-worn."

"Makes no difference," said Mr. Devoy; "with me 'tis a matter of conscience. You lost your money in my place, and there it is. Nayther you nor I know who took it, but I keep a dacent place, and no man shall suffer sich a loss upon my premises."

The Colonel treated all hands again and again, and walked away happily from the premises.

CHAPTER X.

A BASE CONSPIRACY.

THE chief of police was the blacksmith Peter McIntyre, known in Irish political circles as "Peter the Pagan." The Devoy family and the baser brood of Irishmen, who lived upon ward politics and its kindred infamies, entertained for him a relentless hatred, and they "showed their teeth" upon many an occasion, though "they feared to bite," and many of them who would injure him in secret if they could, met him from day to day with all the outward semblances of friendship.

He had an apparent disregard for things that were sacred to many of them. He was something of a mimic; he was bitter in his wit and irony, and his ridicule of the piety which robbed a drunken man on Saturday, while it posed in front pews upon Sunday, was exasperatingly offensive to the Devoys; but there was an undercurrent of charity that would shield the family, while it reached in justice down to the ill-gotten treasure of old Barney.

All manner of rumors became current as to the robbery at the Buchanan Exchange.

The report, as repeated by old Tom Sullivan, was that "Hoggitt had committed shoe-aside," while Miss Victoria O'Toole pronounced it "Susan-side," and Pete McIntyre quietly observed that "the distinguished lawyer had merely suffered hemorrhage of the bowels in his head." Others had heard that the Colonel had robbed old Barney; and others still, putting together isolated facts and probabilities, arrived at the more probable conclusion that old Barney had murdered the Colonel.

But the New York evening papers reduced the story to reasonable certainty, and one of the reporters for a city morning paper came upon the ground to investigate and report the particulars in full. He first became impressed by the fact that no arrest had been made; that the police were making no inquiry; that the plate-glass window had been broken accidentally by the chief of police (it was not broken by the robber, for hundreds had seen it whole and sound late in the forenoon). He interviewed Barney and Tony at the Exchange.

"Who was the person that closed the saloon?"

"I it was," said Tony.

"Who, if any person, except Colonel Hoggitt, did you leave in the Exchange when you closed it?"

"No one but the Colonel."

"Did you lock both doors?"

"I did."

"There are no windows susceptible of being lowered or raised in the Exchange?"

"No, sir."

"Where was the key of the saloon this morning?"

"In my pocket, where it usually is."

"Does any person except yourself occupy your sleeping room?"

Old Barney raised his forefinger to his lip—a signal of silence for Tony; and the younger Devoy responsively hesitated.

"You have a brother called Frank?" said the reporter.

"Yes, a boy called Francis Xavier—the flower of the family, me religious boy," said Barney.

" He slept in Tony's room last night—he did or he did'nt?" said the reporter; "fix it either way—which will you have, he did or he didn't? Where was he last night, and where is he to-day?"

" He retired early last night, as usual," said Barney, "in the room wid Tony afther his evening devotions; and to-day, like every other day, he is down in the woods, engaged in his meditations."

The morning paper represented by this inquisitive reporter gave a very full and graphic account of the robbery, with biographical sketches of the Irish leader and his pious son, and in express terms charged Francis Xavier as the robber. The report added that the story of the plate-glass window being broken and torn out by an accidental contact with the police officer's club was a "fake," pure and simple; and charged the officer as an accessory after the fact, who covered some evidence of the crime by breaking the window.

Francis Xavier spent a day and a night, under cover, with Mr. Isaac Marx, a wholesaler, who supplied the goods for the Buchanan Exchange, and who resided somewhere in the vicinity of Chatham Square, New York; and he then left for parts unknown. It was noticed that soon afterward the Devoy family mailed an occasional letter to one " Timothy Devereux," at Bloody Gulch, in the Territory of Arizona; but the pious face of the ecclesiastical student had vanished from New Limerick.

Peter McIntyre, now chief of police, was in heart

and spirit a religious man. He gave in quiet charity more than his share to the deserving poor; he contributed to every church in New Limerick, including his own; he was a patron of the parochial school, and an intimate friend of Father Ventura. It was known that he had taken the best coat he owned and put it upon the back of an unworthy tramp. "To be poor and worthy," he used to say, "is bad enough; but when a wretch is poor and unworthy, he is indeed an object of charity."

Between himself and the Devoys there existed a natural antipathy. Old Barney declared that hell was not hot enough to scathe, nor deep enough to hide a ruffian who would go back upon the faith by votin' the Republican ticket, as Peter did; and Peter, from his standpoint of reason, asserted that "until the church could master sufficient courage to purge itself of its 'Barney Devoys' in conspicuous places, decent and patriotic men would desert it much faster than ships would carry over new recruits."

On the Sunday morning succeeding the robbery at the Exchange, McIntyre went to mass. On entering the vestibule he heard the melodious voice of Birdelia in the choir; he saw Albert Michael occupying the post of financial cerberus at the door; but overlooking these obstacles to devotion, he entered and knelt behind the last pew in the sacred edifice; but when old Barney entered and uncovered his villainous looking head, and prostrated himself in front of the altar-rail before taking his seat in the purple cushioned pew, the "Pagan" bolted and knelt in a nook of the vestibule so as to conceal the interior of the church from view. After a moment's reflection there, he retired to the chapel-yard, and, kneeling under a shady maple, offered up the Lord's prayer and the *Confeteor Deo* in a spirit of heart-felt devotion, and retired over the rear fence of the church inclosure. He never afterward went to church in New Limerick, though he regularly paid his church dues, and was sometimes discovered in quiet places with the beads in his hands, devoutly repeating his *paters* and *aves*. When Father Ventura urged him to attend at mass, he would reply :

"No, father; so long as the Devoys lead in politics and religion at the same time, I'll never enter a church door. The Devoys, all over the country, are sending my people to death and disgrace and perdition ; while the church, tolerating such men in its front pews, lends them the calcimine of character and enables them to pose in politics as representatives of our race. That they rule and rob is not the greatest evil. The crowning disgrace is that they are forever making a trade of their Irish, to the scandal and disadvantage of the virtuous millions of our people, who share the disgrace, while they do not share the plunder. No, father; if I were old Barney Devoy, and tried as he tries to lie to the living God, I would expect lightning to strike me dead in the pew. Neither could I indulge in the mockery of worship under the same roof with him."

The Devoys resolved to crush the "Pagan ;" and to aid them in their scheme for that purpose, they summoned to their councils Mr. Isaac Marx of New York City. He was a friend of the Devoys, for whom Peter the Pagan entertained a feeling of horror and loathing.

"Joost wait—you joost wait; I fix him," said Isaac.

And so, when Isaac was summoned to the council-board to devise measures for the ruin of the "Pagan," a fiendish fire lighted up his eye, he rubbed his hands with vigor, laughed and laughed his cruel laugh, and said :

"Vell, vell, vell! vait—you joost vait."

Albert Michael's plan was to work some scheme by which the "Pagan" could be convicted of forgery.

Old Barney would make the crime burglary, because Peter was a blacksmith, accustomed to tools and keys; and tools and keys could be disposed so as to aid in convicting him of such a crime.

Isaac here inquired for the exact truth as to the "Pagan's" character for honesty. Albert Michael replied that he was an honest man, a man of some means, a good debt-payer, economical and sober, and above suspicion in the eyes of the public.

"Then," said Isaac, "forgery or burglary vill neffer do. Iss he a married man?"

"No, single," said Barney, "but engaged to be married to Maggie Sullivan, the milliner, ould Tom Sullivan's daughter; and Barney reflectively spelled the hated name: "S-u, soo, l-u, loo, v-a-n, van—Sullivan."

Isaac suggested that he would befoul his character as to social purity; that burglary, forgery, manslaughter, or such crimes of dishonesty or violence were not necessarily fatal to the man's success in local politics; but some foul accusation, no matter how baseless, as to his gallantry, would certainty damn him among his own people.

"Correct," said Albert Michael; "that is the way to do it. At a single stroke you can kill the Pagan's character and humble the pride of the Sullivans. You can kill two birds with one stone. You will cover his mother and sisters with shame and sorrow, and get even wid him for the thousand dollars." And a cruel light appeared in old Barney's eyes; and Albert Michael rolled back the scanty covering from his ponderous teeth as he assumed one of his diabolical smiles.

They opened another bottle of New Jersey champagne and lit their Connecticut Havanas, and drank confusion to Peter the Pagan, to the Republican party, and the whole machinery of liberty and law.

CHAPTER XI.

REVENGE AND A RUINED MAN.

ABOUT a week after the conference held between the Devoy family and Isaac Marx, a certain man and woman took rooms at the Clifton House, a second-class hotel, where Peter the Pagan boarded. The couple registered under the name of "Herman Levi and wife, Philadelphia." The man was of powerful build, two or three-and-twenty years of age, of very dark complexion, with a foreign accent to his speech, and with an eye whose artful and labored smile only half concealed the numerous devils peering out from the "window of his soul." The woman was by many years his senior; nor did her highly colored robes, nor her lavish application of paints and cosmetics, completely obliterate the traces of age and infamy.

These people occupied apartments adjacent to the sleeping room of Peter the Pagan. During their stay, Mr. Isaac Marx came on a business mission from New York, and also occupied a room upon the same floor of the Clifton House.

It was midnight. The peaceful people of New Limerick were at rest. The streets were deserted, save that a solitary carriage stood in front of the Clifton House. Herman Levi and wife, having previously paid their bill, descended the hotel stairs soon after midnight, hastily entered the carriage, and were driven at a gallop out of town. Meanwhile there was great excitement up-stairs in the hotel. A dozen guests with lighted candles stood outside the door of Peter the Pagan, while inside the door lay Peter's body, apparently insensible. The other guests had been aroused by the sound of a blow delivered upon

Peter's head, by his sudden and heavy fall, and by the hasty retreat of his assailant. Mr. Marx was the first to reach the scene of the assault; but though he said he had heard the retreating steps, he did not see the guilty party. A rusty old navy revolver, whose usefulness as a firearm had passed, was found in the hallway; the door of Herman Levi's apartment was wide open. The Levis had hastily fled, so that the spectators reasonably and properly concluded that the deadly assault was committed by a revolver, clubbed in the hand of Mr. Levi. When the Pagan recovered consciousness, he was utterly unable to say who assaulted him. He only knew that as he was entering his door somebody in the darkness felled him with a heavy metallic weapon.

But an incident so mysterious to every person at the hotel, and even to the victim himself, was made perfectly plain, tangible, logical and intelligent to all patrons and visitors at the saloon of Barney Devoy next morning.

A scandalous story was invented—Peter the Pagan was pilloried for his alleged gallantry; and the mysterious stranger Levi was glorified for defending his wounded honor.

The theory took wings, flew to every Irish household in New Limerick, accumulated additional details in its flight, so that before night, at the bar of Irish public opinion, the blacksmith and chief of police was a doomed and a ruined man, convicted without a particle of evidence that would justify a conscientious suspicion.

A surgeon had been summoned to examine and dress the "Pagan's" wound. He discovered a deep cut in the head, and also believed that there was a slight abrasion of the skull. He dressed the wound, administered a little opium, and the patient went to sleep.

Maggie Sullivan, and the whole Sullivan family, were overwhelmed with sorrow, while the "Pagan's" mother and sister were stricken with grief and shame. The "Pagan" was confined to his room for a few days only; because the wound, though severe, was not considered dangerous. Gradually it healed, the hair again grew and covered it; but beneath the re-united skin and the new growth of hair there remained a constant pain, an incessant throbbing of the brain. This, it was said, would pass away; but it did not pass away. It increased into agony and torture.

The "Pagan" re-appeared upon the street, and vainly endeavored to attend to business. Except a very few of his most intimate friends, nobody asked him any questions as to the scandal and misfortune; and to these dear friends he invariably replied that they knew just as much about it as he did. But the mayor of the town, one who had risen as the scum upon "the seething pot of politics," was very active in creating the worst possible opinions, and the little political parasites looked into the "Pagan's" eyes with bitter cruelty, and decent men and women gazed upon him with a look of pity that was to him far more torturing than the hateful glances of his ene-mies, and intimate friends took him kindly by the hand and gave him assurances of continued sympathy and confidence. To all of these people he mani-fested a spirit of indifference. To their disappoint-ment, he neither apo'ogized nor exp'ained. He occasionally smiled, and even joked, as of old; but, while he smiled upon the multitude, his brain was on fire, and his heart was breaking. For himself he did not particularly care; but he had a sweetheart who was his betrothed, and a pious mother and vir-tuous unmarried sisters. There are heroic hearts that sink by slow decay, while they give no outward sign; there are spirits that break, but never bend;

and such were the heart and the spirit of the "Pagan." Gradually the hair above his temples showed streaks of gray. He shunned his old associates, and kept within his room, or wandered in the fields, in their most secluded places. To all he became sullen and uncommunicative.

"And the spirit was broken that never would bend."

Within three months from the date of his misfortune the "Pagan" was a melancholy maniac.

Dr. Barry, the surgeon of the Sisters' Hospital at New York, who was a specialist in such cases, was called to his relief. His malady showed no particular delusion. He simply manifested an immoveable melancholy, with constant and pitiable sobs and sighs.

The public said that "his brain had been turned;" and this vulgar opinion was shared by the local surgeon who attended him. This worthy but ill-informed gentleman spoke of insanity as a disease. To this suggestion Dr. Barry replied:

"My dear sir, insanity is not a disease, but the visible manifestation, the outward indication of a disease. The disease itself is somewhere in the brain."

Dr. Barry's inquiry led to the information that the wound had been inflicted by the heavy revolver, and the "indentation," so called, had been made by that triangular contrivance beneath and behind the muzzle that holds in place the ram-rod of the weapon. Barry caused the scalp over the wound to be shaved, and with a lance he quickly re-opened the site of the wound. Probing for the indentation, he discovered that a slight fracture had been made, and that a fragment of the skull, scarcely one-tenth of an inch in diameter, had become imbedded in the brain, causing a slight mortification in that organ. The fragment of skull and the dead and festering matter surrounding it were skillfully removed, and by careful treatment the healthy condition of the brain and the reason of the patient were restored. Slowly he returned to the pursuit of his business affairs; time removed the physical anguish from his head, but his heart was lacerated, and to heal that organ, time seemed wholly ineffectual. Gradually public opinion turned in his favor, and the probable truth dawned upon the minds of all well-disposed persons, but time brought him no consolation. He closed his affairs, sold his shop, and left for—God knows where.

Many and many a year Maggie Sullivan mourned for him, and the tree of his memory, scorched and blasted to the senses of his enemies, to her mental vision was ever green.

She had felt the beating of his heart, and though he never ventured to vindicate himself with her, though he did not even bid her a parting good-bye, she still cherished his conduct and his memory as she knew them; and though many opportunities were afforded her to become a bride, she continued to live a maid.

CHAPTER XII.

AN IRISH-AMERICAN LAWYER.

JIM Sullivan, having completed his law studies at Columbia College, returned to New Limerick, and "hung out his shingle," as the saying goes. His business at first consisted chiefly in drawing simple contracts, making small collections, and attending to probate matters. None of the old neighbors would trust him with the trial of law-suits until he had fairly demonstrated his capacity for that kind of work, and when his abilities were generally recognized and rewarded, and when he had passed the necessity of Irish patronage, then the old neighbors came to "patronise" him.

One morning he was honored with a visit from Albert Michael Devoy, who desired to sue one Tim Finneran on a promissory note which the said Tim had executed to the aforesaid Albert Michael. The face of the note was for one hundred dollars, and the accrued interest amounted to five dollars. The consideration originally was a bar bill at the Buchanan Exchange, amounting to sixty-five dollars, and under pressure of Barney's anathemas, Tim Finneran had sought relief at the hands of the *gombeen man* (which is the Irish term for usurer), and Albert Michael "accommodated" the distressed creditor of the Exchange by taking Finneran's note for one hundred dollars and handing him sixty-five dollars. To secure the note, the debtor gave the *gombeen man* a bill of sale upon his live stock, consisting of two cows, six pigs, a blind mule, and a lot of chickens. This contract Mr. Devoy desired Captain Sullivan to enforce.

"Mr. Devoy," said the attorney, "in view of the facts and circumstances of your case as stated by yourself, I wish to be excused from the employment which you are so kind as to offer me."

"And why, please, Captain?" inquired the *gombeen man;* "isn't a bargain a bargain? Haven't I a right to my money as conditioned in the note?"

"Mr. Devoy," said the attorney, "I have no desire to discuss the legal or moral questions involved in your case. I simply beg to be excused."

"D'ye mean to say," said Albert Michael, "that its chatin' I am? If that's what you mane, out wid it."

"I haven't said anything of the kind, but since you have driven me to it, I will be plain with you. The law makes fine distinctions in criminal cases, and there are criminal acts for which the criminal law provides no punishment; but from a moral standpoint there is little difference between picking a man's pocket and robbing him under your polite and gentlemanly system. It can make little difference to your victim whether you rob him by the vulgar methods of a professional thief, or obtain his money under your blood-letting system of usury. I give you my word of honor, sir, that I would just as soon share the plunder of a thief as take a retainer from you in the case you have submitted. Now, sir, let this be the end of the controversy; no offense intended; let me bid you a kind good-morning."

"Enough said, sir;" said Albert Michael, "you will hear from me again. I'll show you whether you can insult a gentleman."

Within a hour after this conversation had taken place, it was rumored at the Buchanan Exchange that Tim Finneran, in anticipation of the law-suit indicated, had bought (Irish for bribed) lawyer Sullivan by a promise to present him with the old blind mule. This story was the subject of much hilarity among the members of the bar, and among the respectable citizens generally.

Mr. Cheney observed that "an effort on the part of Mr. Devoy's retainers to thus befoul a man like Captain Sullivan, reminded him of a drove of village curs turned loose upon an African lion."

But a result of the incident was that the Captain thenceforth refused the patronage of his countrymen. He would espouse the cause of a widow or an orphan, or collect the just claims of the worthy poor from wealthy corporations, but in such cases he declined to receive compensation. He succeeded beyond his brightest anticipations, and soon enjoyed a lucrative practice; and while his business came almost exclusively from Americans, he yet cheerfully bore every just obligation demanded of him as an Irishman. He delivered their Patrick's-day speeches, and spent his money at their church fairs, contributed to their parish school, and was foremost in the many works of charity and mercy proposed by Father Ventura. But when it was proposed at an Irish meeting to make Albert Michael Devoy a member of the public school board, for the avowed purpose of seeking a division of the school fund, he denounced the scheme in the most vigorous terms.

"I have no patience with you," he exclaimed. "I can overlook with sorrow your folly and ingratitude in the unclean work of ward politics, but your present proposition is worse than folly. It is madness. The people of this Nation are merciful and patient; but there is such a thing as provoking them too far. The public school is the apple of the American eye, and God help you if you should excite the just wrath of the American people in regard to their most cherished institution. You talk about taxation for school purposes. Why, have ye no reason at all? Doesn't a certain wealthy American in New Limerick pay in taxes for the education of a hundred of your children? If ye must have separate schools, buy them. I am heartily with you for separate schools if you want them, and will go down in my jeans to assist you; but you must keep your hands off the public school. A curse upon the pious knaves and idiots responsible for leading you in this madness!"

And so effective was this appeal that Albert Michael's candidacy "died in the bornin'," and the more thoughtful and patriotic Irishmen in the audience became permanently converted to Captain Sullivan's view on this subject; but it added fresh fuel to the flames of hatred burning in the bosoms of the Devoys.

Lawyer Sullivan was a welcome guest at the homes

of the very best of the Yankee citizens. His empty sleeve, instead of disfiguring him, added a glory and a charm to the man—if we may indulge the paradox that a man may have anything added by the process of subtraction; but so it was, and so it is. There is something almost God-like in every affliction resulting from exalted human sacrifice. He was especially welcome at the home of the Cheney family, and though no word of mutual love in express terms had ever passed between him and Laura Cheney, there was unmistakeably a mutual understanding, not simply tolerated, but evidently encouraged by her parents. She sang for him during his winter evening visits, and by way of compliment to his nationality, she took especial delight in rendering the exquisite melodies of Moore, and other beautiful Irish airs, and on his invitation she assisted the choir of Father Ventura's church upon extraordinary occasions. Often the subject of religious differences naturally arose, and usually terminated in a compromise.

"The difference, Miss Cheney, between your faith and mine, is that I believe a little more than you do; that is to say, you believe something less than I do; but every positive truth in the body of your religion is found floating on the surface of mine;" and he followed up this suggestion with explanations, dispelling her erroneous impressions, and convincing her that, after all, between sincere Christians of different churches, the difference is not so wide as is commonly supposed.

The Sullivan family, by the sale of the old orchard, were now in very comfortable circumstances. Old Tom having washed away the smoke and dust of toil, and donned a suit of substantial American cloth, presented a very neat appearance; and all that he lacked in refinement, he fully made up in the gentleness and simplicity of his manners. He was loyal to the heart's core in his love for America, its people and its institutions, and this was all that they demanded in return for their friendship and affection for him.

Mary Sullivan was a teacher at the high school, and Maggie conducted a prosperous millinery business. Captain Sullivan was proud of his venerable father and his charming sisters, and this avowed pride attracted to him additional respect from the American people. But much as we love to contemplate the lives and characters of this estimable Sullivan family, we are compelled to turn to other lives and characters.

Tom Sullivan lived to a ripe old age; was buried with the rites and ceremonies of his ancient faith; a solid but simple tomb in the grave-yard of New Limerick marks his mortal final resting place; and beside that tomb the sojourner to the cemetery has frequently seen a strong, noble-looking, manly man, with an empty sleeve, kneeling in silent prayer.

Captain James Sullivan became popular with his own people, despite the most potent efforts that malice and ignorance leveled against him. He married Laura Cheney, and at her father's death shared her ample fortune.

But, considering the broad extent and the broader possibilities of the great Republic, he naturally sought a wider and more congenial field for his energies than New Limerick and its vicinage afforded. He found a home in a greater State. Sons and daughters were born for him, inheriting his vigorous frame, and lofty character, and the sweet face and temper of their lovely and loving mother. He was deeply devoted to his profession, and in its line rose to well-won distinction. For many years he entertained, in common with thousands of worthy citizens, an aversion for what is commonly called politics. But when wealth brought him leisure, and afforded him time for reflection, he turned his attention to politics, and its exalted sense, and though steadily declining public office, he devoted the energies of a well-stored mind to what he termed "the creation and fostering of a sound and honest public opinion." He was an ardent lover and persistent hater, and there were two leading articles in his political creed: He loved America with the ardor of a dutiful son for a generous mother; he hated England, not with barbaric and revengeful hate, but with the enlightened hatred that sees in her ascendency conquest, rapine and cruelty, and in her flag the symbol of desecration, selfishness and blood. He devoted much of his leisure hours to a study of her free-trade policy, and in after years, when the great question in American politics became, whether England or America should control the manufacturing and commercial destinies of America, it is needless to state that Captain Sullivan was an ardent champion of American political ascendancy.

CHAPTER XIII.

RULE BRITANNIA.

ENGLAND never had such other faithful subjects as the Irish famine exiles.

While the Devoy family loyally upheld her free-trade banner in Connecticut, another contingent of their generation was shedding upon the British name the glory of military triumph in the Crimea.

On the 21st day of September, 1854, a party of

British soldiers, burying the dead upon the battle-field of Alma, found among the slain one soldier whose feeble moan gave testimony that he was not quite dead. He was covered with the crimson stains of battle, and his face was horribly blood-bespattered and mutilated. They raised him tenderly; for the brave respect the brave. A fragment of a Russian shell had torn out his eyes and a portion of the left cheek-bone. He was still breathing, but the burial party debated among themselves as to whether he had sufficient life to be counted among the living, or whether it would be good military economy to carry him from the field.

"This man is not a soldier," said one of the party. "See, he is without a coat. He must be one of the civil employes from the slaughtering pens. Look at the meat axe."

"Yes, he is a soldier," said another, "and well worthy of the name. I saw him as he entered the battle yesterday. He was with our battalion as we waded the Alma River and charged the Russians up the heights."

"Well," said the first speaker, "but where's his uniform, and how comes that meat axe there?"

"The wounded man," said the other, "is Private John Dillon of the Eighty-seventh Foot—the regimental butcher. As we passed the slaughtering pens on the double-quick yesterday, he was engaged killing sheep. I saw him jump across the inclosure without his coat, but he carried that meat axe in his hand, and an old black pipe, lighted, in his mouth. Bloody into my eyes, if there isn't that old *dudeen!*"—and sure enough, the venerable short clay pipe lay beside the body of the wounded man.

"Pick him up, men, and take him to the field hospital," the sergeant ordered, and his gallant comrades bore him off the field.

In the Dublin daily papers, containing a report of the battle of Alma, among the "mortally wounded" appeared the name of John Dillon, private of the Eighty-seventh Foot. The autumn and winter passed away; and as no letter was received from Dillon, from him who had so regularly written, his wife presumed him dead.

"Surely," she reasoned, "if John were living I would hear from him. Sure, he never failed to write me upon pay days. Didn't he even write letters on pieces of brown paper picked up in the trenches, when he couldn't get letter paper to write upon, and didn't he send me a trifle of money monthly as regular as the watch? God rest his soul."

There were now two children in the family—Andy, ten years old, and little Kathleen, born three months after her father's enlistment; a child whom the soldier had never seen, and whom he was destined never to see. In the cheerless cabin of the family, night and morning during the winter, mother and children joined fervently in their prayers for the repose of the father's soul, and in the village chapel a mass was offered by Father Joseph Lenehan for the same pious purpose.

* * *

In the summer of 1856, in the town of Erinbeg —the birthplace of the Dillons and Devoys—Mrs. Mary Dillon, looking from her cabin door in the direction of the public square, saw a crowd of the townsfolk coming down the street. There was something unusual going on. There were shouts of joy and clapping of hands, and children were romping as if at play, and the dogs even delightedly joined the procession with their "glad to see you" and "how d'ye do's." Older people seemed excited, and at every few steps some one would rush up and bring the procession to a halt. Mrs. Dillon at last discerned her own two children at the head of the procession, leading a tall stranger, who appeared to be blind; and Mrs. Dillon, after closely scrutinizing the stranger, passionately embraced him.

"Oh, John, *acushla macree!* tis you, my own, my long lost husband, my children's father—ye are not dead!"

It was indeed John Dillon—but how changed! The raven locks were turned to iron gray; the strong hand was now shriveled, nerveless and feeble; and the glorious grey-blue eyes, that melted in pity at the sight of suffering, or flashed fire at the mention of his country's wrongs, were gone—forever gone.

An opulent government compensated him with a pension of eighteen pence a day, and the tottering ruin of a once glorious manhood lived once again beneath the thatched roof under which himself and his children were born.

Poor John Dillon became an object of interest and of pity to all the surrounding country. Around his hearth-stone on winter nights, the youth of the village would assemble and listen to the story of his glory and his misfortune. He wou'd occasionally whistle some inspiring marching tune like the "British Grenadiers," or sing a verse of the "Flag that Braved." On summer nights he could be seen seated on the rude bench beside his door, pensively gazing heavenward, as if the sightless sockets were not dead and indifferent to the glorious full moon that gazed in pity upon him now, as it smiled into his manly face in the blessed years gone by, ere the famine came, and he had sought bread and fame in the ranks of the British army. His little Andy gradually became a man, and when he had secured such limited education as the family's slender means and the local schools afforded, he added to the family resources by working when he could as a *spalpeen*, or common laborer.

Agriculture was the only industry—there were neither mills, nor mines, nor factories. The hides and pelts, the wool and flax were exported regularly to England; the wheat and oats, the butter and eggs were sold to pay the landlord, and the men, women and children who toiled through the spring, summer and autumn, lived through the winter upon cornmeal, potatoes and milk, and shivered in cotton and corduroys. The limpid stream that rose in the adjacent hills, and which in former times had turned the great wheels of the woolen and of the linen mills, now rushed on unimpeded and unpolluted to the sea. The wheels were silent, and the spindles still. English manufacturers, under the existing free-trade system, flooded the country with cheap merchandise, and finally bought and destroyed the machinery of the mills.

Andy Dillon for many years had been a familiar figure in the labor market, and the ten pence or the shilling which he received for a hard day's labor had kept the wolf from the door of his mother and sister. Now that his father was the recipient of an army pension, the youth considered himself relieved. One morning he went as usual to the corner of the public square, spade in hand, and was accosted by the principal employer of the village, a gentleman named Mickey Shanley. This village tyrant was what was known as a *shoneen;* a little more affluent than a farmer, a little less respectable than a landlord. He was a middleman, a renter of farms, a grinder of labor, an oppressor of the poor.

"Dillon," he said, "I have kep' you a good long time, gave you work for charity's sake. Yer father is home wid his pinshun. I have always paid you eight pence and ten pence a day. You're a good boy, and I want to patronize ye; but all ye'll get is six pence a day."

"To the devil wid yerself and yer sixpence!" said the youth; "and it's for charity you employ me? While my mother and sister depended on me I was at yer mercy; but now I'm free. By heaven!" he added, "I'd rather die a dog's death, and be buried in the old grave-yard on the other side of the square, than give you a full day's work for a half day's pay, and still be an object of yer charity."

He broke his spade upon the curbstone, and in another hour was traveling in the footsteps of his father, on the road to Athlone, the depot of the Sixteenth Regiment, a candidate for pay and glory in the British army.

CHAPTER XIV.

IN FENIAN TIMES.

SEVENTEEN years had come and gone since the famine exiles had left their island home, with tears in their eyes and curses on their lips, but conditions were little changed. The upper and nether millstones of English rule in Ireland kept grinding human hearts, and the grist of emigration resulted. The life-blood of the ancient nation was being drained at the rate of a million human beings a decade, and the stream of life that flowed across the Atlantic for seventy years was again accelerated. The "Cinderella of the nations," bruised and bleeding in 1848, was quickened into life by the Fenian conspiracy, and Ireland once again, with all her feeble strength, rose up to grapple with the armed power of the British empire.

Thirty thousand armed men, in the service of England, marched and counter-marched through the island, ready to quench in blood any attempted insurrection on the part of the "sister island." Order once more reigned in Warsaw, and England governed Ireland with thirty thousand bayonets.

A battalion of the Sixteenth Infantry, Andy Dillon's regiment, entered the town of Erinbeg. Their band played "The Girl I Left Behind Me," and when the strains of instrumental music had ceased, the leading company broke forth in song, and company after company joined in the chorus until the wooded hills echoed and re-echoed:

"My heart nigh broke when I answered 'No!'
To the girl I left behind me."

There were Englishmen and Scotchmen in the command, and with equal fervor with the Irishmen, the soldiers from the Thames and the Clyde, each doubtless animated by loving memories of a distant maiden in his own land, entered fully into the spirit of the soul-inspiring song.

The command marched past the ruins of an ancient abbey, under the shade of the ancestral elms in the court-yard of the village inn, to an open square, in whose center was a large spring well, protected by a rude stone building. On one side of the square, inclosed by a moss-covered stone wall, and shaded by ancient massive trees, stood the Episcopal church, with its grave-yard. The sacred and venerable edifice was built and occupied, before the days of the Reformation, as a Catholic chapel, but had been adopted by the English settlers under sanction of English law, and had sheltered the faithful of the "established church" for more than two hundred years. On one side of the graveled road-way that led from the iron gate to the main entrance lay the last resting-place of the Episcopalian dead, with ample space, under plain tomb-stones or elegant monuments; while an equal space upon the other side of the graveled road was generously allotted to the Catholics, and consecrated for the burial of their dead.

In this limited space had been deposited the remains of fifteen different generations, and such was the dearth of land that, when certain families interred a departed member, the coffins of those who had gone before were temporarily raised from their narrow beds, so that the grave might be dug more deeply to make room for the new-made coffin. At one corner of the church enclosure stood the little "national school," with its three score of boys and girls, enjoying the privilege of an education—a privilege which had been denied to their fathers, and the acquirement of which was in the days of their grandfathers a felony by English law.

Upon another side of the square stood a massive stone building. Its great oaken doors were closed, many of its windows were broken, swallows built their nests beneath its crumbling eaves, and ravens, bats, and wild pigeons disported themselves in the topmost story and upon its roof. This massive ruin was the same old factory building that had been used as an hospital in 1847. Before the doors of this building the British Lieutenant-Colonel gave the command to halt, and within its ample walls the contingent of the invading army found quarters for the day and night.

When Private Andy Dillon was relieved from duty, in the company of a comrade, he hurried to the home of his father. It was evening, and in the uncertain light he saw two men sitting upon the stone bench beside his father's door. One of these, on close observation, appeared to be what he was—an old man, wrinkled and gray and blind. It was John Dillon, the blind pensioner. The other was Sam Timms, the policeman who made occasional visits as the lover of Kathleen Dillon, the old man's daughter, and sister of Andy Dillon, private of the Sixteenth Foot.

Andy Dillon was member of a so dierly family, himself a soldier of fortune. Though he devoutly hated the government he served, there was one other object that he hated with more burning intensity. This object sat before him in the person and uniform of an Irish policeman. Dillon had just enough liquor in him to arouse his slumbering hatred, and on seeing the policeman sitting beside his father, the young soldier hastily grabbed the close-fitting collar of the peeler, lifted him bodily from the bench, and kicked him violently in the rear. "Get out," he said, "you miserable whelp! A peeler is no company for soldiers."

The irate officer, deeming discretion the better part of valor, did not undertake to defend himself, but strode away, uttering between his teeth: "Dillon, you'll be sorry for this."

Timms made a forced march to the police barracks for reinforcements, and in fifteen minutes a squad of policemen, seven in number, under command of a sergeant, were on their march to the cabin of the blind pensioner. They did not reach the cabin. A very trifling affair interposed, and caused a diversion. In front of a saw-pit, a solitary member of her majesty's Irish constabulary was engaged in a hand-to-hand encounter with a woman, and to this unpretending theater of war all eyes and steps were suddenly turned. Bessie Johnstone, a camp-follower of the Sixteenth Foot, was engaged in mortal combat with a peeler. Bessie was somewhat intoxicated, and while in that condition fell under the observation of the officer. She was not unaccustomed to the attentions of the police, and with true military instinct she prepared to offer resistance. She was in a crouching position as the peeler approached her, and as he seized her rudely by the shoulder, she disengaged his grasp by a sudden jerk, and struck him a blow with an improvised "slungshot," consisting of a stone tightly twisted into a large red handkerchief. He fell as an ox might fall under the well-directed blow of a butcher in a slaughter house, and the unfortunate woman was bracing herself for a renewal of the murderous assault, when the squad from the barracks came to his rescue. Bessie was soon overpowered and tightly grasped by two policemen. By this time some twenty soldiers had been attracted to the spot from the old factory building, and proceeded, according to their general custom in those days, to rescue the woman from the hands of the police. The soldiers used as weapons their leathern pipe-clayed belts, with the heavy brass buckles of the period. The peelers defended themselves with their long heavy batons. The fight was "quick, sharp and decisive." The policemen beat a hasty retreat amid the jeers of the populace, which had now assembled in force, leaving behind them the unfortunate woman as a trophy in the hands of the red-coats. This military melee so diverted the police that Andy Dillon was not arrested that evening. The assembled crowd cheered vigorously for the victorious soldiers, and as vigorously jeered and hooted the police. The policeman has ever been the object of hatred and loathing to the masses of the people. 'Tis his duty to perpetrate upon them a great many injuries and injustices. He will insinuate himself into the confidence of young men, and at the first opportunity betray them; he would meet harmless, well-meaning peasants leaving town slightly intoxicated and goad them into some thoughtless expression, and swear before a magistrate next morning that they were drunk and disorderly. It was his duty to impound the poor man's pig that strayed upon the highway, and wring a fine from the impoverished owner. It was his privilege to indulge in petty oppressions, and his chances of promotion were commensurate with the baseness of his conduct and character in pursuance of his duty. Himself the son of some poor Irishman, he became the pampered enemy of his country and his countrymen; and despite his titles, his emoluments and his airs, he was an Ishmaelite in his own land, with his hand against every man, and every man's hand against him.

Private Andy Dillon remained for the night at the cabin of his father, but his deep sleep was broken at the dawn of the succeeding morning. The house was surrounded by a squad of police, and before sunrise young Dillon was in a cell at the police barracks, on a charge of assaulting Sub-constable Samuel Timms. By nine o'clock he had had his trial before a local magistrate, and, in default of a fine, was sentenced to the county jail for fifteen days; but he did not go to jail. On his return from the magistrate to the police barracks, himself and the two policemen who conducted him were met by a force of his comrade soldiers, upon whose approach one peeler jumped across the ditch to the right of the road, and another scaled the low stone wall to the left, leaving Private Dillon in the hands of his soldier friends. His rescue was not prompted by any desire to avoid the trifling fine, nor to escape a brief jail sentence, but to baffle the malignity of Policeman Timms, who had in store for Dillon a severer vengeance.

Andy Dillon carried under the scarlet uniform of England a heart that was loyal to Ireland; and, indeed, his politics might at that time have been summed up in a single phrase: Hatred of English government. As child and boy he was a person of superior intelligence. He had in his boyhood been a day scholar at the seminary in Erinbeg, where Protestant youths of the aristocratic class received their academic training. He was a Fenian, and had "sworn in" many of the aristocratic youth as members of the Fenian conspiracy. Conviction for the treasonable act of "swearing them in" would mean for Dillon a life-sentence in an English prison, and it was this that Policeman Sam Timms had in mind, when in front of old John Dillon's cottage, on the preceding evening, he had warned young Andy—"You will be sorry for this."

But there were even among the Irish police some few, at least, who were not to be depended on in the service of England against their own country. It was intended that Dillon, at the expiration of his jail sentence for the assault, should be arrested on a charge of treason-felony, but a loyal Irishman revealed the scheme to Dillon's father, who in turn communicated it to the soldiers, which led to the rescue of Dillon from the custody of the two policemen.

CHAPTER XV.

AN EPISCOPALIAN FRIEND.

ON the afternoon of the same day upon which occurred the events related in the preceding chapter, the soldiers of the battalion of the Sixteenth Foot marched out of the town of Erinbeg. The Scotchmen of the command led off in song, and the others joined in the chorus. This time it was: "The Campbells are Coming."

Later in the afternoon, on the dead walls of the town were posted two proclamations, as follows:

> V. R.
>
> A reward of ten pounds (£10) is hereby offered for information that will lead to the arrest of Private Andrew Dillon, a deserter from Her Majesty's Sixteenth Regiment of Infantry. The deserter is twenty-one years of age; five feet eleven inches in height; weight, twelve stone; black hair, dark complexion, bluish-gray eyes. The above reward will be paid for the desired information at any constabulary barracks in Ireland.
>
> EDWARD THORNHILL,
> Sub-Inspector of Constabulary.

A second advertisement offered a reward for the capture of Dillon, charged with the crime of treason-felony, for conspiring with other treasonable persons to levy war upon the Queen of England, and "against the peace and dignity of Her Majesty's government in Ireland." The sum offered in this instance was fifty pounds (£50).

At nightfall of the same day, the Episcopal minister, Rev. Hugh Loyd, was sitting in his study at the parsonage, a mile from the town of Erinbeg, when his reading was interrupted by a gentle tap upon the window pane. Rising from his seat and peering through the window, he perceived a man in the uniform of an English soldier; and responsive to the soldier's sign he hastened to the hall door, and, opening it, recognized his youthful friend, Private Andy Dillon of the Sixteenth Regiment.

Dillon placed a forefinger to the lip as a signal for silence; the minister quietly beckoned him in, and as quietly led him into the study, and softly closed and locked the door behind him.

"Young friend," said Mr. Loyd, "what does this foolish visit mean? Don't you know there is a reward of sixty pounds upon your head? Isn't it said that the ministers of the established religion are a part of the British garrison in Ireland? And why in God's name should you come to me at my house, under all the circumstances?"

"Your Reverence," said the runaway, "what you say must be true, because you say it. It is sadly true that your established church has been a powerful engine for Ireland's oppression. As I often dared to tell you, your institution has fattened upon the substance of our people for two hundred years; but if you are an Episcopal minister, you are also a man. Yes, sir, and more than that, you are an Irishman. Our creeds do differ. There is a wide breach between us, but we are children of a common God, sons of the same sod, each hoping in his way to see salvation. You are a loyal subject of England, but I repeat, you are a Christian and an Irishman, and in the name of Christ and of Ireland I am here to ask your assistance."

"Surely, Dillon," said the preacher, "you would not make me an accessory to the crimes of treason-felony and desertion, by sheltering, aiding or sympathizing with you under the circumstances? and if I desired to do so, what in the world could I do for you?"

"You could give me a suit of old clothes, sir, in exchange for these regimentals, couldn't you?" said Dillon.

"Tut, tut, man," said the minister, "how dare you? In case of your capture, what would be said when a violent rebel was found inclosed in the clerical garb of Rev. Hugh Loyd? Why, man, there isn't a loyal man in the British empire who wouldn't heap reproaches on my head. Now, my good sir, don't impose too far on good nature. It is morally my duty to turn you over to the officers of the law, but I will not do it. God pity you! Now go."

Saying this, Mr. Loyd unlocked the door; Dillon moved as if to go, and did actually enter the hall, when the minister gently touched his arm, and placed ten silver shillings in his hand. Beckoning him back into the study, he added: "Dillon, I can't give you the clothing, for two reasons—first, because it would be unlawful; and, secondly, for the more substantial reason that I haven't a second suit to my name. Just as soon as I get a new suit, some poor fellow solicits the old one. Now, for instance, my last suit I gave to Billy Sheridan, my servant, and by the same token (nudging Dillon's arm), Billy does not wear my livery week-days, but reserves them for a respectable appearance on Sundays, and they are now hanging beside the horse's stall in the stable."

"Very well, your Reverence," said Andy. "A nod is just as good as a wink to a blind horse. Goodbye, Mr. Loyd; God bless you; and if we never meet on earth again, I hope we'll meet in heaven."

Passing from the house, Dillon repaired to the stable, and taking off his English uniform, lifted the preacher's cast-off suit from the peg and suddenly dressed himself in clerical attire. Passing from the stable, he hastily walked down the carriage way towards the main road. The parsonage was separated from the rest of the world by a stone wall, and exit from the rear was through a large "picket" gate. The bright full moon, now nearing the horizon, shone almost horizontally. Coming near the gate, the moon arrested Dillon's attention, and he stood still for a moment to gaze upon it. There is something peculiar in the beautiful objects of the visible universe. Moons are forever beautiful, and yet to all of us it sometimes seems that, when we see a full moon, it looks larger this latest time than it ever seemed before. So it did on this occasion seem larger than ever to the fugitive. Its light was not the splendid blaze of the clear winter night, but the mellow gold and copper mixture of its waning days. It was suggestive, not of illumination, but of shadows; and so still was the night, that the figures of the trees reflected upon the grassy lawn seemed engraven rather than transitory. Standing in the roadway and thus reflecting, Dillon's ear caught the sound of approaching measured steps, and as he turned away to escape observation, he saw a squad of four policemen marching past upon the road.

"Good night, yer Reverence," said the acting constable.

Dillon did not deem it prudent to reply in words, but he surely passing out of range of the peeler's observation, waved his hand gracefully in recognition of the acting constable.

"His Reverence is in rumination on next Sunday's sermon," said the acting constable. "Move on, men, move lively."

They did move, and Dillon made a double-quick from the grounds of the parsonage. Determined upon leaving Ireland, he bent his steps toward the residence of Father Joe Lenehan, that he might enjoy the consolations of religion before his departure.

Billy Sheridan, the parson's factotum, was one of the liveliest boys in the parish. Little was known of his early history. It was said that he was a foundling, neglected by his mother, and having been deposited on the door-step of a wealthy old neighbor in infancy, he was sent to the foundling hospital in Dublin. In after years, when the reasons for his abandonment were presumptively forgotten, his mother, with the maternal yearning for her offspring, started on foot for Dublin, and seeing a number of children, each about Billy's age, then five years old, playing in the yard of the foundling hospital, she selected the one she deemed most probably her Billy, and bore him in triumph from the benevolent institution.

"*Alanna macree*," said she; "is this my Billy?" She presumed that it was, and so returned with her treasure to the birth-place of the original.

Billy was favored with the attentions of the benevolent Parson Loyd. He in time was duly baptized, attended the parson's Sunday school and became a member of the church, and ultimately the trusted servant of his Reverence.

Some two hours after the time that Dillon had exchanged suits in the stable, Billy Sheridan cautiously moved out of his room at the parsonage, and very quietly made his way to the stable. Parson Loyd was by this time sound asleep, and Billy was intent upon having a pleasant time at the dance at Paddy Ryan's, at a distance from the parsonage of four long Irish miles. By this time the moon had gone down behind the hill of Knock-a-doo, and stygian darkness filled the stable. Billy reached for the familiar peg, and hastily exchanged his clothes. The trousers went on all right, but he cou'dn't find the waist-coat, and it seemed to him that the skirt of the coat had shrunken, and the buttons did not feel as smooth and level as they might; but he was in a hurry, and hastily putting on the coat, he hurried out into the night, and across the fields for Paddy Ryan's.

Near the end of his journey he had to cross the public road that led from Clashaganny to Carrick, and on entering the road soon found himself face to face with a squad of six policemen. It was the night patrol from Carrick, returning from their rendezvous with the night patrol from Erinbeg. Between this crowd of peelers and the parson's man there was no personal acquaintance. The sergeant commanded him to halt, at the same time flashing a dark lantern, revealing to the police and to Billy himself the uniform of an English soldier. Billy, unconscious of any crime, halted as commanded.

"Ah ha!" said the sergeant, "we've got you. Hold up your hands."

"In the name of the Queen," said the sergeant, "I arrest you, Andrew Dillon, for the crime of treason-felony, and for desertion from her Majesty's Sixteenth Regiment."

"What the divil d'ye mane," said Billy.

"We mean," said the sergeant, "to take you with us to Carrick, and I warn you to say nothing to criminate yourself; *thiggin thu*—a close mouth catches no flies."

Billy in vain protested his innocence; proclaimed his untarnished loyalty to church and state; begged to be taken back to the parsonage for identification; but all to no purpose. He was securely handcuffed, and, surrounded by six vigilant officers, marched across the Shannon to Carrick, and long before daylight occupied a stone cell in the county jail.

CHAPTER XVI.

ESCAPE OF ANDY DILLON.

A "HORSE Policeman'" arrived at Erinbeg from Carrick, early in the forenoon succeeding the night of Billy Sheridan's arrest, announcing the capture of Andy Dillon, and volunteering the information that Andy would arrive under guard during the day. Great was the consternation of the populace. There was dismay in Nationalist circles. All manner of rumors were afloat to the effect that the arrest of Andy was but a beginning, and that other arrests were to follow. Old John Dillon, Andy's father, was grief-stricken. nor would he be comforted. He well knew the penalty that "treason" brought to the Irish soldier in the service of England, and he felt that the conviction of Andy meant the separation for life of himself and his beloved boy.

A crowd of people from all parts of the village started out on the Carrick road to meet the prisoner, Andy Dillon, and to give him the poor consolation that in his misfortune he was neither friendless nor forgotten. As the crowd proceeded it gathered accessions, so that when it was two miles from town in the direction of Carrick, more than a thousand people were in the procession. Very soon the prisoner and his escort put in an appearance. First came a jaunting car with the driver on the front seat, and the prisoner and three policemen occupying the sides; and around the car, alongside and behind, a troop of cavalry in flaming uniform. At first sight of the military and their prisoner, a cheer went up from the multitude—a cheer for the captive, a shout of scorn and defiance at the captors. Responsive to this shout, a detachment of cavalry were ordered on a gallop to meet the approaching crowd, but when it became evident to the officer in charge of this detachment that the people were unarmed, the drawn sabers were returned to their scabbards, and the road was cleared by the retreat of the people through an open gate to an adjacent field.

The car and its guardians soon passed in front of the great audience, and there, in British regimentals, surrounded by the "pomp and circumstance of war," sat the prisoner, Billy Sheridan—not Private Andy Dillon. When this became apparent, and when upon a closer scrutiny it appeared that Dillon was not there, the mistake was evident, and the cheers and jeers were loftily renewed—jeers for the peelers, cheers for Billy Sheridan.

"*Yerrah*, Billy; well ye may wear your regimentals;" and, "Billy, when did you jine the army?" and, "Bravo, Billy!" and "Catch Andy if you can!" and similar expressions were flung at the peelers as they passed in review before the delighted audience. Soon the military and their prisoner halted in front of the police barracks at Erinbeg, and soon the captors were undeceived. The deep disgust and disappointment of Sam Timms and his brethren at Erinbeg can better be imagined than described. Billy Sheridan was released without form or ceremony, and soon found himself on the shoulders of four stalwart men, surrounded by a cheering multitude. It was then declared, and tradition perpetuates the fact, that "there was nothing too good for Billy;" that if he drank a whole barrel of porter he must have his fill, and "the divil a penny would he be allowed to pay."

As measure after measure of Dublin stout entered the parched lips of Billy, and as he mildly protested in vain that he was "full to the guzzle" and "couldn't howld another drop," he at last resigned himself to his fate, and innocently confessed that he "was as aisily led as a child." But his sense of duty to Parson Loyd remained, and toward sun-down he was loaded into a cart and hauled in triumph to the parsonage, amid the cheers of the multitude.

Rev. Hugh Loyd saw at a glance the comedy of errors that followed his suggestion to Dillon as to the suit of old clothes that was hung up in the stable; but the parson was a man of undoubted loyalty, and of course no suspicion was attached to him in connection with the affair. He assisted in leading Billy to an improvised couch of straw in the stable, where he leisurely slept away the effects of the celebration.

***

When Dillon turned his back upon the policemen, and left the grounds of the parsonage, he carefully avoided the public roads, and by a semi-circular march walked out to the west end of town, and through the open fields, in the direction of Carraghmore, the residence of Father Joe Lenehan. The declining moon gave just sufficient light to guide his steps, and at the same time avoid unfriendly observation. From a hill-top he gazed for the last time upon the roof of his father's cabin—the roof under which he was born. He could see the spire of the church in the venerable grave-yard, where reposed the ashes of ten generations of his people. He passed the trysting spot, under the tall hawthorns, where mutual vows of love had passed between himself and Nancy McHugh, and he passed the cabin of Nancy's parents, though he dared not approach close enough to see Nancy through the window pane, as he had often done before; but he saw the light of the candle burning near the window, and his heart beat audibly, so that he believed he could hear its throb; and he brushed away a tear, with a prayer in his heart for his country and for those he loved, and a curse upon the heads of their oppressors. And he stood for a moment on the crest of a little hill, and lovingly gazed upon the village steeple and the dim lights in the windows of the last house in the village that he passed; and he bade good-bye to his home, his kindred, his comrades, and his love—forever.

Within an hour old Mary Fahey, the house-keeper of Father Lenehan, had opened the kitchen door of the priest's residence, and in a few seconds he stood in the presence of Father Joe.

The story of his trouble and his flight had preceded him; his "crime" of loving Ireland had reached the ears of the *soggarth*. The priest gave a word of caution to old Mary, ordered up a supply of bread and meat and milk, which he placed upon a table in his own bed-room, then hastily closed the blinds and curtains of that room, put out the lights that were burning in others, and hastily led Dillon to a feast in the bed-room.

"Father," said the fugitive, " I have come for——"

"Hush, *ma bouchal*," said the priest. "You have come, first of all, for something to appease your hunger. You must be famished, *a vic machree*. There now, *agra*, say nothing, but eat something."

Dillon obeyed orders; but he had a higher purpose than the appeasement of his hunger, and after filling his mouth, he persisted in saying:

"Father, I have come for——"

But the priest interrupted him with a "Hush, *ma bouchal, na bocklish nish;* wait till you have eaten and then I'll listen to you."

Nothing further was said until the meal was finished, and then the runaway was permitted to finish the sentence.

"Father, I am leaving Ireland, and I have come to say my confession and to ask you for absolution, and your blessing."

The priest, sitting down, put on his stole; the penitent knelt beside him; the priest whispered a prayer in Latin; suggested to the penitent the *Confeteor Deo*, "I confess to Almighty God, etc.;" and then proceeded to hear a recital of the young man's sins. Slowly the young man related his transgressions; told of his spree at the sheebeen house, where he drank more liquor than he could bear; how he kicked policeman Sam Timms; how he once, under provocation, called the name of God in vain in the barrack yard at Athlone; and how, overstepping the law of Heaven, he had sometimes kissed Nancy McHugh; and last, how—contrary, as he understood it, to the rule of the church—he had sworn a solemn oath of eternal hostility to England.

"And now, my son," said the *soggarth*, "is that all?"

"That is all," said the penitent.

"And now," said the priest, "do you feel a hearty sorrow for having so offended God? Do you feel a true contrition for all your sins, and are you disposed not to repeat your sins, but to abandon them, and from out your heart desire to sin no more?"

"Father," said the penitent, "I am heartily sorry for all my sins, and before God and you I can forgive my enemies, all but one—I can make no peace with England. In that case I can neither retract nor repent."

"Then, my son," said the priest, "I cannot give you absolution."

"Father," said the youth, "can you say a mass for my soul, and give me a parting blessing?"

"With a *cree galore*," said the *soggarth*.

"Then a blessing and a mass let it be," said the youth; "I'll never enter the gate of heaven with an English pass."

Father Lenehan placed his hand upon the dark

head of the young man, and offered a fervid blessing for his temporal and eternal welfare. The door was cautiously opened, and the fugitive went out into the night, crossed the stone fence in front of the priest's residence, and turned his face to the west. It was midnight. He traveled all the remainder of the night, and at daylight was safely housed in the home of his friend Ned Duffy, in the neighborhood of Castlerea. Thoroughly rested at nightfall, he started again, guided by a trusty companion, and before daylight on the second morning was again under shelter with a Fenian brother in the town of Tuam.

Resolved upon receiving absolution, he went to the home of the venerable Archbishop McHale at the cathedral. Here he met an aged priest who, in the latter half of the eighteenth century, had to seek his education and ordination in France; the office of a priest being then in Ireland a felony, according to English law.

To this venerable father he told the story of eternal hostility to England, and the old father, with a smile, cheerfully gave him absolution.

"*Ma bouchal*," the *soggarth* added when the youth had made his act of contrition and risen from his knees, "*ma bouchal*, I, myself, have made no peace with England. In my young manhood I taught the boys how Jude and Macabee invoked the wrath of God upon the slave who could forget that God made us free. When rebels were forced into the hills I shared their hardships and their hunger. I was among the poor when every man, woman and child in the western half of my parish was apparently dying of famine and fever, and when I administered the b'essed sacrament to every living soul, deeming each of them in *articulo mortis*, practically. Go your way; God bless you; and wherever you go you must "make no peace with England."

CHAPTER XVII.

ARRANGING FOR DEPARTURE.

THE venerable priest at Tuam furnished Dillon with a suit of corduroy and moleskin, and in the confessional he donned his new suit, and deposited the clerical garb of Rev. Hugh Loyd. Already the *Hue and Cry*, the organ of the police power, had described him as traveling in the guise of an Episcopal clergyman, so that his newest suit of sober gray and mud color was calculated to throw his pursuers "off the scent," if by any chance they were enabled to see him. The extreme western part of Ireland presented to him scenes that were entirely different from those in the Valley of the Shannon. The rich cattle pastures and sheep walks of the interior were behind him; he was now among the western peasants, whose five-acre holdings presented none of the natural richness, the prosperity or thrift occasionally visible in the interior of the island.

The land was primitively sandy and bare, and the system of landlordism was a most effectual handicap to progress. If a peasant planted a tree, the tree was not his; if he built a stone fence, he could lay no claim to that improvement; if his family had carted the sea-weed from out the very ocean and hauled it in "creels" upon their backs, to fertilize the stony places, they merely fattened the land for the benefit of the landlord; and if, in the face of every difficulty, the tenant at last succeeded in beautifying and permanently improving the little holding, his industry and toil were turned to a disadvantage by an increase in the rent.

Was ever a system of political economy devised by man so well calculated to discourage and impoverish a people? Rack-rents, to the utmost capacity of the land and to the limit of human endurance, were exacted for these wretched little farms. If the season was favorable, the tenant managed to raise the rent from an acre of grain, and by fattening a pig or two; and the net profit consisted of half an acre of potatoes and the milk of a couple of cows. The proceeds of the butter went to the landlord. The pig was the honored guest, very often sharing the same sleeping apartment with the family; and yet, under these deplorable conditions, there were, in prosperous years, peace and joy and happiness, begotten of labor and love and virtue. The father of the family, sometimes accompanied by the eldest son, would make his way on foot to Dublin, would cross the sea to England, to save the English hay crop and reap the English harvest, and return in the fall with a few sovereigns in his pocket. These harvest men generally entered the British island in crowds of fifty or a hundred. This massing was necessary to their very lives, because it frequently occurred that a hundred English workmen, brawny and well fed, would sally forth from a factory or a brick yard, and assail an inferior force of these poor, underfed harvest men. On such occasions, and only on such occasions, was the Irish blackthorn put to a meritorious use. Nowhere on earth—neither at Fredericksburg nor at Waterloo—have Irishmen displayed greater valor than in resistance to the cruel onslaughts thus made upon them. England, gentle reader, is said to be a free-trade nation, and this rude warfare of brick and stone and bludgeon, aimed at Irish heads, was but the assertion of the higher law of a people protecting their well-paid labor market against the cheaper labor of a sister island. It was the untutored assertion of the doctrine of protective tariff.

As Dillon in the early morning stepped out of the old ruin, and looked upon the scenes, and listened to the voices of nature, there was neither human being nor human habitation in sight; for far as the eye could reach, a clearing had been made; that is to say, the land had been cleared of its Irish population by process of English law, and sheep and cattle were browsing lazily above the hearthstones of the exiled race.

"Great God!" he exclaimed in the very agony of soul, "is this the destiny of my countrymen? The crows have homes in the trees, the blackbirds and thrushes in the hedge-row, the fishes in the brook, and yet upon the face of Irish earth Providence has allotted no space for man. If this then be the fate of my people, Ireland is the last place on earth for an Irishman. Surely the tallest mountain, the dryest plain, the deadliest swamp in free America is far better than a land where, amid the loveliest scenes, there is human desolation."

So saying, he hastily left the spot, and bent his steps to the town of Galway. On his arrival in "the City of the Tribes," he naturally avoided the principal streets, and undesignedly found his way to the sea-shore suburb of Claddagh. This district was distinctively, peculiarly Irish. Tradition tells us that in the distant times—some hundred of years ago—when Ireland enjoyed a prosperous commerce with Spain, a crew of Spanish sailors were shipwrecked on the Galway coast; were accorded the hospitalities of the Claddagh fishermen; became enamored of the Irish *colleens;* married Irish wives; became "more Irish than the Irish," and a permanent part of the Claddagh population. Tradition is verified in the large dark eyes and the silken black hair of the Claddagh maidens of to-day. Upon a rude bench in front of a white-washed cabin that fronted on the Bay of Galway, sat an aged man, a chieftain among his people, upon whom the unwritten law of the tribe conferred the honors and title of "the King of the Claddagh," and to this aged man the deserter turned for a *senecus* (conference). The talk was in the Celtic tongue; for in those days no aged resident of Claddagh spoke a word of English.

"God save you, friend," said the visitor.

"God save you kindly," said the king.

"Could you give a poor famished *bouchal* a mouthful to eat?" said the stranger.

"With a heart and a half," said the venerable man; "come in. We can give you a drop of *poteen*, a potato and fish *galore*, with a measure of milk or water to wash it down. Poor boy! you look tired and distressed. Where do you come from, and what can we do for you?"

Dillon felt that he had found a friend, and without hesitation, speaking in undertones, told his story to the fisherman, expressed his purpose of leaving Ireland, and added that he was entirely without means.

"Trust in God" said the fisherman; "the darkest hour of night is the hour before dawn. You will rest in this cabin until morning, and meanwhile I will see what can be done for you. If all else fails, we will send you out in a fishing smack, and the boys will land you on the coast of France, where there is always a *caed mille failthe* for a runaway Irishman."

With assurance of his perfect safety, the king led the fugitive to an inner room, and the youth was soon at rest in the deep, dreamless sleep of a healthy innocent man.

From his sleep he did not awake until nightfall, and on re-entering the main apartment of the cottage, he saw several persons, among them a stalwart stranger, with skin as black as coal, and a voice which bespoke him a foreigner.

"This man," said the king of Claddagh, "is Anthony Sexton, an American negro, a cook upon the ship *Hibernia*, which sails out of Galway for New York to-morrow afternoon. His face is black, but his heart is true. He belongs to a race of men who have suffered long in slavery. He says that a great many Irishmen fought in the American war which resulted in the freedom of his people, and in return he has sympathy for our suffering countrymen."

Dillon grasped the black man's hand. He had read a good deal of the negro. He had read and re-read "Uncle Tom's Cabin," and was thoroughly familiar with the attitude of Daniel O'Connell toward the institution of slavery in America. He proudly repeated to his new acquaintance how the great O'Connell had spurned the proffered gold of the slave power, declaring that if Ireland's freedom depended upon money drawn from the blood and sweat of the African slave in America, Ireland would prefer to clank her chains until the crack of doom.

"A thousand times I have wished," said Dillon, "that I might be privileged to reach America before the close of the war, so that I might strike a blow for the freedom of the negro."

"And is that the sentiment in Ireland?" inquired the black man.

"That," replied Dillon," "is the sentiment among the younger and more enlightened generation of Irishmen; among all of us who know enough to entertain a sentiment, there is a deep desire for world-wide freedom and universal emancipation."

"Golly!" said the black man, "a voyage on the ocean makes an awful change in Irish sentiment; for while a great many of your countrymen love liberty, and fight for it in America, there is a big majority of 'em in the States that hate the niggers, as they call us, and who work and vote against our every right and privilege."

A blush of shame mantled the face of the Fenian when he learned that any of his countrymen could be basely recreant to freedom, and he vowed to Heaven then and there, with uplifted hand, that if he reached American soil, he would take the side of freedom.

Sexton rose, and proceeded to take his leave with an all-round hand-shake. "Meet me," he said to Dillon, "at Salt Hill by sunrise in the mawnin', and I'll try and assist you to America. The old man or one of his boys will take you to the appointed spot, and I be thar sure."

It was so agreed, and the party separated for the night—Sexton to his ship, and Dillon to the cottage of the king of Claddagh.

CHAPTER XVIII.

THE EXILES OF ERIN.

AFTER the departure of the negro, the family of the fisherman, Dalton by name, lighted their candles, and busied themselves—the father and his wife mending and adjusting the nets. The two sons, young men, entered a little later. They had just returned from a fishing voyage.

"What luck, my boys?" said the father.

"Poor luck, sir," responded the oldest of the boys. "The French vessels were in force to-day a few miles outside the bay, and it's a sorry chance we stand fishing in competition with them and their splendid vessels and perfect tackle."

Dillon inquired whether fishermen came all the way from France to fish upon the Irish coast.

"Oh, yes, sir," said one of the Dalton boys; "the French, the English and the Scotch find profitable fishing on the western coast of Ireland; and our mackerel are sold in the markets of Paris, London and Glasgow. Want of capital compels us to use unsafe and inferior fishing boats and tackle. We have no proper wharves or other landing places, and compelled as we are to fish inshore, our catch is small, and small as it is, there is no market for it."

"I would think," said Dillon, "that Galway City alone, with its thousands of population, would afford a very good market."

"Bless your soul!" responded the fisherman, "if you leave out the Queen's College, the railway hotel, the police and the poor-house, there is little left in the way of a market. As a majority of the poor have no other employment, they do their own fishing."

"Have you no mills, or mines, or factories?" said Dillon.

"Nothing of the sort, sir, except a flouring mill. In the matter of factories, Galway is like the rest of Ireland. Since we lost our native government, and the power to protect our industries, England has done our manufacturing."

"But," said Dillon, "I see a great many ships in the harbor. You must have considerable commerce."

"Oh, *Dea!*" said the old man. "We have some shipping, sir. There are ships from America, that bring us yellow meal, and export from us, in return, the bone and sinew of our people, the young and hearty, leaving behind them the old and the helpless; and there are ships from England, that bring us clothing and hardware and farming tools, and take away in return our beef and bacon and butter, the finest that the world yields."

"But you certainly receive some money for your farming produce?"

"Yes, sir; but it doesn't get time to warm in our pockets till off it goes again, into the pockets of the landlords, who spend it in England, or squander it in gambling houses, and worse houses than that, on the Continent of Europe."

From this the topic of conversation turned upon the work at which the young girls were engaged. They were dextrously sewing on what appeared like a miniature tambourine—upon muslin drawn tightly over a little wooden hoop, and held in its place by an outer hoop, closely fitting the inner one.

"It is spriggin' they call it," said Mrs. Dalton. "By working day and evenings, the poor *cailins* earn a rag of clothes for themselves and their parents."

"By spriggin'," said Dillon, "you mean embroidery; and what can the girls earn at that?"

"The youngest one, Bridget," said the mother, "earns four pence a day, and when Mary, the eldest, can put her whole time to it, she earns as much as five pence a day. They obtain the work from a Scotchman, who works for an English house, and when he is in good humor, and doesn't "dock" them, the wages of both amount to something like five shillings a week. But what can the poor craythurs do? There is no other employment for them. Meself and father are growing old, and we cannot be wid them long. It's hard to part them, but, hard as it is, when the girls can save enough, they are both thinkin' of goin' to America. We have some relations in a place cal'ed Waterbury, in the State of Connecticut, and their letters say that girls working there in the factories earn in a single day as much as my two poor girls can both earn in a week."

The fishing nets and the sprigging were at last put aside, and the girls, at the bidding of their mother, favored the stranger with a song: *"Gra macree ma cailin oge ma Mairie bawn astore."*

The pile of bog turf, or peat, was now reduced to living coals; the candles were extinguished, the firelight being deemed all-sufficient and appropriate for the time and the occasion. The rosary was announced, and, the father leading in prayer, all offered up their hearts to God, and repeated the prayers in a language that for fourteen centuries had voiced the devotions of the people of Galway.

A little before daylight next morning, Dillon, guided by old man Dalton, passed through the silent streets of the quaint old town to Salt Hill, at the other extreme of the city. The negro was waiting with his small boat, and after many a mutual " God be with you," the black man and his new-found friend set out across the bay, and by daylight had boarded the *Hibernia*.

"What flag is that," inquired Dillon, "floating from that pretty little vessel near the mouth of the bay?"

"That," said the black man, "is the tri-color of France. The boat is a French fishing vessel. And that," he added, "is the Union Jack of England, that flutters from the black gunboat over yonder; this, to the right of us is the German flag; and the flag that floats above our heads is the Stars and Stripes of America. She's a dandy, isn't she?"

"She is, indeed," said Dillon.

"That is the flag," said the negro, "that gave shelter to millions of your Irish people. It is the flag that was borne by the Union army that routed the old slave power, and it is the flag that in the famine years waved over the ships that carried bread and meat to the starving Irish."

"God bless that flag, its country and its people!" said the exile, with all the fervor of an uncontaminated Irish heart.

As early as seven o'clock, the lighter commenced

discharging its cargoes upon the ocean ship. Three hundred emigrants came on board. There were few old persons or infants among them. There was the oldest son of a family, leaving a country that afforded neither labor for his hands nor scope for any honorable ambition. There was the oldest daughter of another family, a young creature scarcely out of her teens, playing the heroic part of pioneer for the rest of the family, animated by the ambition to save her wages and "pay the passages" of all the other children. They came by rail from several counties, or they came on carts for distances of twenty or thirty miles, accompanied by friends and parents and lovers. Ah, merciful God, what sad processions, and sadder partings! Mother and daughter take the last embrace. The gray-haired father is torn away from the throbbing breast of the stalwart son, never to meet him on earth again. The tender youth bids a tearful farewell to a weeping girl, to whom he has plighted his troth, and the vow is renewed that they will soon meet again upon the other side of the Atlantic. Their mingled prayers go up to heaven; their longing eyes look westward to the new land of their hopes and homes, and they picture to themselves the great Republic, strong and gentle mother that she is, opening wide her arms and receiving the guiltless outcasts to her warm young breast; and look with the eye of faith upon the finger of God's angel beckoning them across the Atlantic. And there is a parting piercing wail as the lighter leaves the wharf, and bitter weeping as she steams across the bay. There are waving of handkerchiefs, and a parting cheer from the vessel, answered by a farewell wail from shore; the anchor is weighed, the pilot comes on board, the sails are set, and the emigrant vessel bears away the young and the innocent, the youth and the beauty, the blood and the bone, the heart and soul of an ancient and sadly decimated nation. There is a lingering look at the Irish coast as the vessel heads southwestward past the cliffs of Clare, and three hundred pairs of Irish eyes have seen for the last time their own green land, the "Cinderella of the nations," their island home of beauty, of love and of sorrow.

Dillon is not permitted to witness these scenes, for his friend Sexton has stowed him in the hold. He is a "dead-head" in the strictest sense of the word. He has neither a passage ticket nor a pound in his pocket.

For four days he remained securely in the hold, regularly supplied with food from the galley at the hands of his friend, the black man. But during the fifth day out from Galway, the stowaway was discovered by some of the sailors working in the hold, and they reported to the first mate, who immediately descended and, with the aid of the sailors, suddenly dragged him on deck. If he had tamely submitted, he might have escaped severe physical punishment; but irritated by the unnecessary violence of one of the sailors, he broke their grasp upon him, and with a blow from the shoulder knocked his tormentor down. In another instant the second mate approached, armed with a belaying pin, and striking him upon the head, felled him to the deck. Blood streamed from his wound, and sailors and passengers gathered around the prostrate man. Slowly regaining consciousness, he rose from his position and feebly staggered toward the galley. The second mate followed, and raised the murderous weapon to give him another blow, when suddenly Anthony Sexton, the colored cook, rushed from the galley, and standing back to back with the wounded stowaway, stood face to face with the second mate, with carving knife in hand.

"You jus' luf him alone," said the black man.

"You just stand aside, you black son-of-a-seacook," said the enraged mate, or I break in your——head."

"You jus' try it on," said the negro.

The mate accepted the challenge, and proceeded to blows, without exchange of courtesies. By a rapid blow he shivered the blade of the carving knife and detached its handle from the grasp of the negro.

Sexton in a second made a dash for the mate; with one hand grasped the belaying pin, and with another seized his assailant by the throat.

Both were powerful men, and after wrestling for a moment the mate went down, with the black man on top. But it was a momentary ascendancy. Half a dozen sailors proceeded to kick him. The mate sprang to his feet, belaying pin in hand, and was rushing at the prostrate black man, when the captain came upon the scene, armed with a revolver, and commanded a cessation of hostilities. The stowaway and his defender were placed in irons, and the mate ordered to his quarters. Next morning an investigation of the affair was made by the captain, with the result that mate and cook were severely reprimanded, and ordered to their respective duties, the services of each being indispensable.

Dillon's wound, at first supposed to be a fracture of the skull, proved upon examination to be a dangerous contusion. The steerage passengers set apart for him the most comfortable berth in the steerage, and there was no dearth of kindly attention from the men, or of tender nursing on the part of the women.

He became delirious, and for days, at intervals, raved in most pitiable forms. He imagined that he was in America; that he had entered the Union army; that he was leading forlorn hopes and bayonet charges, animated by his heart's desire to "strike a blow for the freedom of the negro."

"Forward, boys!" he would say at times, wildly plunging from his bed. On these occasions two strong men were required to keep him down.

At other times he would sing snatches of Irish "treason songs," such as "Who Fears to Speak of Ninety-eight?" "Paddies Evermore," "O'Donnell Aboo," or "The Green Above the Red."

The bed-quilt, composed of many colors, chiefly of red, white and blue, to his disordered mind was an American flag. He at times would frantically kiss its hem, or, seizing it by a corner, would attempt to wave it.

In his calmer moments his fancy would run to Nancy McHugh.

"*Cailin macree*," he would tenderly say, "when this war is over, won't we return and strike a blow for Ireland? and when the old sod is free, won't you and I be happy?"

And finally, exhausted, he would raise the right hand to his wounded head, and, supposing himself dying on a battle-field, would utter, in tones scarcely audible: "Oh, that this was for Ireland!"

By the tenderest care and nursing, he was restored to life before the end of the voyage. Dillon had made friends of the three hundred emigrants, but his dearest friend was the American negro. To him he bade his most heartfelt and tender farewell.

CHAPTER XIX.

GETTING ACCLIMATED.

AS Dillon stepped on shore, his negro friend handed him a five-dollar greenback, warmly shook his hand, and the two friends mutually expressed the hope that they would soon meet again. Three hundred Irish immigrants were added to the American population; three hundred strangers, male and female, were marched into Castle Garden. Many of them were met by friends, and as their names were loudly called by an officer at the immigration bureau, they passed out through a gate and into the arms of their relatives. There were others called, who received letters containing railway tickets or money remittances, to enable them to join their friends in Pennsylvania, New York, New Jersey, and New England. There were others who hoped to meet some friend, to recognize some face in the new land, but hoped in vain ; and there was more than half of the whole three hundred who saw no friend and who received no letter, but who stood in Castle Garden, strangers in a strange land ; whose possessions in many cases amounted to a bundle of clothing and a shilling or a pound in English money. Some few of them were absolutely penniless. They were all anxious to obtain employment. A majority had been raised upon farms (so-called) in Ireland, but of this agricultural class, not one in five had ever formed the intimate acquaintance of a plow. Some of them had never harnessed a horse, and not one in ten had learned how to manage a team. Horse-teams, plows and wagons were only possessed by the wealthier farmers in Ireland then. The donkey, the cart and the spade, the reaping hook and the scythe were the

Irish aids in agriculture. As to mechanical trades, they were at a still greater disadvantage. Among them were a few tailors, shoe-makers, stone-masons and blacksmiths; good mechanics in their way, for Irish heads and hands are susceptible of mechanical knowledge, and with fair opportunities the Irishman, trained to any given employment, will favorably compare with the man of any other nationality. There was not one machinist among the whole three hundred; not one man who could put the parts of a watch together; not a man who could make a pistol, a gun or a gun-cap; not one who had ever seen a yard of cotton cloth manufactured, and not ten who had ever worked in a brick-yard or a saw-mill. They came from a country whose industries had been destroyed by legislation; whose capital is annually drained out of the pockets of the agriculturist; whose trade and commerce are paralyzed, and whose children are sent adrift upon the world, handicapped by the curse of industrial ignorance, with heads and hands deprived of the skill and cunning that, in this age of mechanism, give to men and nations an equal chance in the race of life.

That which was true of the men, was more forcibly true of the women. They had strong and willing hands, brave and virtuous souls, but their industrial skill fitted them only for the humbler tasks of domestic service. British law had not only impoverished them at home; it pursued them into exile. It had made in former times the task of the schoolmaster a felony; it had driven industrial knowledge from the island, and then mercilessly pursued them with its press and its lecturers to taunt them with accusations of ignorance. Thus handicapped, they were compelled to commence life in the new world at the lowest round of the ladder; and when their circumstances are fully considered, it is marvelous how they climb, and how many of them reach the top.

Dillon had no training in any regular employment. He had a good common school education; he had some knowledge of Latin, and the rudiments of French; he could read and write and cipher, but his education did not equip him to earn a living. He had studied arithmetic, the elements of Euclid and geography; but he was neither a land surveyor, a navigator nor a book-keeper. He was willing to work at anything, but he was utterly unused to tools or labor of any kind.

Leaving Castle Garden, he sauntered up Washington street, and attracted by some of his fellow emigrants who had preceded him, he entered a lodging house in the third or fourth block from the lower end of the street. Retiring to a dingy, dirty little room on the third floor, he soon undressed himself and went to bed, for he was tired, having spent the preceding night on the deck of the *Hibernia* without sleep. He had locked his door, and closed his eyes, and was entering upon his coveted sleep, when he was suddenly aroused by a scraping noise upon the wall. Looking in the direction of the noise, he saw that somebody had inserted a fishing pole through the transom-light, and was lifting his pantaloons from the peg on which they hung. The fisher for pants had succeeded so far as to drag the garment through the transom, when Dillon sprang from the bed, suddenly unlocked the door, and recapturing his pants, kicked the thief down stairs into the bar-room of the lodging house. The robber was no less a person than the proprietor of the hotel, a prominent politician, president of the famous "Hickory Club"—the most influential citizen in the ward!

"Police! police! police!"

A member of the famous force responded, and on complaint of the landlord, took Dillon in charge for the distinct offenses of assault and battery, and drunk and disorderly.

He spent the night at the station-house, and next morning was arraigned at the Tombs Police Court. He was duly convicted upon the testimony of the landlord; and the presiding magistrate was opening his precious mouth to pronounce sentence, when a fine-looking gentleman, dressed in broadcloth, approached the bench and begged for a moment's conference with his Honor. The request was cheerfully granted; they retired to the judge's private room, and on the return of his Honor to the bench, Dillon was severely reprimanded and discharged.

"You must be careful for the future," said Justice Divvy, "how you disregard the peace and person of such an honored citizen as the complaining witness."

The gentleman in British broadcloth led the stranger out of court and into a fashionable saloon on Chambers street. They drank a couple of times, and the man of broadcloth proceeded to scrutinize the emigrant. He lifted Dillon's little narrow-brimmed hat from off his head, kicked it into the street, and, leading the hatless man to a store on Broadway, "rigged him out" in a splendid five-dollar broad-brimmed Stetson hat.

"These nasty little English hats are no ornament to the head of an American citizen," he observed.

He then led the stranger to a clothing store, and fitted him out with new underclothes and a suit of American tweed.

Dillon was astonished, and twenty times, while in process of renovation, earnestly exclaimed: "Free America! generous Americans!"

Finally, the man of broadcloth took him to the restaurant at Sweeny's Hotel, and "rounded him out," as he expressed it, with such a meal as Dillon had never eaten before, with Dublin stout galore to wash it down.

"Andy," said the gentleman in broadcloth, "don't you know me?"

Dillon taxed his vision and his memory to their utmost, but he couldn't recognize his friend. He gave it up.

"Don't you know Pat Byrne, from Abbey Cartron?" said his friend.

"How the devil could I know you?" said Dillon. "They have been calling you Mr. John P. Burns, and Alderman Burns."

"Oh," said the alderman, "it was Byrne at home, but it is Burns here, and I have stuck on the 'John' in front; it's a little more fashionable than Pat."

Sure enough, it was Patsy Byrne, an old schoolmate of Dillon, some five years older than himself. He had emigrated seven years before; had done a very prosperous business, first as a bar-tender, and then as a liquor dealer on his own account; and being young, smart and handsome, and highly influential on account of his business, he soon climbed the ladder of fortune and fame in New York City politics. He had been in the police court on political business on the morning of Dillon's conviction, and, recognizing the youth, came to his rescue. He now brought the emigrant to his place of business, on one of the busy streets running eastward from the Bowery. Dillon thought it a beautiful establishment. Above the door and beside it there were gilded signs: "John P. Burns, dealer in foreign and domestic whiskies, brandies, wines, liquors and cigars." There were rosewood counters, and shelving laden with the bottled goods, silver-mounted faucets and beer-pumps. This palace occupied a corner. There was also a "private entrance" through a hall door, over whose portals ran the legend: "Bottled wines and liquors for family use." To this private entrance there came a procession of shabbily-dressed women, boys and girls, with empty bottles, pitchers and tin cans. A special bar-tender waited on these through an opening in the wall at the end of the bar. Dillon was astonished at the run for whisky and beer for family use. He did not remain long, however, to witness it. He was tired. His friend, the alderman, made arrangements for him in a neighboring house, and here he may be said to have commenced life in the city of New York.

CHAPTER XX.

HOW DEMOCRATS ARE MADE.

ACCORDING to appointment, "the greenhorn," Dillon, appeared at the establishment of Alderman Burns. The alderman himself seemed to bear no part in the business of the house, except to draw moneys from the tills and to hold informal receptions. Three bar-tenders, in white aprons and wearing diamond pins, were there to do the heavy work.

Laboring men, shabbily dressed, appeared at the bar from time to time, drank their liquor, deposited fractional currency, and greeted the elegant proprietor, who in turn beamed upon each customer a most benignant smile. He would even condescend to shake hands and crack jokes with some of them.

"A pleasant mornin' this mornin', Alderman."

"A delightful mornin'. How are you this mornin', Briney?"

Sometimes his great mind would be diverted by an application for credit in "the family department." He would dispose of these customers with a smile and a refusal. He did a cash business, but he would give the lady who called "the wettin' of her whistle" as a balm for her wounded feelings. This particular morning he was deeply laden with the affairs of state. "The Registration Bureau" was open for business on Chatham street. To this bureau he led Dillon and several other recent arrivals.

"And what do he be takin' us to the bureau for?" said one of the emigrants.

"He do be takin' us," explained another, "to get us our papers and make us Democrats."

"And what do we do wid our papers?" said the first speaker; "and what is a Democrat?"

"A Democrat," said the alderman, "is a Democrat—one who votes the Democratic ticket and belongs to the Democratic party. The Democratic party is the white man's party, the party that's agin the nigger. It is the Irishman's party, and any Irishman who kicks on votin' the ticket is a thraithor and a turncoat."

The procession started for the "naturalization bureau," and Dillon and the other emigrants were duly enrolled as members of the Democratic party. Each of the new members was furnished with a certificate of naturalization; they all drank hearty to the party and its friends, and confusion and defeat to Abe Lincoln, the nigger and the radical party.

Alderman Burns gave to each of the new recruits a five-dollar bill, or provided him with a week's board and lodging, giving precise directions as to the rallying point on the morning of election.

Dillon was not entirely satisfied. He had a vague idea that a man could not become a citizen of the United States within a week of his arrival.

"Patsy," said he, addressing the great leader. The alderman scowled. "I beg pardon," said the Democratic recruit; "Alderman Burns, I mane. Will you tell me what's a citizen?"

"A citizen," said the alderman, "a citizen, you *omathaum*, is a citizen—a man who votes."

"Doesn't he," said Andy, " have to take an oath, or swear allegiance or somethin' of the sort?"

"He does," replied the alderman, "if he's suspected of favorin' the Republicans. Now, Andy, darlin', a close mouth catches no flies. If you'll ask me no questions, I'll tell you no lies. You're a citizen and a Democrat—a Jacksonian Democrat; and maybe, it's a policeman I'd make of you one of these days."

That evening there was a great procession. It started from City Hall place, and marched up the Bowery, to the Cooper Institute. A great meeting was arranged, to take place in the great hall of the Cooper Union.

There were several German bands; a body of of business men; European importers and their clerks, porters and salesmen; clothing men from Chatham street and the Bowery, with little in their language or appearance suggestive of American birth or sentiment. Then came the young men's Hickory Club—a stalwart set, five or six hundred, chiefly Irish-Americans. Then came the Laborers' Democratic Union, and in the rear came the White Man's Government Club. This club numbered about four hundred, the members presenting an appearance repulsive in the extreme.

Dillon inquired of his friend, the alderman, who the White Men's Government Club were.

"Them," said the aldermen proudly, "are my boys; every black-leg, pick-pocket, shop-lifter, burglar and cut-throat in my ward, as far as I know."

"Them," said Dillon, "are the Republicans, I suppose?"

"Andy, jewel," said the alderman, "don't be so inquisitive. They are my friends on election day, and I never look a gift horse in the mouth. One of their votes is just as good as the vote of Peter Cooper or John Jacob Astor."

There was a great meeting at Cooper Union. The hall was filled to overflowing, with five hundred men standing near the doors, and the very doorways crowded to suffocation. Every square foot upon the platform was occupied. The audience, including those upon the platform, was composed chiefly of Irish-Americans. A fine-looking audience, too. Four thousand men, perhaps. All in all, it was a splendid meeting. One hundred prominent citizens occupied the platform; and as Dillon gazed upon that vast assembly he could not control the pride of his heart that he was an Irishman and a Democrat.

Richard O'Gorman was the orator. He was Corporation Counsel of the city of New York, and was then in the very fullness of his mental and physical power; a man of splendid presence, and in his day one of the foremost political orators of the Democratic party. He had borne some part in the abortive revolution in Ireland in 1848; had fled from the Green Island in his youth, and became in New York City "an Irishman by trade."

After the preliminaries Hon. Richard O'Gorman was introduced, and was greeted with tremendous cheering. He commented severely on Mr. Lincoln's administration; deplored the emancipation of the negro as a violation of constitutional right; predicted disastrous results from the freedom of the black man, and ingeniously confounded social and political equality. But it was his sympathetic plea for the conquered Confederacy, of mercy for the stricken South, that evoked the cheers of the audience; and as he drew comparisons between a persecuted Ireland and a stricken South, in language touchingly pathetic and eloquent, there were tears and sobs interspersed with cheers from the audience. He reminded Irishmen of the early history of the Democratic party, when the Irish were few and feeble in America; how the Democracy gave them their rights and protected their persons and their liberties; how the great Democratic organization, in its friendliness for foreigners, was true to principle as needle to pole.

That speech made Dillon a Democrat. It appealed to his sympathies and his reason, and in after years, under every different circumstance and completely different issues, when every feeling, every reason, and every motive of love, hatred, enlightened selfishness and patriotic duty told him that he could no longer vote the Democratic ticket, he found it hard to efface from his affections his Democratic love as painted by Richard O'Gorman.

He left the hall of the Cooper Union that night a Democrat. He would repay by devotion the Irish debt of gratitude to the Democratic party, and he did.

Alderman John P. Burns presented to him ample opportunity for the exercise of his suffrage and his generosity.

Election morning arrived, with its brass bands, banners, carriages, mottoes and election booths.

Dillon was seated with three other recruits in an open carriage. With the driver sat a "worker," whose business it was to "vote" the emigrants. There was difficulty with one of the recruits. He was an Italian, named Diego Rosacco, and he could not understand why he should vote as David Brown, Richard Williams and Jacob Schnauber; but he voted all the same, and successfully personated three Republicans who had died in the city since the last election. Dillon, by casting three different ballots in as many precincts, testified his gratitude and devotion to the Democratic party, and he did it with a clear conscience. He was an Irishman, and if by virtue of that fact he was in duty bound to vote the Democratic ticket, and if by doing so he was circumventing the Republican tyrants and the Knownothings, he had performed a noble duty and a virtuous act.

With all the light he had upon the subject, he was eminently conscientious and patriotic. It was not his crime. It was the crime of Alderman Burns and the great organization of which he was a shining light and influential member. If Andrew Dillon, on his arrival, had met no Democratic worker, and had entered no Democratic recruiting shop, but had been favored by the acquaintance of some good citizen, who would enlighten him as to his duties and rights under the law, and who would appeal to all that was wise, patriotic and generous in his nature, he might have easily become a devoted Republican and a law-abiding man.

But he was an Irishman. He had landed at Castle Garden, had entered the devil's political net, and became charged to the teeth with the virus of the so-called Democracy.

CHAPTER XXI.

"GREATER IRELAND."

THE war of the Rebellion was at an end, and the streets of New York were enlivened by dissolving views of the victorious army. Remnants of regiments, men with bleared faces, ragged regimentals and tattered battle-flags, marched along Broadway to the music of military bands. Crippled veterans, some who had lost a leg, some who had ost an arm, some hobbling along on crutches, others tottering on wounded or enfeebled limbs, were familiar figures. There was joy over the return of husbands, fathers and sons, and commensurate grief in the households of those whose beloved ones were missing from the ranks of the living, and mustered in upon "the eternal camping ground of fame."

The heroic remnant of Lee's once powerful army had surrendered to General Grant. The Confederacy died as it had lived, heroically, true to its solemn pledge that it would "die in the last ditch," and so it died. The Confederacy was not merely conquered, as other great rebellions were. Its forces were not merely outnumbered. The Confederacy disappeared only when its civil government and military power were literally annihilated. Neither history nor fiction nor time can obliterate the record. The Confederacy bravely fought and heroically perished. There is nothing in the record of the fighting men to shame the valor of the American people.

There was joy throughout the North, and though the bitterness of defeat rankled at the Southern heart, it was a blessed hour for North and South when the angel of peace spread its wings above Grant and Lee at Appomattox. Amid the general rejoicing that followed the surrender of Lee came the terrible news of the assassination of Lincoln; and again the land was steeped in gloom, and again the Nation wept sad, bitter tears, and dressed itself in deepest mourning. Among the wise, the virtuous and the merciful, there was no difference of opinion as to the cruel murder. It was generally deplored. Since Christ had died on Calvary, no nobler figure passed from earth. But in the slums of New York City there was rejoicing over the death of Lincoln. The chief demon of the Republicans had been killed, and great was the joy in the breathing-places of hell at Gotham.

The public buildings, the great business houses, churches, residences and squares were draped in mourning, and a general gloom pervaded the countenance of every law-abiding and liberty-loving man.

The Irish emigrant found it difficult to comprehend how there could be a divided public opinion as to the death of Lincoln. The native American people generally deplored it, and among them there were heard expressions of sorrow, anxiety, rage and revenge. Among the industrious and respectable Irish, too, there was scarcely a division of opinion. They condemned the assassination as a wanton, cruel, uncalled-for murder, contrary to their Christian feelings and patriotic instincts.

Andy Dillon's sweetest consolation in exile was the contemplation of a "Greater Ireland." His liberty-loving soul yearned to gaze upon his exiled race in its trans-Atlantic home, where free institutions, unlimited opportunities and equality before the law afforded ample scope for the exercise of the "cloudy and lightning genius of the Gael." His countrymen were all friends of liberty, of course, and no doubt they had hoarded up to the credit side of their honor a burning sympathy with the emancipation of the black man.

One morning, while his soul was filled with these delightful fancies, he saw, at the corner of Chambers street and Broadway, a little yellow man engaged in a hand-to-hand fight with a crowd of boot-blacks.

"Hit 'im agin, Patsy!" "Go it, Micky!" "Give it to de bloke!" "Murder de dam Chinaman!" "Smash him, Tommy!" "Dat's right—hit him wid de box!" These were the sounds that disturbed his reverie. He hurried to the rescue of the stranger, and succeeded in scaring away the Chinaman's tormentors. He then extended to the little yellow man the right hand of fellowship, and advanced in his most eloquent words the doctrine of the universal brotherhood of man; but the Chinaman "feared the Greeks, even when bearing gifts," and, with a continued aspect of fear, declined the proffered hand.

"Don't be afraid o' me, darlin'," said Dillon. "I'm a friend of the foreigner. I'm a Democrat. I am your friend."

"Hellee! Me no takee hand. You no Melican man—you Ilishman." But the voice and manner of the emigrant were so persuasive that the Chinaman at last believed him sincere, and gave him his confidence.

"Why," said Dillon, "don't you be an *omathaun*. I'm your friend; I'll protect you. I'm a Democrat; and I suppose you, bein' a foreigner, are also a Democrat."

"You bettee me no Limoclat!" said the Chinaman. "Me no Ilishman. Ebelee Ilishman a Limoclat, an' ebelee Limoclat an Ilishman." And the Chinaman explained that he was not a citizen. He had only one idea in politics—a hatred of the Democratic party; for, as he understood it, every Irishman was a Democrat, and every Democrat an Irishman.

Somewhat discouraged at this first exhibition of liberality, as preached by the tongues and blacking-boxes of the gamins, he turned back on Chambers street, and on up Chatham street toward the business place of Alderman Burns. There surely would he hear the gospel of liberty—in that center of civilization, in that hotbed of Democracy. On approaching the place, he was surprised and delighted to see his friend of the *Hibernia*, Tony Sexton, the black man, who had traced him from the boarding house; but his friend looked greatly excited, and as Dillon warmly grasped the hand of his benefactor, a murmur of dissent and a derisive laugh went up from the crowd around the bar. Alderman Burns gave an overpowering though somewhat dignified scowl; but Dillon begged their attention for a moment, and supposed he would excite the proverbial generosity of the race by reciting the story of the negro's manly and heroic treatment of himself.

"And now, there," he concluded; "doesn't that beat Damon and Pythias?"

"It doesn't make a pinch of difference, Andy," said the alderman, "if he suffered crucifixion for ye; he's a nigger, and out he goes!" and half a dozen voices echoed the dictate of the alderman: "Out wid him!" "Out wid the bloody nigger!"

"Gentlemen," said Dillon, "this black man is my friend—my dearest friend on earth. He found me penniless in Galway; he stowed me away in his ship, and afterwards, when I was discovered, he risked his life to defend me."

"No matter; he's a nigger!" said one.

"You're whistlin'; he's a naygur!" said another.

"Out he goes!" said a third one.

"Bounce him!" added the third fellow at the lunch counter.

"But, gentlemen, said Dillon, "he's my friend, and poorly it becomes an Irishman to turn his back upon one who in need befriended him."

But Alderman Burns' word was law, and the black man turned and went out.

"Very well," said Dillon; "if he goes, I'll go; good night. Grateful for past favors, alderman, I may lose you as a friend, but I'll not be false to human nature. I'll never be guilty of ingratitude."

"Stop awhile," said several voices. "Andy, don't be a fool. Let the damn nigger go. You are actin' like an abolitionist."

But Andy disregarded their entreaties, and hurried into the street, in company with his friend.

But before he went away, he returned to the door, and facing the crowd, he said:

"A day will come when a generation of Irishmen, yet unborn, will blush for deeds like this. The schoolmaster is abroad in Ireland, and is doing the work that will give to the world a newer and a nobler generation. And is this your love of liberty, that came to us in wails across the ocean? And is this your Democracy? If so, may the devil fly away wid Democracy!"

CHAPTER XXII.

STILL CHASING HIS "ERIN MOR."

"BUY a shovel, young man; here's a two-dollar note. Buy a shovel."

This was the advice Andy Dillon received from Horace Greeley, with whom he had obtained an interview.

During Sunday night he became possessed with an idea which he regarded as an inspiration. He could not live upon freedom's air alone, so he must find employment, and the occupation most congenial to his taste, most harmonious with his lofty desires, was editorial writing. On Monday he sought the office of the New York *Tribune*, edited by Horace Greeley. Learning that Mr. Greeley had not yet arrived, he loitered in the vicinity until the great editor mounted the stairs to the editorial sanctum of the *Tribune*. He followed closely behind, and was confronted at the door of Mr. Greeley's office by a savage-looking youth with a triangular mouth and a crop of hair that stood upon his head as if he had seen a ghost.

"What d'ye want?" inquired the door-keeper.

"I want to see Mr. Greeley."

"He isn't in."

"Oh, yes, he is. I saw him come up the stairs."

"Naw, you didn't. He isn't in, and you can't see him, which amounts to the same thing. You git!"

This was the same youth who had threatened to throw Vice-President Wilson, of Massachusetts, down the stairway of the *Tribune;* but Dillon was unconscious of his combative character, and so he persisted.

"Will you git?" queried the human mastiff.

"I want to get into Mr. Greeley's office," said the greenhorn.

The door-keeper reached his right hand for the collar of the intruder, and jerked him in the direction of the stairway. The greenhorn reached his left hand for the throat of the door-keeper, and hurled him against the office door. Mr. Greeley stepped out into the hall-way; and as a pair of menagerie animals are awed into submission by the presence of the keeper, at sight of the editor the combatants stood apart.

The remarks made by Mr. Greeley would not bear publication. When the rage of the great man had expended itself, he demanded:

"What is it? be brief—what do you want?"

"I am a young man lately landed from Ireland, and want to be an editor."

Mr. Greeley's face presented the appearance of a Frenchman's countenance when he has smelled something disagreeable. He hurriedly thrust his fingers into his vest pocket, extracted a two-dollar bill, handed it to the aspirant for editorial honors, and with a tone which was never forgotten by the party addressed, said: "Here is a two-dollar note, young man; buy a shovel."

"But a word, Mr. Greeley. I want to tell you my scheme as to 'Greater Ireland.'"

"Not a word," said Mr. Greeley, as he slammed the door and locked it on the inside.

The ferocious door-keeper posted a chair in another room overlooking the hall-way, looked over the transom light as Andy descended the stairway, and shouted after him triumphantly: "You git, greeny! you git!"

He turned from the *Tribune* building to the office of the *Irish-American*. Mr. Meehan received him kindly and courteously; and while he unfolded his scheme as to *Erin Mor*, the calculating editor regarded him with mingled feelings of doubt, curiosity and pity—doubted his sanity, enjoyed his simplicity, and pitied his foolishness.

"Mr. Meehan," ne said, "I am a day-dreamer. In fancy I have turned my eyes a thousand times to the American side of the Atlantic; and as I thought of Little Ireland bleeding to death, I thought of a Greater Ireland in America. I am a trifle disappointed at appearances, but I am hopeful of the future. Knowledge is a wondrous power, and I am turning my eyes to the good time coming, when our race—more numerous, more enlightened and more prosperous—will harmonize with the American people in building up a great nation in America, wise enough, strong enough and sufficiently respected to hinder England from placing an unfriendly hand on Ireland."

Mr. Meehan laughed. "Well, well, Mr. Dillon, that's a most delightful dream. But why should you come to me with your scheme, Mr. Dillon?"

"Because, sir, I knew you to be an Irishman, and suspected you of patriotism."

"Very good, young man; thank you for your esteem. But, while I am an Irishman, and, if you please, a patriot, I am also a Democrat—the editor of a Democratic paper in New York City. Our countrymen, especially those who came in famine times, are Democrats—natural Democrats, sir; and—and—and—well, in short, Mr. Dillon, what d'ye take me for?" and the veteran patriot rose and, after the manner of princes, diplomats and busy men, retreated slowly a step or two, as a signal for the departure of his visitor; and the visitor took his leave; and as he slowly and sadly walked up Park Row he remembered the command of God to Adam; paraphrased the language of Horace Greeley, "Buy a shovel, young man, buy a shovel;" and he realized that dreams are dreams, and it seemed as if his delightful picture of *Erin Mor*, in a gilded frame with purest glass, had fallen on the rude stones of New York City.

Next morning, thanks to the influence of Alderman Burns, he found himself standing twenty feet below the level of the street, with a shovel in his fist, digging a sewer-trench in Third avenue.

With his first sixty days' savings he bought a passage ticket for Nancy McHugh, and in due time he heard the joyful news that the *Britannia* had arrived, was anchored in the harbor, and would land her passengers on the following morning.

He was at Castle Garden before its doors were opened, and by eight o'clock, in response to the call of her name, his heart went bounding at the cheerful answer of Nancy. In a moment they were in each other's arms, and had exchanged every loving salutation in the Irish vocabulary.

A thousand inquiries were made and answered in relation to old friends, and a thousand tales unfolded as to the dances and the wakes, the patterns and the fairs, the hurlin's, the marriages and matchmakings.

"As to old Ireland itself," said Andy, "there is no hope for her, while there is a British gun-boat on the Irish coast, or an English flag on Dublin Castle."

Andy proposed an immediate marriage, but to this proposition the *cailin* demurred. She was the oldest of her mother's family. There were three other children, and she would never get married, she said, until she had paid the passages, or otherwise relieved the helpless ones at home. Nancy had a brave heart, but her form was frail. She was a pure Celt, with coal-black hair, a sweet hazel eye, with lips like little rose buds, and Andy, in poetic terms, often compared her neck and brow, as contrasted with her raven hair, to a snow drift underneath a bank of coal; and "her soul," he said, "was pure as the waters of the blessed spring at *Tubber-Patrick.*"

She was faithful to her purpose. She was soon receiving a dollar a day—four shillings she always reckoned it. She "batched" with a fellow-working-girl, and, by self-denial and close economy, was enabled to save something like three dollars a week, which she regularly deposited in the local savings bank.

Andy labored earnestly at his own task. Very often at night, at the close of the Fenian circle meetings, the "brothers" would invite him to the bar-room on the ground floor of "Military Hall," where the meetings were held, but he steadily declined. He saved his dollars, and every delve of his pick, every upward turn of his shovel received an impetus from the blessed hope that he would soon be able to make a home for the prospective Mrs. Dillon.

The moral dry-rot had already taken possession of Fenianism. It was a losing cause, to which the faithful and devoted still ardently clung; but its petty leadership had become a regular profession for what it might be worth. Every circle had its unofficial commissary, and when the meeting terminated in the hall above, the circle usually descended in a body to the bar below. There the political captains turned aside from their pretensions to Irish patriotism, and discussed the glories of Democracy and the shining virtues of alderman so-and-so, or senator this and that.

The merits of O'Sullivan for alderman usurped the place of Ireland's hope for liberty. A vast majority of the members were men of good character, and labored for a living; but there were some few who fed upon various forms of human misfortune, and who scoffed at all forms of religion. All this was sullenly tolerated by the majority, for "conscience sake," and in the interest of fraternity; but there was one unpardonable crime—the crime of "Black Republicanism." For this there was no toleration. Not one Irishman in a hundred would dare to avow a Republican sentiment.

There was Patsy Bradley, of the Wolf Tone Circle, a very giant in stature, who had seen four long years service in the army, who had his lower jaw torn out in front of Fredericksburg, who time after time had borne a part in forlorn hopes, and went with a cheer up to the very muzzles of artillery; but in Captain O'Grady's bar-room he did not have the moral courage to say that his soul was his own, nor would he dare to avow his sympathy with the Republican party. He would secretly vote the Republican ticket; and when Colonel Denny Burke endeavored to have him proclaim his political sentiments, he would beg his old comrade to spare him the consequent torture.

"I'm all right for the ticket and the party, Colonel," he would say; "but for the love of God, don't put the boys on to me."

Captain O'Grady was especially severe on Dillon. He suspected him of sentiments inharmonious with the workings of Democracy. He had actually heard the greenhorn declare that "in the sight of God the color of a man's face made no difference." In debating with Captain O'Grady, who was a devout Christian, Dillon was heard to say that "before God's altar, in receiving the Blessed Sacrament, in the pews of the church, there is no distinction as to color. And what'll you do, Captain, when you go to heaven? There you'll have to associate with the souls of negroes—aye, even with the souls of African saints and martyrs."

And the captain would end the controversy by arrguing that God, in his omnipotence, would color the nigger white before he admitted him into the society of gentlemen in heaven.

These incidents went far to shake the Democratic faith of Dillon; yet he would not be tempted by any earthly consideration to express the slightest doubt as to the everlasting rectitude of Democracy, and he would rather suffer the loss of an eye or an arm than have some heeler put upon his track to denounce him as a turn-coat.

CHAPTER XXIII.

IRISH INCONSISTENCY.

ON Fenian times England once again asserted her ancient doctrine of "Once a citizen, always a citizen." John Warren, Thomas Francis Burke, Edward O'Meagher Condon and other American citizens, ex-officers of the Union army, had been tried in England and Ireland for treason-felony, and many of them were convicted for acts done and words spoken on American soil. James G. Blaine, a member of Congress from the State of Maine, resented this doctrine upon the floor of the House, and excited among his fellow members a determination to insist upon the doctrine that naturalized citizens of the United States were entitled to the same privileges and protection as native citizens. He contended and insisted that no American, native or naturalized, might be convicted in a British court for acts done or words spoken on American soil. His efforts led to the immediate release of Costello, and ultimately to an international understanding, by which England abandoned the doctrine of perpetual allegiance, and which guaranteed to adopted citizens the same privileges accorded to native citizens abroad, and worked the release of many of the convicted American Fenians. Thaddeus Stevens, of Pennsylvania, was chairman of the Committee on Foreign Relations of the House of Representatives. A committee of Fenians was appointed to wait on the Foreign Relations Committee, to urge the action of the American government for the release of certain American citizens then in English prisons. The leader of this Fenian delegation was John F. Scanlan, of Illinois, a member of an Irish family distinguished for its devotion to liberty in Ireland and America. He was then a young man, full of enthusiasm, and very thoroughly informed as to the history of his native and adopted countries. Of the whole Fenian delegation of ten, he was the only man who called himself a Republican. He entertained a highly enlightened love for America, and a commensurate hatred of England. He knew that, from the battle of Bunker Hill to the surrender of Appomattox, the sympathies of England had been against America. He kept thoroughly informed on the secret efforts of the English on behalf of the Confederacy in an effort to destroy the Union, and when he essayed to address the distinguished committee of Congress, his words were listened to with respectful consideration. If the Fenian delegation had been wise, it would have rested its case when this man had spoken; but it was not wise. A number of New York City men, including Andy Dillon, were "loaded" for the occasion, and several eloquent speeches were discharged into the minds of the Congressional committee. The speakers dilated on the services of Irishmen in the Union army. They rung the changes on "freedom, liberty and patriotism."

Thaddeus Stevens was evidently very restless. He was a man who abhorred false pretenses. He had devoted many years to the cause of liberty and union. A man of iron will, of violent temper, of controlling mind, he swayed, in his day, the Republican majority in Congress, and moulded much of national legislation during the war and reconstruction periods. He was evidently irritated by the Irish delegation, but he bore with them patiently until the close of the speeches. He was disabled in his legs, and rose to a standing position with pain and difficulty.

"You are all great friends of liberty, are you?" said he.

"We are, indeed, sir; we are."

"You are all patriots—all devoted to the cause of human liberty in America, are you?"

"We are!" "We are!" "We are!"

Then Thaddeus clenched his teeth and his fists, and looked at them bitterly and scornfully.

"I hate you!" said he. "Confound you, I hate you! You are always deafening the ears of mankind with your whine for liberty—for Irishmen only; but you are forever ready to jump on the bodies of every other human being battling for liberty. You are always snarling at England, but you are ever ready with your ballots to do her work in America, to the detriment of this Nation and its people. You land upon our shores, and find employment in our factories, and you then join the English interest in America, to vote for the destruction of the factories. You have persistently voted against the Republican party, and you are now voting against the liberties of four millions of black men who never did you any wrong. I hate you, confound you! I hate you! But your countrymen now confined in the prison-pens of England are American citizens, among them gallant fellows who risked their lives in defense of the government, and the Republican party will protect them. But I hate you, confound you; I hate you!"

The hot blush of shame mantled the face of every Irishman present. If the question of negro suffrage had been submitted to them before Mr. Stevens had spoken, nine to one would have voted against it. If the question were then and there submitted, they would have voted unanimously for enfranchisement. They had heard the truth for once. Some of them had never in their lives before listened to the voice of a representative American. They regarded it as high treason to hear a Republican speech or read a Republican newspaper. As they descended the steps of the Capitol building, the Illinois man gave a hearty laugh. He had often deplored the inconsistency of Irishmen in American politics, but neither he nor any of his brother delegates had ever heard that inconsistency so powerfully presented.

"Here you are," he said, "moping like bats and owls to shun the light of day, when this magnificent American draws the curtain of your hiding-place and exposes you to the full glare of God's sunlight. You remind me of ostriches, which, when hotly pursued, bury their heads in the sand, and supposing themselves hidden because they have blinded themselves, expose their hind parts to the weapons of their pursuers."

They saw the force of the argument; and though some of them did not for years muster courage to vote according to their judgment and their conscience, in the year 1884 every man of the nine save two, who were then dead, was a conspicuous fighting advocate of Blaine for President, and for protection to American industry.

"Young man, what do you think?" said the Illinoisan to Dillon.

"I dunno what to think," said Dillon. "Of course, I am a Democrat—never voted anything but a Democratic ticket—but on principle I agree with the Republicans. If I was not a Democrat I would be a Republican; but, being an Irishman, you see, I must be a Democrat, though God knows I cannot agree on principle with my party."

"For shame!" responded the citizen of Illinois. "If you were some ignorant creature, who never saw the inside of a school-house; if you were some broken-down wretch, whose soul was in the keeping of some little ward politician; if you received your morning drink for sweeping out some bar-room, I could pity and excuse you; but you, a man, created, as you believe, in the likeness of God—you, who have worked and prayed and run the career of an outlaw for Ireland's liberty—for you and such as you I have no mercy. You are moral cowards, who deserve and receive the contempt of the American people."

"Well," replied Dillon, "I cannot dispute what you say. The Republicans have the right of it; but bein', as I am, a Democrat, I must be a Democrat. If it were known that I was to vote in accordance with the opinions that I entertain, the boys would make life unbearable for me. I'm a Democrat, of course, and so being, I must be a Democrat; but, between ourselves, the next time I vote I'll think about it. But, for God's sake, sir, don't say that I told you so. I couldn't live in the ward nor hold my job if I was anything but a Democrat."

"Thad. Stevens' creed is good Fenian doctrine, isn't it?" said Scanlan.

"I can't deny that," said Dillon.

"Then," responded his friend, "don't be a bat or an owl. The doctrine of liberty is universal in its application, and there is little consistency in claiming liberty for Irishmen, while denying it to any other race of men; and there is just as little consistency in taking an oath to fight England, and on your arrival in this country casting your ballot to advance her interests—her commercial interests, I mean. But here we are at the depot."

"I'll think about it," said Dillon.

And he did think about it. Neither prejudice nor sophistry, nor moral cowardice, could ever cancel the truth of Thad. Stevens' argument on Irish inconsistency.

It was thus that Irishmen became Republicans—shamed into a sense and confession of their inconsistency by the burning words and heroic deeds of liberty-loving Americans. The change has been painfully slow. But it is only the courageous man who *honestly* changes sides in politics; and no man fully realizes the strength of political ties until he has broken them.

CHAPTER XXIV.

PETTY POLITICAL REVENGE.

DILLON reported to the Fenian circle the result of the trip to Washington; repeated substantially the remarks of Thaddeus Stevens, and offered a resolution of thanks to the Republican leader. A growl of dissent rose in chorus from the circle.

"To the devil wid Thad. Stevens!"

Half a dozen members rose at once to speak, and loud and bitter were the denunciations poured out upon the action and the motives of Dillon. From that moment his influence in the circle was gone, and his brother members denounced him as a "turn-coat and a traitor," an enemy of their blessed religion, a receiver of Republican "goold." If he had entered a church, and dashed a chalice from the hands of an officiating priest, his sin would be more readily forgiven. He might have taken a club and smashed a picture of the crucifixion, and be excused by some of the members; but in speaking in favor of the Republican party, he had made himself an Ishmaelite. His resolution was voted down, and hissed down unanimously. By an unwritten law of the Fenian brotherhood, American politics were excluded from discussion at their meetings, and so a fitting expression of their feelings on the subject was reserved until they had informally re-assembled in the back room of Captain O'Grady. There Dillon was vigorously denounced. They would listen to no defence, explanation or apology. Next morning he was discharged from his employment in the sewer trenches.

"Sorry for you," said the foreman; "but no one suspected of using a pencil on the Democratic ticket can hould a job upon the public works of New York."

In the private office of Isaac Marx, near Chatham Square, three men were engaged conversing in undertones on the evening of Dillon's discharge. Frequent mention was made of Andy's name. The trinity consisted of Isaac Marx, Alderman Burns, and Mr. Barney Devoy, of New Limerick. The subject of the conference was to devise ways and means to injure or disgrace Dillon. Alderman Burns was at first unwilling to lend himself to the scheme. He could not, he said, willingly injure the friend of his youth, a young man who, aside from his sin against the Democratic party, was a very worthy fellow, industrious, honest, and a good Irishman.

"He's no Irishman," said Devoy. "Any man who has love or likin' for the Republican party is no Irishman. He's a turn-coat, a back-slider and a thraithor, and he ought to be run out o' town."

"Right, *mine freund*," said Mr. Isaac Marx; and turning to Alderman Burns, he added: "Pisness is pisness, mine dear Alderman. You lof your *freund*, but you better lof the Democratish barty. Your *freund* Dillon ish no goot. You need not do the vork yourself. You leaf him to me—I fix him."

The alderman felt as if his heart turned upside down. He hated to injure and betray the friend of his youth; but he was a Democrat—his first duty was to the party. That duty was very simple. He was commanded to induce Dillon to take a few drinks, and then lead him down to Mr. Marx's establishment. This task he quickly accomplished. He met the victim at his own place of business, took him into the private office, and gave him honied words and loving sentiments; and to water the tree of memory, saturated him with several drinks of whisky. He then led him to Mr. Marx's saloon and turned him over to the tender mercies of Isaac and Barney.

"Ah, mine dear *freund*, I vas so very glad to meet you—so very glad," said Mr. Marx; and Barney talked Irish with him; sang "*Acushla gal macree*" for him; and by request, Dillon favored his new friends with an old Irish air: "Let Erin Remember the Days of Old;" and the whisky flowed, and the two new friends wouldn't permit him to spend a cent. And they drank and sang and smoked until after midnight; and they laid him out upon a sofa, and they danced attendance upon him. At daylight in the morning other friends joined the company in the shape of relays to relieve old Barney and Isaac, until on the second day Dillon passed through the several stages of royally drunk, gloriously drunk and dead drunk. Since he came to America he had been abstemious, as a matter of self-respect and of economy; but in his younger days he had been convivial, and when fairly started on the spree, like many of the bravest, the wisest and the best of men, he did not know when to stop. Many a time he feebly resolved to quit, but the dear friends (?) clung to him and overthrew his resolutions; and when the expert judgment of Isaac and Barney pronounced him on the verge of delirium tremens, they carefully searched his pockets, finding only a fraction of a dollar, for he had left his wallet with more than two hundred dollars in the safe of Alderman Burns. They next loaded him into a cab, with instructions to the driver to "dump him in Central Park."

If there is any one condition more than another in which the human soul fights an unequal battle with the devil, it is when a man is incompletely sober, after a protracted drunk. His reason, his understanding and his sense of duty are all engaged in urging him to become sober; but his will is enfeebled, his appetite for liquor inflamed, and the power of body absent, as well as the power of spirit.

In this condition Dillon found himself at daylight—chilly, spiritless, hungry, thirsty, reckless. If he had not an immortal soul and a hope of the hereafter, and a loyal love for Nancy McHugh, he would just as soon sink his body in a river or walk into the crater of a volcano. He had reached his lowest depth of degradation—had lost his self-respect and self-esteem. A drowsy, dreamy feeling came over him. He tried to move, but found it at first impossible. The earth reeled, the trees and buildings appeared to be dancing; the tall grass seemed a thing of life—or rather ten thousand things: frogs, snakes, cockroaches, eels, crawling things with fiery eyes, jumping at him and crawling over him. Thus tortured and pursued, he dashed away down one of the shaded avenues, and headlong from a high stone arch to the granite pavement thirty feet below.

* * *

Late in the afternoon of the same day he opened his eyes in a state of semi-consciousness. He was in a large room. There were beds ranged around the walls. Pale-faced women, clothed in plain dark garments and great white linen bonnets, moved silently among the inmates of the beds. One of them stood calmly at the foot of his couch, and beside him, crucifix in hand, stood Father O'Connell, a priest of the Catholic church. When he opened his eyes, the priest placed a hand upon his forehead and smoothed his fevered brow; then sprinkled his face, and placed a glass of water to his lips. He recognized the priest.

"Where am I, Father, and how did I come here?"

"Patience, my son," said the priest; "you are among friends. You are very ill. Keep quiet a little while. Be contented, and feel assured that you are with friends. To-morrow you will know the rest."

"Oh, Father, my right leg is terribly sore, and I have no strength to move it."

"True, my son, your leg is in a bad condition—very lame. It is of the utmost importance that you do not try to move it. The fact is, you have suffered an accident. Well, if you must know, your leg is broken, and you must keep perfectly still."

"Then, Father, you can tell me where I am."

"My son," said the priest, "you are in the Sisters' Hospital. You came here early this morning."

"Father," said the patient, "tell me all. Why am I here, and how did I get here?"

"My son," said the priest, "I would prefer not to talk about your affairs now; but if you are sure you can bear it, I will tell you all."

"Do, please," said the wounded man.

"So be it, then," said the priest. "At daylight this morning I was crossing Central Park, returning from a sick call. I found you lying on one of the drive-ways, apparently lifeless. Opening your shirt collar, in the hope of restoring you to conciousness, I found that you wore a scapular, from which I inferred that you were a Catholic, probably an Irishman. I called an ambulance, and brought you here. You are in the Sisters' Hospital, and these two angels of mercy, Sisters Mary Isidore and Mary Bertha, have nursed you back to life."

For weary months Andy Dillon occupied his cot in the Sisters' Hospital. During all this time these two sisters, under whose special care he was placed, were almost constantly with him. Mary Isidore was a tall, æsthetic, highly intellectual woman, "wise as a serpent, and harmless as a dove." She knew this man better than he knew himself. She knew his weaknesses and his sorrows, and his struggles against temptation, and yet she never made a single suggestion that would remind him of those weaknesses. Irresistibly he confided to her his follies and his sins, but instead of rebuking him and chiding him, she simply shared in his contrition, told him of the efficacy of prayer, and reminded him of the goodness and mercy of God. Mary Bertha was as pious as her elder sister, fully as divine, but a trifle more human. Nature did it. She was far below the middle height, but very strongly built, and her sweet little face exercised the vivifying influence of a summer sun. She was an organized smile. She did more hard manual labor than any two sisters in the institution, but "God fitted the back for the burthen." She never complained, rarely talked religion, but she constantly ministed to the material wants of the suffering and the dying. The fever patient calling at midnight for water, found little Bertha suddenly appear at his bed-side, and the consumptive craving for his stimulant at the dawn of day, also found her standing at his side.

Two marvelous women, these! Yet no; nothing extraordinary. The world abounds in sisters just like them. You find them in the stifling tenement, among the paupers of calamity, and the paupers of iniquity. You see them hurriedly moving along the forbidding alleys of the great cities. You find them in the institutions of charity, bathing the feet of the aged, and eating the refuse of the pauper's meal. You find them in the fever hospital, in the plague-stricken city, under fire of artillery, close behind the front rank of the army in battle, binding the bleeding wounds of suffering soldiers, and quenching the burning thirst of dying men. You would probably find them in purgatory, ministering to the temporarily condemned; and so surely as there is a God and an eternity, they will be found in heaven rejoicing with those whose dying eyes they closed, while they whispered the blessed consolation of immortality.

The two sisters knew that whisky had been the immediate cause of Dillon's misfortune.

Mary Isidore would frequently say: "If it were not for the curse of liquor, I could conceive no such thing as a hell for the Irish. I have seen men and women," she continued, "who had qualities to equip them for sainthood or martyrdom, converted into human fiends and hideous hags by the demon of alcohol."

"There is no half-way house," little Bertha would say. "The proximate occasion of sin is sin. Where one is liable to intoxication the sin is in the first glass. Repentance is precious, but it is much better not to sin." She would ask him to contemplate the blessed thirst of the Redeemer, and resolve to drink no more intoxicants.

The pious teachings were effective. He took the total abstinence pledge before he left the hospital, and went out into the world a sober man.

CHAPTER XXV.

THE BELFAST OF AMERICA.

DURING his stay at the hospital, Dillon had become the intimate friend and confidant of Dr. Patrick Barry, the surgeon who attended him. It was his good fortune, also, to secure the friendship of Dr. William McNevin, an Irish Methodist preacher from the State of Ohio, who, on his return from Ireland, had visited the hospital. It was in the early days of September, about eleven o'clock in the forenoon, that these two friends left the Sisters' Hospital. They walked down Broadway and into Fifth avenue at Madison Square.

"Curious," said the Western preacher; "all your principal hotels have English names."

"No, not all of them," said Dr. Barry, "but enough of them. We have, as you see, the Buckingham, the Marlborough and the Victoria, but no Washington Hotel, no Jackson Hotel and no Grant Hotel. These things are in demand. The names are attractive cards for foreign tourists, and our own gilded youth and shoddy aristocracy delight in the association of the distinguished or pretentious foreigners."

Several beefy-looking young gentlemen were observed riding up the avenue on horseback, the tails of the horses trimmed, and each rider armed with a whip-stock without a lash.

"These," said the preacher, "I suppose, are distinguished Englishmen?"

"No, indeed," replied the doctor. "They are commonplace Americans, aping, to the best of their ability, the manners and habits of the British aristocracy; and the most pronouncedly British-looking man among them is the over-fed, beefy-looking fellow, who is the son of an Irish contractor."

Their attention was attracted by the elaborate display of elegant "gents' furnishing goods" in one of the store windows on Madison Square. Beside the window was a gilded sign bearing this legend: "No goods sold here but imported goods."

"Well, well!" said the preacher. "If any man out west had told me of an establishment in an American city bearing such a sign as that, I would not have believed him."

Animated by feelings of mingled anger and disgust, the pair crossed the avenue and promenaded the walks under the generous shade of the trees in Madison Square. Their minds were temporarily diverted by the noisy twitter of numerous little birds.

A number of them were engaged in an effort to kill another little bird, of a different species and of somewhat highly colored plumage.

"What birds are these?" inquired the preacher.

"These," said Dr. Barry, "are English sparrows, engaged at their congenial task of killing off some little domestic bird. How typical of the spirit of the British nation! They were imported here as friends, for the purpose of aiding the farmers to destroy bugs, worms, insects and other pests af agriculture; but they have abandoned their mission, taken to our centers of population, where food is plenty, and in securing their plunder they kill every living thing weaker than themselves in the land to which they have come, that in any way interferes with the gratification of their appetites. I understand that the man who first imported them is now 'doing time' in a Pennsylvania penitentiary; and whatever the guilt or innocence of the man of the crime for which he was convicted, if he imported the English sparrow 'willfully and with malice aforethought,' he ought to be in the penitentiary."

"They have not yet reached the West," said the preacher, with a sigh of relief.

"No," replied Dr. Barry; "but they will get there some day. You will have the British free-trader and the English sparrow out west pretty soon, and it will require your forbearance, courage, caution, industry and patriotism to head them off and circumvent them."

Turning out of Madison Square, the two gentlemen walked down Broadway to Union Square, a little more than a quarter of a mile.

"Here," said Dr. Barry, "step into this open carriage. Let us ride a couple of miles. Let me show you the Belfast of America."

"The Belfast of America?" said the preacher. "I

would prefer to call it the Dublin of America. It was in turn the New Amsterdam of the Dutch and the New York of the British. With its Irish population, it ought now to be called New Dublin."

"No," said Barry; "I insist on Belfast, and in so calling it I mean no unkindness to the hustling city of Northern Ireland. New York, like Belfast, is a great city—only, of course, immensely greater than Belfast. It is great in commerce, great in manufactures, great in its newspapers, finances, charitable institutions and churches. It is a splendid place to live, if one is rich and has the means to select his locality. But its commercial, financial and political life is not merely un-American—it is anti-American. Look at the signs above the doors of these mercantile houses. The names are not American, and the owners are not American. They are a European colony of traders, intrenched at the gateway of national commerce, and, in the very nature and necessity of their business, hostile to the development of American manufacturing industries. They are a great people, but they are not Americans, nor of the American people. This is your American Belfast, fattening on the commerce of a land to whose political and industrial aspirations it is bitterly hostile."

"I have heard numerous reasons," said the preacher, "why New York is Democratic, but I never saw it in that light until now."

"Now," said Dr. Barry, "let me show you the grave-yard of the Irish race. We will discharge the carriage at Chambers street, and turn to the left. Before leaving Broadway, let me impress one fact particularly on your mind. Whenever I call the attention of Irishmen to the evils that afflict a portion of our people, I am accused of 'slandering the Irish.' Almighty God forbid! When I was a boy I fondly hoped to fight for Irish independence, and to be rewarded by six feet of Irish earth for a grave. In later years, in my humble way, I've tried to do a man's share for her in every way that opportunity suggested. Even my enemies know all this, and why should I slander the Irish? I know their virtues and their elements of strength; and it warms my heart to contemplate them and discuss them. You see this mass of splendid men and comely women passing up and down Broadway. Very nearly one-half of these are our people—Irish-Americans. These men are the salesmen, porters, laborers, lawyers, editors, telegraph operators of the city, and the women are engaged in stores and factories and offices. Of these men and women we are all justly proud. But there is another side of the picture, and to this darker side I will call your attention, and the attention of all decent Irishmen, and the attention of this great American nation, in which it is our privilege to live, and I propose to do this even at the expense of being accused of 'slandering the Irish.'

"Here we are in Chatham Square. Look at that sign—'Black eyes and broken noses repaired and restored to natural color and appearance.' That is the sign of a doctor who makes a specialty of repairs. Now let me take you through the gate of the grave-yard—the Democrat factory of Mr. Isaac Marx."

"Vell, vell, shentlemens, this is an honor. Vell, vell, Dr. Mac—I vorgots the name; und mein goot vreund Dr. Barry. Coom in, shentlemens; vat vill you haf?"

They took cigars, and Mr. Marx seemed deeply grieved that they would not have a little of his "Kinihan's Double L" whisky (from Peoria) or a bottle of champagne (from Jersey). Mr. Marx's establishment was indeed a variety shop, both in its stock and the scope of its business. There was a bar, and a family department liquor store. There was also a bucket-shop department, where the man of large appetite and modest means could regale himself with a "tumbler" of whisky for a nickel. In addition to these varied industries, Mr. Marx stood ready to buy for cash, at his own price, any watches, jewelry, or other valuable articles offered by the light-fingered gentlemen of the metropolis; and he did an extensive business as bondsman for thieves and other criminals in the courts. He was also president of the "Marx Guard," a formidable political organization, composed of the Democracy of four blocks in that vicinity.

It was as President Marx, chief of the "Marx Club," that Dr. Barry addressed him; and there was a visible swell in his portly stomach as he modestly acknowledged the compliment.

"Mein boys are goot boys," Mr. Marx proudly remarked. "Ninety-seven per cent of the vote of mein precinct is Democratic. I gif mein boys a picnic at Coney Island next Soonday. Mein Irish freunds are mein customers, und the boys of mein club, und I gif them und the ladies of their families a leetle airing Soonday."

Mr. Marx was firmly intrenched in the hearts, the appetites and the ruins of his constituency. He had held his present corner for fifteen years. In his voting precinct there were one hundred and fifty Irish families, mostly exiles of the great famine of 1846–47. They were not fair specimens of the race. They were the weaklings, flung by adverse fate from their island home into the wretched tenements of the dirtiest part of the dirtiest city of America, and destitute of the power, the knowledge, or the ambition to elevate themselves. They were originally pious, rash and irascible. For years they attended mass and their religious duty; but as old age, disease, drunkenness and their attendant miseries overtook them, Mr. Marx became their high priest, his establishment their temple, and his politics their study and their worship. A vast majority preserved the virtue of their race, but through the gateway of the grave-yard—through the establishment of Mr. Marx—many of themselves and their children went to the grave, steeped in those miseries that rot the body and damn the human soul.

Dr. Barry called professionally on one of Mr. Marx's constituents—an old man named Murphy, once a brave, generous and virtuous Irishman. Mr. Marx, on the recommendation of Alderman Burns, secured employment for Murphy on the street-sweeping force, where he held his place until the city government of New York reluctantly yielded to the inevitable, by the employment of sweeping machines. For years he had suffered at times from dysentery. Of this disease Dr. Barry had succeeded in curing him. Suddenly he sent for the doctor again. This time it was diphtheria. The family lived upon the ground floor in a rear building.

"You have a cellar under this floor?" inquired the doctor.

"We have, Doctor," repied Mrs. Murphy. A lantern was obtained, and the doctor and the preacher descended into the damp, dark, foul-smelling cellar; and in a corner, directly beneath the spot where poor Murphy lay, there was an open privy vault, "smelling to heaven for vengeance," as Dr. Barry expressed it.

"To heaven for mercy," said the preacher.

"No; to heaven for vengeance," repeated the doctor. "For vengeance upon the powers that rule and rob and rot this city—upon the accursed system that neglects the first and simplest duties of municipal government; that permits the virtuous poor to suffer and to die from disease engendered in these lazar-houses. I say again, 'To heaven for vengeance.' 'It is mine,' saith the Lord; and these plague-spots will prove the avengers of the poor. You will hear of deaths among the rich—politely attributed to pneumonia, influenza and heart disease, but in truth from fevers and other disorders engendered in the homes of the poor, and rising like God's wrath to the homes of upper-tendom, becoming God's avengers of the poor."

Upon his bed, in a dark, damp corner, lay poor Murphy, dying (so Dr. Barry said). No power on earth could save him. He was in high fever, and delirious. He was calling for "Johnny" and for "Norah"—his "*bouchal bawn*, Johnny," and his "*cushla macree*, Norah."

And where were they? Where was Johnny? He was on Blackwell's Island. "He had a discussion with a Dutchman," the mother explained. "He had an iron bar in his hand at the time. It was down at Mr. Marx's grocery on election night—he had been celebratin' the victory of O'Reilley for assemblyman; and he raised the bar above the head of the Dutchman—and the bar fell over agin' the head of the Dutchman, loike." For a time it seemed as if the Dutchman would die, but he finally recovered, and, through the influence of Mr. Marx, Johnny got off with a jail sentence. And Norah—who and where was she? Norah was the oldest daughter. She was dead? "No—worse than dead," said the poor mother, with sobs and tears and groans, as she covered her face with her apron and hastily left the room.

The party took their leave—not until Dr. McNevin had placed a gold coin in the wasted hand of the afflicted Mrs. Murphy.

Dillon, who had joined the party at Chatham Square, was a silent spectator at Murphy's residence. On reaching the street, he said to Dr. Barry:

"I humbly hope that cases like this are rare."

"I grieve and blush to say they are not," said Dr. Barry. "This is a sample of the wretchedness among thousands of New York City's poor. This is the condition to which human avarice, operating through whisky and politics, has degraded them."

"And is this your Greater Ireland—my *Erin Mor?*" said Dillon.

"Young man," said Dr. Barry, passionately, "don't repeat that question. You know that this is not Greater Ireland. Greater Ireland is scattered all over the world. It comprises millions of strong, brave and virtuous men and women. It has passed through a long, dark, bitter, bloody night, and 'will have an inevitable day.' It is like a giant waking from a troubled dream, stretching its limbs, opening its eyes and hoping for greater things. No, my brother; this is not Greater Ireland. This is the great American Democrat Factory—the grave-yard of the Irish race. This is the mire into which the weak and the unfortunate have fallen. It is the narrow strip of quicksands across which Greater Ireland passes on the road to liberty and affluence. The head and heart of Greater Ireland are above the sands, and are making gallant effort to drag up the lower limbs."

The preacher listened with a tear in his eyes, and he looked at Dr. Barry and at Dillon. "This," he said, "is the bitter fruit of English rule in Ireland— the product of famine, rack-renting and free-trade; and this is the power that England now seeks to use in obtaining free-trade in the United States of America, and controlling the commerce of this continent. I am a minister of the gospel, but I am a citizen and a man; and I swear by the throne of God that England will not accomplish her ends without a struggle, in which Greater Ireland will bear a part. What say you, Doctor? What say you, Dillon?

"I simply say, amen," said Dr. Barry. "And I repeat, amen," said Dillon. "Until this hour I bore some slight allegiance to the Democratic party, 'but now my soul's my own.' Situated as I am now, I am of small account. I am lame, down-hearted and penniless; but I'll turn up some day. I'll go to California on the *Coronado* with Anthony Sexton. If fortune favors, I'll return and bear a part in the contest that confronts America in her free-trade struggle with England."

And the friends separated, Dr. Barry returning to his home, and Dr. McNevin and Dillon to the Astor House.

CHAPTER XXVI.

DEATH OF NANCY McHUGH.

DILLON, on parting with his friends, took the train for New Limerick; but the story of his misfortunes had preceded him. Mr. Marx and Mr. Devoy had visited Nancy McHugh, and told her all the details of Dillon's spree, with several insinuations and evil suggestions added. They would not vouch, they said, for the horrible story that he had been drugged and robbed in Central Park, but such was the rumor. Whenever they had occasion to reinforce the bitter truth with lies, they were "so sorry," and "it was too bad," and they themselves didn't know, but "somebody had said so."

These worthies did not intend to commit the particular crime which they were then perpetrating. Murder was no part of the programme. They only intended moral assassination—to destroy the character of Dillon, to rob him of Nancy's love, and deprive him of an intended bride. But the result was graver than the crime anticipated. At the end of their visit the enfeebled girl fainted, and retired to the bed of sickness, never to press the earth again. During all the time that Dillon lay in the hospital, Nancy was slowly but certainly dying at New Limerick. Consumption would probably have caused her death in a few years; but Messrs. Marx and Devoy sent her to eternity by a shorter route. Her lover had been informed of her illness, but had no thought that death would so speedily claim her for his own.

On approaching the cottage where Nancy resided, it became apparent that all was not well. Numerous women of doleful and subdued appearance were sitting in the little front parlor. As Dillon entered he found these women conversing in whispers. One young woman was silently shedding tears, and she, arising from her chair, suggested to him to walk softly and to remain in the outer room until she had first announced his coming. He waited some minutes, and receiving no sign to enter the sick-room, he opened the connecting door in his anxiety and peeped into the room. As he did this, Father Ventura walked out of Nancy's room. On entering he found two sisters of charity kneeling by the bed-side, with bended heads, and deeply engaged in silent prayer. A blessed candle lighted, upon a little table, stood beside the large crucifix at the foot of the bed; and upon the bed, with eyes closed and hands devoutly clasped above her heaving breast, lay the emaciated form of Nancy McHugh. She was pale as death, and pitifully wasted; but something—his imagination, perhaps, or more probably the touch of the guardian angel invisibly watching beside her—had made her seem lovelier than ever. A thousand bitter pangs crowded his aching heart. If he had only foreseen it; if he had been all that he ought to have been; if human malice had even confined itself to the bitter truth respecting his follies and misfortunes; if the politicians and their wives had only spared the tender heart of Nancy the suffering for him of a vicarious atonement; if he had left her in Ireland; if he had never met her; if he had never been born; if the waters of the Atlantic had afforded him a grave; if—if—if—"Oh God of Mercy, you know best!" he exclaimed in passionate and bitter agony, and the gentle, tender eyes of Nancy looked calmly into his agonized face.

Here the sisters arose from the bed-side and motioned Dillon to approach. They whispered the truth, that Nancy had received the last rites of the church; had made her peace with God, and would probably have been in heaven some hours ago, if she had not struggled with death in the hope of seeing him before she died. He bent his form and kissed her forehead, now clammy with the cold sweat of her dying agony. She tried to raise her wasted little arms to embrace him, but no power remained. Tenderly he lifted her hands until the fingers clasped upon his neck. Her eyes slowly closed, but the hands remained in their embrace; the patient, pure and constant heart had ceased to beat—poor Nancy McHugh was dead.

There was abundant, heart-felt sorrow at New Limerick, and in the limited circles in New York City where Nancy McHugh was known. All that is loving, noble, generous and tender in the Irish nature asserts itself in the presence of death. The remains of the departed girl were tenderly prepared by loving hands for the solemn, silent hours that intervene between death and the grave. The sisters had prepared the habiliments of death. There was the plain brown habit, with its melancholy adornments; the wreath of flowers and green vines to festoon the coffin; the white beads, with the little silver crucifix that Nancy brought from home—the gift of Father Joseph Lenehan. No bride was ever decked for the wedding feast with better grace than the poor, pale form of the dead girl was prepared for her last long rest in alien but not ungenerous earth, in the parish cemetery at New Limerick.

All this was the heritage of the dead at the hands of Christian Ireland. There was the requiem mass and the funeral sermon, the tender tears, the eternal farewells; but poor Nancy was not exempt from the penalty that seems inseparable from Irish burials in America. There was the funeral—the heartless pagan pageant that follows the corpse in hollow mockery to the grave. There were some real friends in the procession. There was a long line of livery-stable buggies; and every little politician, from the road supervisor to the village peeler and pound-master, was out in force. Mr. Isaac Marx and Mr. Barney Devoy and the old white horse were near the head of the procession; and when the grave had closed over all that was mortal of poor Nancy McHugh, the Chatham-street "fence" and his evil Irish factotum, Devoy, were among the first to extend the mockery of their condolence to the afflicted Andy Dillon.

This is "the most unkindest cut of all" to an Irishman, when the hand of God falls heavily on him by the death of some one dearly beloved—the presence and the condolence of those who have neither mercy nor pity nor charity for their living fellow-creatures. And the livery carriages; and the sad-looking "funeral director" (as the coffin-seller is now called); and the days and nights of sorrow for his dead.

But such is life, and such is death.

In a secluded corner of the little cemetery of New Limerick, under the shadow of the tall elms, under the mist and the dew, the cloud and the sunshine, the storm and the rain; under the blue sky and the watchful stars, and under the omniscient eye of a pitiful God, lie the ashes of Nancy McHugh.

May her pure soul rest in peace.

Quickly the carriages and buggies rushed back to the village—from the resting-place of the dead to the homes of the living. As Dillon stood bewildered by the side of the new-made grave, three persons only remained with him—the Rev. William McNevin, the black man, Tony Sexton, and Dr. Patrick Barry, the surgeon who had attended him at the Sisters' Hospital.

In all the sounds of earth and air, there is nothing so saddening as the dull, cold, heavy, heart-shocking fall of the clods upon the coffin of one sincerely beloved. These sounds had fallen upon his heart with crushing severity. He felt as if a dark, impenetrable, immovable shadow had fallen across his path in life, and that from out that shadow his soul

"Should be lifted nevermore."

CHAPTER XXVII.

GLORIA IN EXCELSIS DEO!

NOW that the heart and hopes of Dillon were thoroughly crushed, courtesy demanded that he receive a balm for his wounded feelings. There is some small spark of human nature in every human heart that even crime cannot entirely destroy. Mr. Marx and Mr. Devoy felt that they had done this man cruel wrong, and they concluded to make his visit at New Limerick pleasant as possible. Mr. Marx remained over Sunday for that special purpose.

On Sunday morning they escorted him to the Church of St. Loyola; and as he entered the sacred edifice, and before the mass commenced, he feasted his eyes upon the congregation. They were his people—bone of his bone, flesh of his flesh—and he was one of them—every fibre of his body, every pulse of his heart; and as he saw hundreds of men, young and old, arrayed in fine clothing, and hundreds of comely women, mothers and *cailins*, dressed in cashmeres, poplins and silks, and a score of Irish-American boys in surplice at the foot of the altar, it seemed (as he expressed it) as if "his ribs were sugar-candy, and his heart was lickin' them." The mass proceeded. Father Ventura sang, in the full, soft, melodious voice of the Italian that he was; and the choir, consisting of a dozen voices, sang the responses in soul-inspiring tones that might have awakened the souls in purgatory. Nine times was the divine clemency invoked in the *Kyrie eleison, Christe eleison* (Lord have mercy on us, Christ have mercy on us); and then arose from the dozen voices in the choir the *Gloria in excelsis Deo* (Glory be to God on high), the most ancient and sublime of all Christian doxologies, which has ascended from every vale in Christendom for thirteen hundred years.

The divine service was interrupted. The people turned round in their pews, and every eye was fixed on the door. Men rushed hurriedly into the street. A panic ensued, and in ten minutes the priest and one attendant were the only occupants of the building. The pastor concluded the mass as if nothing had occurred. Father Ventura divested himself of his vestments and proceeded across the street, forcing his way through a dense throng that had assembled in front of Bill Percival's keno room.

"What is the matter, my good friend?" the Father inquired.

"Oh, nothing, Father; a slight disturbance."

Bill Percival had merely stabbed young Teddy O'Connor, the oldest son of a prominent church member, with a dirk-knife; but the good Father went to see, and there lay the form of a seventeen-year-old youth in the agonies of death.

Percival had a "big pull" in his ward. He was innocently running a turkey raffle, when Teddy, in a state of intoxication, had interrupted the proceedings, and had threatened to lick the proprietor ; and as Father Ventura entered the Exchange, Mr. Percival was touching glasses with Colonel Hoggitt, and outlining his defense upon the ground that Teddy O'Connor had made a motion of the right hand in the direction of his hip pocket. Poor Teddy had no weapon upon him; but "that would make no difference," Judge Hoggitt explained, "if Teddy had put him in reasonable apprehension of great bodily harm." Dillon and his friends followed Mr. Percival when the sheriff arrested him, and when at the sheriff's office the reporter of the *Daily Times* inquired into the particulars, Mr. Percival modestly requested the newspaper man: "Couldn't you kindly leave my name out of the paper?"

Mr. Percival was in the hands of his friends, and morning and evening came and went, and "good citizens" discussed the probabilities of the November election ; and the steady tide of tin cans poured in upon "the family department" of the keno hall, "rushing the growler," as if the now famous proprietor were himself personally present.

Monday evening Messrs. Marx and Devoy insisted upon introducing Dillon to the leading citizens of New Limerick.

This, Dillon thought, would be highly interesting,

as it would include a trip to the factories, banks, stores and newspaper offices; but his friends shook their heads and explained that they wouldn't visit the factories.

"There's nobody there," Mr. Devoy explained, "except greasy mechanics and factory hands. We'll steer you agin' the *craim de la craim, thiggin thu?*"

They visited Mr. Bungstarter, of the Hessian brewery, and Mr. Funk, agent of the Peoria distilleries, and Mr. Albert Michael Devoy, the banker (bless the mark!), and Mr. Bowell, of the Fourth; and Mr. Marx proudly asserted that these were the political princes of New Limerick, with the votes of a thousand workingmen in their pockets.

"And don't these fine-looking Irish workingmen that I saw at mass yesterday—five hundred of them—have something to say in politics?" inquired Dillon.

"Oh, certainly," replied Mr. Marx. "They vote their ticket—their Democratic ticket; them's the boys that go it straight; not one of 'em was ever known to use a pencil. Devoy just hands 'em the ticket, and they cast a freeman's ballot, every one of 'em.

"You're whistlin'," said Mr. Devoy, by way of an amen. "They're all for Democracy, every mother's sowl of 'em; all nathural Dimocrats."

In their round of visiting, Dillon was introduced to several of the "nathural Dimocrats"—fine, broad-shouldered, vigorous-looking fellows, with eyes and ears and brawny hands, looking in every detail and outline just like men—and he sighed for his *Erin Mor*.

The little party spent the evening at the hospitable mansion of Mr. Devoy, up stairs, over the Buchanan Exchange building. Champagne and whisky flowed, but a melancholy drawback to the festivities was the persistent refusal of Dillon to drink; and when they realized his firmness they applauded his virtuous resolution, Mr. Marx observing that "no man who liked whisky ought to drink it," and Mr. Devoy adding that "no one who didn't like champagne ought to touch it."

After the festivities came the music and dancing. Professor Crapoo, who was instructing Birdelia in music, dancing and French, played the accompaniments upon the piano, while the pride of the Devoy household rendered songs from famous operas. Her favorite was, as the professor explained, a *morceau* from "Il Trovatore;" but when she rung the changes on the

"*Non ti scordar ti me,*"

old Mrs. Devoy's nerves became unstrung, and she fervently prayed "A plague upon yer *tee-mee!*" and "Bad luck to yer Italianos." Miss Birdelia, in deference to her mother's prejudices, sang

"The harp that once thro' Tara's halls,"

but in such unfamiliar "maw-claw-claws," that Dillon expressed his sorrow that she had not sung it in English.

"Oh, that was English," Mrs. Devoy explained; "but Birdelia sings by note."

On the next day Dillon was a familiar figure in town; and numerous Irish politicians, who were informed of his misfortunes, commencing with his "goin' back on the party," extended to him their condolence and sympathy; and as he looked into their eyes and realized the cruel deceit and mockery of the sympathizers, he longed

"For a lodge in some vast wilderness,"

and a hundred times he wished that some of them would kick him out doors, or openly insult him, or do anything but offer him their sympathies. At last he escaped from them, but only for a little while. He could walk some unfrequented street, or retire into his room and escape their sympathy and condolence, but he could not escape them in his dreams. He left Devoy's mansion toward midnight, and hurrying to his hotel, retired at precisely twelve o'clock. He slept and dreamt—dreamt that the wake of Nancy McHugh was being held in a damp cellar, and that Devoy and Marx were there, and that they and numerous of their henchmen extended him their condolence, and he thought each eye that looked on him was fiery, and sent forth slender columns of flame that burned into his breast; and it seemed to him as if the fingers of old Barney were cold as icicles, strong as ox-hide, and hard as steel, and that the fingers grew until each was several feet in length, extending up his sleeve and around his back, until they clutched him in deadly embrace, and that out of this terrible dilemma he made an effort to retreat; and that, as he ascended the first step, young Tony Devoy felled him with a hickory club; and that, while he lay helplessly on the stone steps, Isaac Marx picked his pockets, and Mr. Bungstarter, of the Hessian brewery, poured a bucketful of cold stale beer in at his coat collar and down his back. He awoke in a cold sweat, looked at his watch, which indicated twelve-fifteen. He had been in bed just fifteen minutes. Returning to bed, he lay awake for several hours, warming over dead thoughts of happier times, and indulging bitter memories of "the might have been." And he then and there resolved that he would place three thousand miles between him and his political friends; that he would seek obscurity and peace, and never return until the soul of American nationality animated the breasts of the Irish in America.

CHAPTER XXVIII.

AN IRISH EVICTION.

WHEN death became certain to Nancy McHugh, she promptly disposed of her temporal effects. She dictated a letter and committed it to the hands of Sister Mary Isidore. It ran as follows:

"NEW LIMERICK, Sept. 4, 1869.

"DEAR MOTHER—It is Heaven's will that I must die, and the will of God be done. I grieve only that you and my brother and sisters must be deprived of the assistance that I could lend you if I were to live. I send you twenty pounds—about all that I possess. I intended to use this money for the payment of passage tickets for yourself and the children, but I send you the money instead, so that, if you conclude to remain at home, you can use it as you please; but I advise you to come to America. The children will find employment, and Dr. Patrick Barry, whose address is Number —— West Thirty-fifth street, New York City, has promised to assist you in settling down and finding work for the children on your arrival. You may depend on him. Now, God be with you! We must never meet again on earth, but tell the children to be good and pious, and we will all meet in heaven. Your loving daughther,

NANCY McHUGH."

The letter contained, in addition to the draft for twenty pounds, the little silver crucifix, an *Agnes Dei*, soiled and worn, and a braid of the silken coal-black hair of the dying girl. The page itself was stained with the precious tears of Sister Mary Isidore, which copiously fell as she read and folded the touching epistle.

The letter never reached the hand of the widow.

Mrs. McHugh and her children had resided for many years on the outskirts of the town of Erinbeg. They cultivated two acres of boggy land, and when the seasons were favorable found no difficulty in paying the rack-rent; but the season of 1868 was disastrously rainy and cold. The potato crop failed; the rent became in arrears. Then came the process server with the decree of eviction, and the sheriff and his deputies to enforce it. Trouble was anticipated. It was intimated that resistance would be made, and on eviction day a very large force of the neighboring peasantry assembled for the purpose of giving battle to the sheriff's officers. There were arsenals of scythes, pitchforks, axes and spades hidden behind the ditches in the neighborhood for use against the officers; but when the forces of the sheriff appeared upon the scene, resistance was evidently hopeless. Four hundred police had been drawn from the counties of Leitrim, Sligo and Roscommon, and there was a company of English cavalry from Longford.

Father Joseph Lenehan was fortunately present. His mind immediately comprehended the situation. He felt the impossibility of defending the widow in her cabin, and so, at the critical moment, he preached the gospel of peace, and advised the people to disperse. They were reluctant to comply, for they stood in the presence of a spectacle of extraordinary cruelty.

The Widow McHugh had lain for many days struggling between life and death, in the horrors of typhus fever. The disease is highly infectious, and neither the sheriff nor his bailiffs, nor the members of the police force, nor the cavalry soldiers, could be induced to enter the cabin for the purpose of removing her. It was not mercy for the apparently dying widow, but terror of the dread disease, that deterred her Majesty's forces from executing the dread sentence of eviction by removing the fever patient by force from the cabin.

But the British empire is wonderfully resourceful. The great mind of Horatio Nelson Curran, her Majesty's stipendiary magistrate, conceived a scheme which embraced the execution of the law and the exercise of mercy.

Oh, merciful magistrate! merciful England! and ah, merciful God! His proposition was simply this: that the bailiffs and the emergency men should tear the roof from the cabin first, then level the walls, remove the *debris*, and then spread a sheet of canvas as a tent over the prostrate form of the typhus-stricken woman. The order was given, and the work of demolition commenced.

The infuriated peasantry surged up to the very bayonets of the police. Mr. Curran read the riot act, and ordered the people to disperse; the cavalry stood in line with drawn sabres; the police received the command, "Load carbines."

Not a peasant moved. Though merciless slaughter would have been the result, these peasants stood ready, with naked hands, to grapple with her Majesty's forces in defense of the widow's cabin.

Father Lenehan held a brief consultation with the sheriff and the magistrate, and stepping on a little mound in front of the cabin, requested the attention of the people. He said:

"My brethren, as an Irishman and a priest I ask you, in the name of God, to disperse. I need not assure you that I am as eager as you are to shield our neighbor, Widow McHugh, from the violence called law in Ireland; and if the sacrifice of one life —of mine or of any one of yours—could save the dying widow from this merciless outrage, that life might be profitably sacrificed; but it is not the question of one life. You see the power here ready to slaughter you. Now, boys, take your pastor's advice and disperse."

The mass of scowling men fell back, and the priest

resumed his consultation with the sheriff and the magistrate.

"Gentlemen," he said, "the demolition of the cabin is unnecessary. Call off your bailiffs, and I will remove the dying widow."

So saying he entered the cabin, wrapped the insensible form of Widow McHugh in a blanket, and lifting her, as one might lift a child, to his breast, tenderly bore her from the cabin.

Widow McHugh became conscious for a little while; but within a week from the date of the eviction scene she was laid to rest beside the ashes of her husband in the venerable grave-yard near the village square.

The widow's children were homeless orphans, but even in Ireland "Heaven tempers the wind to the shorn lamb." They were temporarily cared for at the homes of poor, kind neighbors, and with the twenty pounds sent by sister Nancy they purchased passage tickets for America.

Dr. Barry was informed of their coming, and met them at Castle Garden on their arrival. Maggie, the oldest, was a girl of fifteen, Johnny twelve, and Mary, the youngest, a child of nine years.

After a few days rest at Dr. Barry's, he brought them to New Limerick. Here they found old friends and profitable employment. Maggie went to work at the linen mill of McCook & Son; Johnny at the rolling mills; and little Mary became domiciled with a good family, who sent her to school.

Dr. Barry inquired of Mr. McCook how wages in Ireland compared with wages in New Limerick.

"In Ireland," replied Mr. McCook, "we employ at our mills eleven hundred hands; here in New Limerick we employ six hundred, and *the wages paid to the six hundred hands in New Limerick weekly is only a few dollars less than the amount paid to eleven hundred operatives in Ireland.*"

"Here," he continued, "the sober and the industrious buy building sites and own their own homes. If they are unmarried and desire to save money, we borrow their savings, pay them five per cent interest, and use the money in our business. There are two Irish girls here, sisters, who in three years have saved eleven hundred dollars. They might live in Ireland to be as old as Methusalch's goat, and never be able to save that amount. Every time I go to the old country the mill hands swarm around me, and beg me to take them to America; but I never yet found one of our New Limerick employees anxious to return to the Irish mills."

"Did you ever see an American looking for employment in Ireland?" asked the doctor.

"Never," said Mr. McCook. "I do not care to enter into discussion on politics with my employees, many of whom are active free-traders; but an ounce of fact is worth a ton of theory, and the fact that the millions of our race who come over generally remain is an unanswerable argument in favor of our industrial system, and knocks the most seductive theories of political economy into a cocked hat. The greatest annoyance to the American manufacturer in our days comes from your *Irish vote.* Agents of the Cobden Club from New York City and college professors from New Haven come down here every fall, preaching free-trade. And while the peeler and the sheriff, with crow-bar and battering-ram, are leveling the cabins of the Irish in Donegal and Conemara, their Irish children and kindred are doing loyal service for England in American elections."

CHAPTER XXIX.

TRAGIC DEATH OF DEVOY.

AT a secluded spot near Newton Creek, Long Island, there stood a large rude frame building, oblong in shape, surrounded by a high board fence. A dense volume of smoke ascending from its chimney, and its powerful smells permeating the air indicated that animal flesh was the material handled there. This institution was known as "The Horse Factory." Mr. Barney Devoy and his two sons, Albert Michael and Tony, were among its principal owners. As great oaks grow from little acorns, this important establishment was but the expansion of an unpretentious beginning. Young Tony Devoy was superintendent of the New Limerick pound. It is needless to add that the office was a sinecure. Mr. Devoy and Mr. Isaac Marx united their influence in obtaining for Andy Dillon an appointment as Third Assistant Deputy Pound-master; but Dillon declined, saying that personally he had no ambition for political office, and had other and different aims in life; and when the two distinguished leaders found that he firmly declined public honors, then they generously offered to make him assistant entry clerk at the horse factory. Messrs. Marx and Devoy gloried in the institution, not alone as a money-making concern, but also as a living monument to their benevolence and patriotism. To the minds of these two gentlemen, aided by the political economy ideas of their friend, the college professor, was due the realization of the scheme embracing some of the loftiest purposes of the human mind. Mr. Devoy, for many years, had contributed to the poor at each Christmas two barrels of pigs' feet, which were unostentatiously distributed from the Buchanan Exchange. Some few days before one of these Christmas festivals Mr. Marx, who had been reading a Polish newspaper, informed Mr. Devoy that horse-flesh had become a regular article of diet among working people in certain European cities, where beef and mutton were beyond the purchasing power of the toilers' wages. Now it so happened that at the New Limerick pound there was a young horse with a broken leg ; and this animal was skinned and dressed by order of Mr. Devoy, and in due time a round of the horse-meat was served by way of free lunch at the Buchanan Exchange. It was eaten as a matter of course by the regular customers, and many of the free-lunch veterans, men to whom regular meals were a "fading reminiscence," pronounced it excellent. New England college professors were at this period active in disseminating the doctrine of free-trade or tariff reform, the fundamental idea of which was cheapness. Messrs. Marx and Devoy, after a conference with the college professor, concluded to start a horse factory, not so much for the purpose of gain as in the maintenance of a great principle—the cheapening of animal food, and to carry out Mr. Devoy's lofty purpose of benevolence toward the laboring people of Europe. Thus originated the "horse factory" on Long Island. Here thousands of aged and crippled horses were annually driven or carried from the horse-car barns and livery-stables of New York, Jersey City and Brooklyn, to be converted into corn beef and sausages for the European market; and here from time to time the elder Devoy made his pilgrimages. Old inhabitants of Newton Creek still cherish Barney's memory for what they deemed the great sympathetic soul that was in him. They still affectionately describe him as contemplating the wretched horses, with his head uncovered. His eyes were weak

and watery, and the voluntary flow of moisture from
those eyes these good people mistook for tears; and
when he bared his ample teeth by an involuntary
contraction of his upper lip, the villagers mistook it
for a smile; and so Mr. Devoy created upon the rural
mind at Newton Creek the impression made by a
sunny shower, of smiling tearfully, in sympathy with
the raw material for his factory. Mr. Marx and Mr.
Devoy insisted that Dillon should accompany them
to Newton Creek and see the factory. Dillon was
not informed as to the precise character of the business, and supposed that Mr. Devoy, like some other
prosperous politicians, was a horse-fancier, and was
leading him to his breeding pastures. Great was his
astonishment, on entering the corral at Newton Creek,
to behold a drove of equine skeletons.

"Ah, now, Mr. Devoy," he said, "I understand.
This is your factory, and these are the frames that
you propose to build up into horses."

"No, indeed; we don't build them up. We boil
'em down, and ship 'em to the Youropyan market
as corn-beef and sausages. Chape merchandise
manes chape labor, and to keep labor chape you must
feed it chape, d'ye moind. That's what our friend the
college professor calls 'political aiconomy.'"

Here Mr. Devoy uncovered his most economical
forehead, and displayed his teeth, and shed something
like a tear, and when Dillon whispered an inquiry to
Mr. Marx as to the cause of Mr. Devoy's emotion,
Mr. Marx confidentially replied: "'Tis his nature, my
dear *freund*. Mr. Devoy alvays breaks down in the
presence of suffering old age, disease and misfortune."

From this affecting exhibition they led Dillon to
inspect the machinery. They had recently imported
from Belgium a mammoth sausage machine, into
which a' whole carcass was dumped, and ground into
sausage meat with amazing rapidity. Mr. Devoy led

the way. While he stood at the edge of the wonderful machine, explaining its merits in detail, the skirt of his Prince Albert coat was grabbed and drawn down into the hopper, and with the skirt, the body of Mr. Devoy. Mr. Marx clutched wildly at the fleeting form of his friend, but in vain; for quick as thought almost, the victim was carried down and mingled with the mass of meat in the great receiving vat of the factory

The precise manner of Mr. Devoy's retirement was kept profoundly secret from the afflicted family, and the sorrowing community. The coroner's jury, upon the evidence of Mr. Marx, returned their verdict of "death from natural causes;" and when the beautiful rosewood coffin, with its massive silver mountings, was lowered into the grave, not one of the tearful multitude doubted that the wooden dummy which filled the casket was the body of the lamented Devoy, in *persona propria.*

It was a wonderful funeral. Four dark horses drew the richly decorated hearse, and the little white horse which Mr. Devoy had driven to funerals so often was caparisoned in mourning, and led in advance of the *cortegé.* There was an immense procession of livery teams. If the soul of Mr. Devoy escaped in angelic form from his body, and if that soul was conscious of things transpiring on this mundane sphere, it is not unnatural to suppose that contemplation of that splendid funeral procession somewhat reconciled the immortal part of the departed leader to the sudden separation from its house of clay.

There was mourning in the family, of course, and heart-felt sorrow among his intimate political friends; but very many of the good citizens and tax-payers, whom courtesy and custom led to the grave of Mr. Devoy, accepted the decree of heaven with fortitude and becoming resignation. It is needless to add that a magnificent tomb marks the spot which, by a polite and merciful fiction, is regarded as his last resting place. His death was tragic in the extreme; and still, to the minds of those who believed with him in the doctrine of cheapness, there must appear a touch of the heroic in his taking off.

CHAPTER XXX.

THE VOYAGE AROUND CAPE HORN.

ON the month of October the sailing vessel *Coronado* hove up her anchor, sailed down the North River and through New York harbor to the ocean. The voyage of a merchant vessel around Cape Horn, however interesting to read about, is to those aboard a commonplace experience—a thing of toil, unpoetic and monotonous. The same everlasting, unbeginning, endless sea; the clock-work regularity of the watches; the patient drudgery of all on board, the absolute sway of the officers, the shifting breezes, the occasional storms, and the consequent calls for all hands on deck. There is the gradual increase of warmth, until the equator has been crossed, and then the gradual lowering of the temperature, until cold and fogs and storms are encountered at and around Cape Horn. Then the shifting and the tacking, and the battling against adverse winds, and at last again the smooth sailing under the genial suns and gentle breezes of the Pacific Ocean. There are occasional glimpses of land along the coasts of Chile, Peru, Central America and Mexico; the landing for water at Juan Fernandez, and brief delays at one or two points on the coast of Lower California.

One of these points is Ensenada. Here the *Coronado* anchored, and some few passengers were brought in row boats to the ship, bound for San Diego. Among the passengers was a woman with a three-year-old child. The woman was a full-blooded Indian, dark almost as an African, with black flashing eyes, and coal-black hair. The lips were full and pouting, while there was a total absence of that ferocity of appearance which characterizes the aborigines in the northwest. The child, though of dark complexion, was fair when compared with the woman; its eyes were also dark, but its hair was fair and light and soft—the very antithesis of the raven locks of the Indian woman. They were mother and daughter. The woman was Juanita Woerner, the wife of Martin Woerner, a pioneer *ranchero* of the San Diego Mountains. Martin had taken a homestead on *Mesa Grande*, near the border of the *rancho* of *San Jose del Valle*, and only a few miles distant from the camping grounds of the *Agua Caliente* Indians. Entirely destitute of capital, he labored patiently and was in a fair way to succeed upon his homestead, when, like the wisest and bravest of his sex, he fell desperately in love with the dark-eyed Juanita, the reigning belle of the Agua Caliente band of Indians. Martin was fair as Juanita was dark. He had the typical blue eyes, fair skin and light soft hair of the Northern Teuton.

Juanita was a fair specimen of her race, gracefully formed, domestic in her training, skilled in the rude house-keeping of her tribe, virtuous and devoted. Martin wooed and won her, but she failed to fulfill the ideal of a wife which Martin's fancy painted. She stoutly maintained that she was neither a donkey nor an ox, nor could the most persuasive eloquence of

Martin induce her to take her place beside a heifer at the plow. All this he discovered after the marriage ceremony that united his soul to the soul of this Indian maiden.

One great purpose occupied his waking thoughts and his nightly dreams: to sell on any terms the personal improvements on his homestead, so that he might be severed, corporeally at least, from his newly married wife, Juanita. This he at last succeeded in accomplishing, and he started with a team of donkeys into Lower California, in quest of the copper mines said to exist in the mountains back of Ensenada. After his departure for California Baja, a child was born to Juanita, and this child was duly baptized *Marcellina*. When she was three years old, the mother and little daughter traveled into Lower California in pursuit of the runaway father, and found him near Ensenada, living, as married people live, with a woman of his own nationality. This discovery, coupled with his refusal to recognize his wife and child, broke the heart and dethroned the reason of the devoted Juanita, and so we find them on the ship *Coronado*, returning to their home in the San Diego County mountains.

The vessel was sailing before a light breeze, some ten miles west of the Lower California coast, about midway between Ensenada and San Diego. It was morning of a delightful day in March. The sailors were engaged in the various little tasks incident to their lives as seamen. Tony Sexton in the galley was smoking his pipe, and Dillon sitting aft enjoying the delightful breath of the Southern Sea, when everybody on deck was startled with the cry, "Man overboard!" All hands rushed aft, and pitiable to behold: the Indian woman, Juanita, and the fair-haired child Marcellina were tossing in the waves abaft of the *Coronado*. The demented mother, with child in her arms, had flung herself overboard. The shock had doubtless temporarily restored her senses, for she appeared to be endeavoring to save the child, whom but a moment before she was determined to destroy. With the left arm she held the little one above the waves, while she used the right arm in swimming. Dillon, divesting himself of coat and slippers, jumped into the sea and swam in the direction of the mother and child; and before the vessel had slackened its speed, and before a boat had been lowered, he had relieved the mother by grasping the child in the embrace of his left arm. At the same instant a huge man-eating shark was seen to rise above the surface of the water and suddenly dash in the direction of the struggling Juanita. Simultaneously the cook, Tony Sexton, carving knife in hand, jumped into the waves and swam to the rescue of the woman. It was too late, for though he succeeded in terminating the unequal contest by inflicting mortal wounds upon the shark, the ferocious monster had done its cruel work, and woman and shark, both dead or dying, disappeared beneath the waves, leaving for a moment some bloody streaks to mark the spot above the ocean-grave of Juanita.

Dillon, with the fair-haired child, and Sexton the black man, with carving knife still in hand, were rescued by the boats; sails were re-set, and the *Coronado* plowed its way to San Diego Bay, anchoring at night in shelter of Point Loma. When day dawned, and the silvery sun, stealing over the mountains, lit up the land and sea, all eyes upon the *Coronado* enjoyed a feast in contemplating the wonderful scenery. To the northward, the promontory of Point Loma extended from the ocean, sheltering the harbor from wind and wave. From old town on the north to Chula Vista on the south, along the margin of the bay, for fifteen miles, stood human habitations.

Around the town rose gently sloping circling hills, green as emerald; and behind the hills lay the *mesa*, or table land, the connecting link between the coast valleys and the mountain foot; and above and beyond the *mesa*, in wider and loftier circle, rose the bold highlands of Mexico to the south, and the towering form of San Miguel, fifteen miles to the east, with its green summit bathed in sunlight, and its foot refreshing itself in the leaping, laughing waters of the Sweetwater River. East and north the mountains form a perfect amphitheater; and the naked eye follows the panorama until the light green is blended in a darker green, and this darker green in turn is lost in the black and white presented by the pine forests, and the snow-clad peaks of the Cuyamaca Mountains, forty miles to the east. Somewhere amid these mountains were the relatives of the motherless child, Marcellina; and when Dillon found himself relieved from service on the ship, he hastened up town, intent upon finding the relatives of little Marcellina, and restoring her to her kindred. He found little difficulty in locating them. He learned that Marcellina's grandfather, Francisco, resided at the base of the Vulcan Mountain, near Agua Caliente, some sixty miles inland from San Diego.

On the *plaza* (public square) of San Diego, there was assembled a crowd of sun-browned men, composed of ranchmen, Mexicans, cowboys, Indians and tramps, listening to an aged gentleman who stood in a wagon and distributed tracts, while he explained, in singularly persuasive tones, the contents of the printed matter. The central figure was "Old Pridmore," a benevolent-looking, bald-headed Englishman; the literature which he distributed was a tract called "The Western Farmer of America," written by Augustus Mongredien, published in London, England, and bearing on its title-page the maxim of the Cobden Club: "Free trade; peace; good-will among the nations." "Verily," said Dillon to himself, "this is refreshing: '*Peace; good-will among the nations.*' This is a loving message, coming from England, a nation which within a century has employed the merciless Indians to use the scalping knife on American women and children; which, within the memory of living men, sent its vandal sailors to burn this Nation's capital, without even the poor excuse of military necessity; which has recently blown the Hindoo in bundles from the cannon's mouth; which poisons the Chinese with opium and the African with rum; and which is to-day, with battering-ram and soldier, bailiff and peeler, leveling the cabins of my kindred in Ireland—all in the interest of 'peace, good-will among the nations'—*moryah*. And this accursed power is the friend, co-laborer and ally of the Democratic party in America."

CHAPTER XXXI.

THE DEMOCRATIC "ROUND-UP."

A PARTY of miners were "out-fitting" at San Diego for a trip to the Julian Mines; and as the relatives of Dillon's little ward, Marcellina, were supposed to reside somewhere in the Julian country, he joined the party on the southern bank of the San Diego River. He arranged with a member of the party for the transportation of himself and the little girl. That evening he climbed the rugged bluffs, three hundred feet in height, to the table-land that stretches between the city and the valley of the San Diego River. From this elevated mesa there was presented a magnificent view of the ocean, the bay, the valley, and the circling mountains in the background. The San Diego Bay region lay beneath him, stretching along the sea, a distance of five-and-twenty miles, from the ocean caves of La Jolla upon the north to the border line of Old Mexico upon the south, and eastward until the flower-carpeted *mesa* was merged in the shadows of the granite mountains beyond the valley of El Cajon. The sun was slowly setting far out upon the Pacific Ocean, and men and women, civilized and savage, paused from their toil to gaze on the picture painted upon the western sky by the hand of God, as the Christian peasant in the fields of Europe paused at the sound of the Angelus bell; and the sense of gratification gives way to feelings of regret as the sun sinks to rest in the bosom of the Pacific. He had relaped into his waking dream of *Erin Mor*, his greater Ireland in America, picturing the good time coming when the manhood of his race would realize the dignity of American citizenship; and he thanked kind Heaven that he was removed from the hot-beds of local politics, and the vulgar wiles, the treacheries, cruelties and deceits of the baser sort of politicians, when he was startled from his reverie by a voice that was unmistakeably Irish, saying:

"Hello, Fogarty! is that you, Fogarty?"

There was "a tear in the voice," as the French say, a tone of anxiety and a trace of dread; and as the stranger approached him, Dillon, stating that he was not Fogarty, inquired into the cause of the speaker's distress.

"I was lookin' for Fogarty," he said, "to attend the corkus. We are short jist three votes to overcome the Missourians and the Dutch; and seein', as I believe, that you're an Irishman, and a Democrat, of coorse, wouldn't it be jist as convanient for you to come over and give us a lift? The Irish, sir, are battlin' for their rights. They think themselves entitled to the office of constable in Old Town, and it's meself is the candidate. Come over and give us a lift."

"But I am not a citizen of California, and I have no right to vote in your caucus."

"*Och*, botheration to the right. That makes no difference. Think of Democracy, and your race and religion. Come down *avic* and give us a lift. Come down, darlin', to the assistance of the holy cause of Dimocracy and me, and may ye never be sick until I'm a docthor to cure ye."

"But, my friend, suppose I'm not a Democrat?"

"Ah, give us a rest! it's jokin' you are. An Irishman not a Dimocrat? Ha! ha! ha! begorra, that's good."

"Oh, you go to the devil!" said Dillon, as he rose and walked down the winding path leading from the hilltop to the river, wondering whether there was not some spot within the borders of the republic in which an Irishman could escape from the roll-call and the "round-up" of the Democratic party, and as he reached the valley he could still hear the voice penetrating the chaparral thickets, and searching the dark ravines: "Hello, Fogarty! where are you, Fogarty?"

Dillon, having carefully folded Marcellina in her blanket in the shelter of the stunted pepper trees, laid himself down to rest; but it was late at night before he slept, for memory called up many a vision, and when his eyelids closed, imagination assailed his senses with the Spartan cry of "Fogarty, come over and give us a lift, for Democracy and me."

The first day's march led the cavalcade up the valley of the San Diego River to the mountain foot now known as Foster's, where numerous mountain rills unite in the broad shallow river, and the mountain wall rises almost perpendicularly, its granite face presenting an apparently impassable barrier; but appearances are deceptive, for Nature in the bygone ages had chiseled out a winding ravine, which in our day the hand of man has utilized into a public road across the mountains. This passage had been leveled by strong and patient hands over the numerous gorges that were chiseled by mountain torrents, the products of the excavation serving to pave the outer margin of the roadway, a safe and solid road withal; and up this winding way the party traveled at a slow but steady pace. To the right of the road, and a hundred feet lower than its level, a rapid, narrow stream dashed over massive boulders, and anon peacefully glided over a level bed among the roots of the gigantic sycamores that lined its margin, and sought their life in the richness and moisture of its narrow bed. Great live oaks and cottonwoods abounded near the entrance to the pass, but as the party ascended the mountain became bolder and balder, its rock-ribbed slopes but scantily relieved by vines and flowering shrubs, and by masses of the dark green chaparral. White sage was abundant; and upon its stems and leaves myriads of wild honey-bees were swarming. The tiny birds nestled and twittered in the shrubs. Rabbits and covies of mountain quail were abundant. Toward evening, a small hunting party rode up a deep ravine, and were rewarded by a pair of young deer. An old hunter climbed among masses of rock and returned with a pail full of wild honey, amber-colored and richly flavored; and when the party camped for the night, there was a rich feast for all upon bacon, venison, pancakes, coffee and wild honey. The encampment was made in a valley studded with massive live-oaks, and covered with grasses and wild oats. A pretty little stream wended through the valley, and springs of pure water were everywhere abundant.

The next morning the cavalcade entered the *Rancho Santa Maria*, traveled up the valley of the Ballena, and down into the *Rancho Santa Ysabel*. It was sundown when the party entered the little village of Julian, "the metropolis of the mountain belt." While the warm breath of the desert stole across the mountains lying eastward, the peaks of the Cuyamaca, ten miles distant to the south, were deeply clad in snow; and while great white and red roses bloomed in the gardens and along the cottage walls at San Diego, and in all the sea-coast valleys, it was wintry still among the mountains; and great was the gratification of Dillon when himself and little Marcellina were housed for the night in the corner of a large rude one-story frame building, heated by a cheerful log fire burning in an old-fashioned open fireplace; and before supper was announced, Dillon and his child companion were both asleep.

CHAPTER XXXII.

A SMALL POLITICIAN'S REVENGE.

DILLON was awakened sometime in the night by sounds of revelry in the other end of the building that gave him shelter. There was somebody rasping on a violin, and a voice, that sounded like a cracked bugle, was endeavoring to sing a beautiful song from the opera, "The Bohemian Girl":

"When other lips and other hearts
 Their tales of love shall tell"—

As the singer repeated the refrain, "Then you'll remember me," there was vigorous applause; and thus encouraged, the singer, perhaps in a spirit of enthusiasm, and perhaps in pure forgetfulness, repeated again his

"You'll remember me,
Then you'll remember,
Then you'll remember,
Then you'll remember me."

Dillon, finding sleep impossible, rose from his blankets, put on his coat, clenched his fist, and moulded an anathema upon the singer, but did not utter it, merely saying: "By——, but no, I won't swear; but I will remember you. If I live to be a hundred years old, I'll never forget you." He then walked to the bar-room, which was separated from the rest of the great enclosure by a canvas tent cover, and in this *sanctum sanctorum* twenty men were seated on boxes and barrels, drinking and carousing. The singer was the central figure, a veritable Bacchus, still imploring them to "remember him;" and as he closed his eyes, threw back his head and opened his capacious mouth, he was a never-to-be-forgotten object. He was dressed in an old Prince Albert black cloth coat, that might have been new at the beginning of the century, worn and glossy with age, mud-bespattered by mountain travel, and disclosing from its skirt pocket an old red bandana handkerchief. His head was surmounted by a tall silk hat, which, from appearances, had been sometimes kicked and often sat upon; for the crown leaned to the right at an angle of forty-five degrees. His coat collar was tightly buttoned or pinned, and a stand-up paper collar, reversed, so as to be fastened behind, encompassed his long and wasted looking neck. He was altogether such a caricature of a Catholic priest as did duty in *Harper's Weekly* before that paper became the organ of tariff reform. As Dillon listened to his voice, and gazed into his cadaverous face, there seemed to him a striking similarity between the singer and some one he had heard and seen before, but the name Tim Devereaux, and the nick-name "Slippery Tim" being to him unfamiliar, he failed to connect his man with those that he supposed him to resemble.

This "Slippery Tim" was a familiar and yet a mysterious character. He had come from Bloody Gulch, Arizona. He was never known to do any kind of labor, nor had he any profession or regular means of support. He was reputed to be a man of great learning; and the rude miners and ranch men, especially the Irish, viewed him with amazement, as he rattled off in Latin the opening sentences of Cicero's denunciation of Cataline, "How long, O Cataline," etc., and the first paragraph of Pio Nono's anathema against the Fenians. It was said that Irishmen, suspecting him of being a cast-off clergyman, occasionally gave him a silver coin for charity's sake, and he was reputed to have earned fees by pretending to work miracles on the sickly children of poor, credulous Mexicans at San Diego.

When Dillon had returned to his rest, and found opportunity for reflection, he remembered that this "Slippery Tim" was the same person who made night hideous on the hilltop at Old Town some three days before, by shouting for "Fogarty," and imploring Dillon himself to assist him at the Democratic caucus. Failing in his ambition politically, he attached himself to a mining expedition, and arrived at Julian sometime during the night of Dillon's arrival, and he devoted his vocal powers to the entertainment of a party of miners, who had, as reported, made a rich discovery of gold north of the Vulcan Mountain, three miles from the Indian settlement at Agua Caliente.

Everybody in Julian was excited over this most recent gold discovery, and before daylight a party had assembled for the purpose of forming an expedition to the mines. Dillon learned that the grandparents of Marcellina dwelt near Agua Caliente, and himself and his little ward were ready at daylight to join the procession. The party started, mounted on horses and mules, and leading pack animals laden with provisions and mining tools. Some few marched on foot, leading *burros* for freight purposes, and some few others with naked hands and empty purses followed the train, animated by the universal thirst for gold. At evening the party camped upon the north side of Agua Caliente Creek, in sight of the promised land. "Slippery Tim," mounted on an aged mule, was among the latest arrivals, but he did not remain with the miners. He went over to the Indian settlement.

These Indians were an innocent, peaceable and pious people before civilization proceeded to destroy them. They had received the Christian faith from the earlier Spanish missionaries, but neglected in more recent times, their religion was little more than a fading memory, a diminishing inspiration. Still, a brass crucifix in the hands of a pious fraud, who could recite the *Pater Noster*, awakened the treasured faith, and "Slippery Tim" was received with veneration and with awe. They feasted him on roasted kid and milk, cracked wheat and acorns, and the softest of their ox-hide couches and their most comfortable *adobe* cabin was placed at his disposal; and so highly gratified was Tim at this Indian hospitality, that he decided to make his home among them; and with this scheme in view, he made his headquarters under a bowery in the old vineyard in the shadow of the mountain. He joined the prospectors every day while the whisky held out, and then settled permanently in the old vineyard.

The famous "discovery" near Agua Caliente was

very soon prospected and abandoned. There were traces of gold, but nowhere was the yellow metal found in paying quantities. The real purpose of the organizers was, not to dig for gold, but to sell whisky; and with the crowds that came to prospect, they did a flourishing business. Villainous *mescal* (a drink distilled from the cactus plant by Mexicans) sold for two "long bits," that is twenty-five cents a drink, and at the close of the excitement the brace of border ruffians who ran the "discovery" had "cleaned up" more than a thousand dollars.

Dillon, having restored little Marcellina to her grandparents, settled down at Agua Caliente for a few days rest at the adobe dwelling of old Francisco, the grandfather. During these days he sometimes wandered through the vineyard to the mountain foot, and in these wanderings he frequently met "Slippery Tim," who had now become a permanent resident of the vineyard. There was mutual recognition, and Tim reproached Dillon as "a vile turn-coat, a traitor to Democracy, to race and religion," because he had declined to support "Slippery Tim" at the Democratic caucus in Old Town; and when Tim exposed his teeth in that horrid grimace intended for a smile, and snapped his watery eyes in the spirit of revenge, Dillon could not resist the feeling that "Slippery Tim" intended to do him some serious injury.

One morning, as Dillon lay dozing in his *adobe* shanty, he was aroused by the foot-falls of horses that suddenly halted in front of his abode. Slowly opening his eyes, he saw standing at the foot of his couch two powerful, brutal-looking men, armed with navy revolvers and well-filled cartridge belts.

"Stranger," said one of them, "we understand that you have been lookin' for us, and we have been lookin' for you. You're a detective revenue officer, you are. You have got warrants for us, you have. Let's see yer warrants."

"My friends," said Dillon, "there is a mistake somewhere. I am not a revenue officer. I have no warrants for anybody. Kindly tell me who you are, and who is your informant."

"We are the gentlemen, sah, who led the expedition from Julian to Agua Caliente. We have it on the information of a gentleman—a high-toned gentleman, sah—an Irishman, sah, and a Democrat, sah, and of your own religion, sah—a man who wouldn't lie nor wrong his own countryman, sah. We learn from him that you are addicted to wearing biled shirts, and won't drink whisky; and you must be a guvament officer, sah."

"But, gentlemen——"

"Not a word, sah; up and out!" And Colonel Doniphant seized him by the collar, while Captain Marmaduke covered him with a revolver, and in three minutes he was mounted on a horse, strapped and bound to the saddle, and hurried eastward to the border of the desert.

There he was confronted by "Slippery Tim," and accused of being a revenue detective, on the grounds that he was "no Dimocrat," and wore biled shirts, and wouldn't drink whisky. Colonel Doniphant demanded if he had anything to say before the sentence was executed.

"Nothing," he said, "only that the accusation against me is a lie, and the accuser a liar."

"Won't you say a prayer for yer sowl?" demanded "Slippery Tim." "Wouldn't ye like to die in the state of grace, like a Christian and a Dimocrat?" and Tim produced from the revolver pocket of his pants a beads with a large brass crucifix. "Down on yer knees now, me lad," he continued, "and I'll jine ye in a *Pather* and *Ave;*" and suiting the action to the word, he dragged Dillon by the collar to a kneeling position, and skinning his awful teeth, lifted his watery eyes to heaven in a prayer for the repose of Dillon's soul.

When prayers were ended they bound him to a tree with thongs of raw-hide, and left him, as they supposed, to die. Before leaving him, however, "Slippery Tim" carefully searched his pockets, but was unrewarded, because Dillon had hidden his purse under a boulder near Francisco's adobe dwelling.

His term of bondage was brief but terrible. The warm southern sun, gleaming through the leafless limbs of the dead cottonwood to which he was bound, and reflected by the granite sands, tortured his eyes; red ants innumerable crawled up his legs and over his body; a rattle-snake once approached within striking distance of him, but did not strike; and the small, but cruel and cowardly, coyotes congregated and chilled his blood with their unearthly yelping. The lone dead cottonwood tree to which he was bound stood in the desert so close to the mountain side that he could see the waters glistening in the sun, as they leaped over the rocks at the head of *Arroya del Diabolo* (the devil's ravine); and he suffered with consuming thirst, and the raw-hide thongs cut into his swelling limbs as the cold night succeeded the genial sunny day. 'Twas a night of awful suffering and suspense, and he often wished that his enemies had shot him dead, rather than subject him to the slow and cruel torture that must precede his death upon the desert.

A beautiful morning followed that awful night; and the sun rose in all its southern splendor, and kissed the mountain, which smiled in return; but the sparkling rivulet rushing down the *arroya*, as if in mockery, sank in the parched sands of the desert. The coyotes, emboldened by his helplessness, were snapping at his feet, and strong, black vultures swept down from the mountains and hovered above him, perching at times upon the dead limbs of the dry cottonwood above his head, awaiting an anticipated feast.

And he prayed to God for mercy on his soul; and he struggled with his right hand with superhuman effort to strike his breast, while his parched lips uttered the "*Mea culpa, mea culpa, mea maxima culpa;*" and somehow—by a miracle, perhaps, for God is everywhere, and omnipotent—he felt a loosening of the thong that bound his right arm, and another effort to strike his breast released the worshipping hand. A minute later he was free. He staggered in the direction of the waterfall, slaked his thirst, and stretching himself upon a shelving rock, was soon in a deep sleep.

And the setting sun was sinking beyond the summit of the San Bernardino Mountains, to the west, when he opened his eyes to meet the pitying gaze of the child Marcellina, who had sat beside him as he slept, while the patriarch Francisco, gun in hand, stood beside a pair of ponies higher up in the *arroya*. They had not seen him forced away from their cabin, but, suspecting foul play, had started on the trail, and traveling across the mountain had tracked him to the desert.

CHAPTER XXXIII.

AMONG CALIFORNIA INDIANS.

THE Indian village of Agua Caliente is situated near a creek that runs along the northern border of the great valley now known as Warner's ranch. The cabin of old Francisco occupied a commanding position upon a strip of elevated table land above the bed of the creek. Almost perpendicularly the Vulcan Mountain lifts its giant head between the cabin and the desert. Mount Palomar, with its verdant slopes, deep ravines, broad table lands and dark green forests, bounds the great valley on the west, and southward lie the foot-hills of the Mesa Grande. Northwestward only seemed there to be a break in the mountain chain surrounding the immense depression. In this direction, at the close of day, the eyes of the old Indian were directed, following the setting sun, whose rays created in the meadows and grain fields a succession of lights and shades, and lighted up the shallow streams into sheets of polished silver. And oh! the sunsets in these southern mountains; and oh! the brief and blissful twilight that cools and charms in this sultry clime; and oh! the myriad stars of the ideal nights, and the soft winds that whisper through the tall cottonwoods beside the stream, and the sweet and sleepful nights that follow the brilliant days. The southern morning is too bright and brief. There is the gray twilight of fifteen minutes duration that separates the night from day; and suddenly the sun appears above the mountain top in all the dazzling splendor of a northern summer noon.

At sunrise the Indian maids and mothers were down at the washing stones—a laundry which Nature had kindly created for them. Ridges of granite rise above the water in the middle of the stream, and the washer-women sit astride these ridges, leaving one foot in the cold water, and washing their clothes in the hot water that runs at the other side of the rocky ridge from the hot springs that gush from the bed of the creek. Near the bank of the creek, upon a huge granite boulder, sits old Marcellina, wife of the aged Francisco, pulverizing acorns into flour, using a heavy oblong stone for a pestle and a hollow in the great rock for a mortar. Down along the stream the Indian men are planting their corn patches, or milking cows, or driving flocks of goats into the foot-hills.

Above the hot springs, and between them and the mountain foot, lay the orchard and the vineyard of the Indian settlement. It was common property. It is watered by many springs and rivulets, and sheltered by the mountain which rises abruptly above it, so steep and lofty that the tall pines upon its summit seem no larger than corn-stalks to eyes that behold them from the valley. For more than half a century that land had been cultivated by the Indians. There was a precious growth of grape-vines, prunes and peaches, and a pear orchard old as the nineteenth century. A thousand feet higher than the level of this orchard, midway between it and the summit of the mountain, there was a green patch containing perhaps ten acres, but seeming from the valley no larger than a billiard table. On the border of this mountain oasis, a tiny stream, a tributary of Agua Caliente Creek, leaped over the rocks and glistened in the morning sun. Above this green table-land the mountain pines nodded in the morning breeze. Some adventurous Indian boys had climbed to that delightful spot when rounding up the flocks of goats, but so far as anybody knew, no white man had hitherto attempted the toilsome journey. Upon that green spot, high up on the Vulcan Mountain, Dillon concluded to make his home. "There," he said to himself, "I will be secure from association with politicians. No ward rounder of the Democratic party would ever be tempted to that spot by the vote of a solitary Irishman."

His intention as to making his home upon the mountain side having been fully settled, he resolved to consult Francisco, the patriarch of the tribe. Francisco's venerable limbs still trod their native heath in eloquent dissent from the usages of civilization. Instinctively, but unconsciously, he was a Democrat of the Democrats. He had seen the beginning of the nineteenth century. The United States of America had grown from a feeble nation of five millions to a great nation of forty millions. Map makers had changed the boundary lines of almost every nation in Europe since he was a boy. The American slave had been emancipated, the serfs of Russia had been freed, the steamship and the telegraph and the telephone had been invented or applied. Political parties had arisen and had fallen, human hands had been carving the Sierra Nevadas, and cattle pastures had become cities, and wild wastes had been converted into factory towns; but to all these changes Francisco was indifferent. The music of a glorious American nationality awakened in his bosom no sympathetic chord. He was a "natural Democrat"—just as "natural" as if he had first opened his eyes in the wilds of Conemara. He would not wear pantaloons. He was a giant in stature; and Nature had nowhere reproduced him among his tribe. His skinny limbs were larger than the fattest legs of the present generation. He would sit upon a great rock, within easy distance of the village school, to the great scandal of the Indian *señoritas*, and to the horror of the pious lady teacher from Washington City. He would make himself conspicuous, if not agreeable, in a circle of native maidens, or stalk unconcernedly into the dwellings of the white visitors at the springs. All efforts to clothe him in pantaloons had invariably failed. The good ladies of the Indian aid society at Philadelphia had sent him an assortment of pants; but no effort on the part of their agent could seduce him from his lofty devotion to an idea. The lady teacher, deeply veiled in a cotton apron, had often approached him, pantaloons in hand, but she could not make him waver in his devotion to his own political economy, the gospel of consistency. Protective tariffs fell powerless at his feet. He remained faithful to his faith in naked limbs, and to the day of his death he continued a shining example of the boasted virtue of consistency.

Dillon consulted this venerable man and his aged wife, Marcellina, in relation to building upon the green spot on the mountain side.

"*Mañana*," said Francisco, "to-morrow." They do all things on to-morrow in that lazy clime; and to-morrow they would lend their grandson Pedro to guide him up the mountain side.

And on the morning of the morrow, at sunrise, Dillon and his guide clambered up the winding path leading over fissures, rocks, gulches and *arroyas* to *Erin Beg* (Little Ireland), as Dillon affectionately called it. There, with the assistance of Indian friends, he built him a neat log shanty, with stone fire-place and chimney; and provided with arms and provisions, and a small flock of kids and goats, settled down in his mountain home. Copying the rude agriculture of his Indian neighbors, he planted him a garden of peas, potatoes, and other vegetables in a rich delta of pulverized granite soil formed by the freshets of converging rills; and with his rifle, his dog and his goats, and a few books, he was happy amid the charms of solitude. He next proceeded to build him a reservoir by constructing a rude stone dam at the outlet of a very narrow, deep ravine, through which a mountain streamlet poured, and when the summer suns threatened to parch his growing vegetables, he conducted this water in irrigating ditches to the miniature garden on the delta. He enjoyed a magnificent view of the great ranch and the mountain foot-hills from Palomar to Mesa Grande. He could see the tree tops and the vines in the old orchard beneath him; on summer evenings he could see the flocks of goats and sheep gather for their nightly rest on the hillocks at the Indian dwellings in the valley, and in the stillness of the summer nights he could hear the barking of the dogs in the settlement; but except by occasional visits from the boy Pedro, grandson of Francisco, he suffered no disturbance from the human race. He had ample scope for the play of his imagination and deep indulgence in dreams. So he dreamt in the day-time, in waking dreams; and while his body slept, the sleepless soul took up the thread of mind, and carried him back in fancy to the fields of his youth and the scenes of his sufferings, and his spiritual eye dwelt upon lovely visions of his *Erin Mor*—his Greater Ireland that was to be.

CHAPTER XXXIV.

"BLESSED ARE THE MERCIFUL."

THE feast of St. John, the 24th of June, is the day of days among the Christian Indians of Southern California. There was joyous anticipation at Agua Caliente. Ground was selected, the stakes were set, and a commodious bowery erected, crowned with the greenest boughs of the forest. The *padre* from San Diego was expected to be present, and Indian mothers devoutly bathed their babies in the waters of Agua Caliente, preparing them for the sacrament of baptism; but deep was the disappointment when on the morning of the *fiesta* it was announced that the *padre* would not come. Deprived of its religious features, the *fiesta* at Agua Caliente degenerated into a country fair. There was spirited horse racing, dancing to the music of the guitar and violin, and the dusky youths circled the dark-eyed maidens in the poetry of motion bequeathed to these Indians by the Spanish *caballeros* in the brave days of old. There was gambling galore. "One-eyed Jake," a Missourian from *Arroya del Diabolo*, brought over a keno outfit, and the Indians themselves, liberally provided with poker cards, sat around in shady places, where everybody, men and women, young and old, took a hand in Mexican poker.

Andy Dillon started from his mountain cabin in the morning to join in the celebration. His heroism in rescuing little Marcellina had been reported and been praised in every Indian home through Southern California, and he was everywhere a welcome guest. Coming down the mountain side, a mile or so above the old orchard, he noticed, some fifty paces from his path, a heap of clay thrown up from an excavation. Approaching the spot, he discovered an oblong pit, six or seven feet in length, unmistakeably a grave, with a spade and shovel placed in the form of a crucifix across it, after the manner of Christendom. He was not a little surprised, for he knew that the Indians had their consecrated cemetery, and that there were no other persons interred in that vicinity; but he resolved to keep his own counsel and await developments. On reaching the bowery of the *fiesta*, imagine his astonishment when he beheld "Slippery Tim" engaged in a game of draw-poker with "One-eyed Jake" and "The Bald-headed Snipe of Mount Palomar." Slippery Tim had disappeared after the attempted murder in the desert, but had returned to Agua Caliente on a business mission. A few days preceding the June *fiesta*, he appeared at the old orchard with a pair of burros, laden with provisions, and in the wealth of fire-arms he was a walking arsenal. He "jumped" the Indian orchard, and took possession of it as a homestead under color of United States law. He had barricaded the adobe dwelling on the premises, and stood, if necessary, prepared for a siege; but finding that the Indians did not risk their lives in an effort to oust him, and animated by the greed of gain, he joined the gamblers at the *fiesta*, armed only with a pair of navy revolvers and a long-bladed bowie-knife. A little after night-fall Dillon retired with the venerable Francisco to that patriarch's home, and after feasting on roasted kid, green peas and goat's milk, lay down upon his ox-hide for the night.

Sometime after the hour of midnight the Francisco household was startled by a vigorous barking of the dogs, and this noise seeming to be echoed all along the valley, the old man and his wife arose and went out into the night. Dillon hastily dressed and followed them. A group of dark figures, twenty or thirty in number, stood near the trunk of a massive live oak in quiet but earnest debate. As he approached the tree and heard the voices speaking the mongrel Spanish of the tribe, he knew they were Indians; but there was one white man among them, and as the waning moon shed its soft light upon the face of the white man, he recognized the livid face of "Slippery Tim," with its affrighted eyes and gaping mouth. The Indians had permitted him to enjoy the fun and gambling at the *fiesta*, but had resolved on the morning of the feast to hang him, and had already dug his grave in the glen upon the mountain foot. Dillon took in the situation at a glance, and hastily advanced to the outer edge of the crowd. Being recognized, he was greeted with a "*Bravo, Señor! bravo, amigo!*" The culprit produced his beads as a certificate of Christian character, and also a letter with the request that his friends, whose address the letter contained, be advised of his death. The Indian leader handed the letter to Dillon. It was dated at "New Limerick, Connecticut," was addressed to "My Beloved Brother, Francis Xavier," and signed "Birdelia Devoy," though the envelope bore the address: "Timothy Devereaux, Bloody Gulch, Arizona."

The mind of Dillon immediately reverted to the sweet singer at Julian, and the injunction, "You'll remember me," was realized. Memory connected the faces at New Limerick with the face of Tim. The voice of the culprit was the voice of Birdelia, and the face was Nature's reproduction of Birdelia's lamented father, Barney Devoy.

While Andy thus reflected, the Indians had lifted their prisoner upon a granite rock, and one of them had fastened the rope upon a limb of the live oak, and had dropped the noose end so that it dangled before the face of the victim. A nimble youth mounted the rock and adjusted the hempen neck-tie around the throat of Francis Xavier Devoy (for it was he), and two others approached with arms extended to push him from the rock into eternity, when Dillon pressed between them and the victim, and lifting his hand and raising his voice, begged his Indian friends to listen to him. The half-breed Miguel acted as interpreter.

"My dear friends," said Dillon, "you are a Christian people. Do not stain your souls with the blood of this man. 'Blessed are the merciful, for they shall obtain mercy,' are the words of the Savior, whom you hope to meet in heaven."

"No, no, no; it is no murder. He is a robber; and since the Great Father will not protect us, we will protect ourselves. Hang him! hang him! let him swing!" was repeated by several voices.

"Now listen, brothers," said Dillon. "I saved your little Señorita Marcellina at the risk of my life, did I not?"

"*Si, si, Señor; bravo, Señor!*"

"Then be patient with me. Be merciful, as you hope for mercy."

"No, no; he is a robber. He would rob us of the trees planted by our grandfathers. Let him die."

"But it is murder, my friends."

"No, no; it is no murder. There is no law to protect us Indians. It is not murder to protect ourselves."

"And are you willing to face the jugdment seat of God with this man's blood upon your head?"

"*Si, si, Señor.* He is a robber; to hang him is no sin."

"Yes, my dear friends; but you know he is a very great sinner, do you not?"

They laughed an ironical laugh, and admitted that he was.

"Very well; if you hang "Slippery Tim," he will die in mortal sin, unforgiven. He will be damned, and you will be damned for sending him to eternity in a state of sin."

This last argument caused them to hesitate. The leaders retired for consultation, and concluded not to hang him. They would be satisfied to scourge him and let him go, and for this purpose they tore off his "Roman collar" and his clerical garb, and exposed his body naked upward from the waist; for Tim was *sans chemise.*

"No, my dear friends," said Dillon, "you must not scourge him. He is one against fifty. You know that he assisted in an effort to murder me. Now, leave him to me."

They knew the circumstances of the attempted murder, and took Dillon's "Leave him to me" as an intimation that he himself desired to punish him; and as the rescued and the rescuer moved in the direction of the mountain, the Indians dispersed to their homes down the valley, with a parting goodnight and a *"Bravo, Señor! bravo, amigo!"*

The two Irishmen toiled up the mountain path, and reached the log-cabin in the gray hours of the morning. Dillon with his own hands bathed the wasted, trembling body of his would-be murderer; dried and chafed him with the tenderness of a mother; and having roasted a joint of fatted kid upon a spit before a fire of blazing logs, he pressed the unfortunate Tim to eat, and eat Tim did with a will. Dillon dressed him in a flannel shirt and a coat of tweed (the only coat he possessed); and the gilding of the sky far east above the desert indicated the approach of day as he led him back adown the mountain and across the great ranch to the Mesa Grande trail that led to the Julian and San Diego road.

CHAPTER XXXV.

TEN YEARS OF SOLITUDE.

IT was high noon when Dillon returned to his mountain home, and it sorely grieved and disappointed him to discover that his potato patch upon the delta had been washed out of existence. A stone in the dam of the reservoir had given way, and the water, rushing down in a torrent, had not only swept away his potato vines, but had also washed away the earth, so that the granite rock was laid bare. For a few moments he gazed regretfully on the wreck, when something glistening on the naked rock attracted his attention. He picked up a shining pebble. It was rough and black, with specks of brightness, like the sunbeams in a summer shower peeping through a dark cloud. Scraping the outer surface with his knife exposed more of the shining substance, and industrious effort revealed a solid little lump of yellow metal, which, when compared with a five-dollar coin, proved with reasonable certainty to be gold. He repeated the experiment upon another and another of the pebbles with the same result, and arrived at the true conclusion that he was the owner of a placer gold mine. Taking a whisk-broom from his satchel he patiently swept the naked rock, gathering in dust and pebbles, the full of a quart tin cup. This he carefully washed again and again, successfully removing all particles of sand; but there was mingled with the gold some black sandy mineral substance, which he could remove only by actually picking the gold particles out of it. This he found so tedious and difficult that he abandoned the task of separation. He dried his treasure on a tin plate in the sun, sewed it into the pocket of his vest, and resolved upon a journey to Los Angeles, that he might formally enter his homestead at the government land office.

Arriving at Los Angeles, he first entered his homestead at the land office, and then proceeded to the office of an assayer, where he received the assurance that his yellow sand was gold.

"This dark stuff," said the assayer, "is cassiterite."

"And what is cassiterite?" inquired the discoverer.

"Cassiterite," replied the assayer, "is stream tin—the dust of tin. You will find that mineral somewhere, at a higher level, near where you found this gold. It may be of little value now, but some day the people of this country will make their own tin-plates, for there is little doubt that somewhere in America the block tin will yet be found; and of course we have the iron for the plates, and the limestone and the coal, and labor and skill. I hope you'll strike it."

Having separated his gold from the cassiterite, by a process known to the assayer, he converted it into cash and started for his home, returning by way of San Diego. There he made a small investment in land, purchasing a five-acre *pueblo* lot adjacent to the great park reservation of the future city. Having purchased a shovel, pick, pan and light crowbar, he resumed his journey, returning by way of the *Rancho Santa Ysabel*, and across the delightful highlands of Mesa Grande. That region was to him a veritable wonderland—a valley soil with a mountain climate, rich in wild oats and grasses, with deep dark soil in the valleys, and forests of various hardwoods clothing the mountains to their very summits. Streams of the purest water bubbled everywhere out of the mountain slopes, and traversed in streamlets his roadway through the winding valleys over which he passed.

Pioneer settlers and Indians were cultivating garden patches, or planting orchards of pears, peaches, cherries and apricots; and the tender sprouts of the young vineyards were occasionally seen on the hillsides. Miners, too, were making "prospect holes," for gold had been discovered at Mesa Grande; but he did not halt to investigate. One gold mine at a time was enough for him. Returning to the homestead, he repaired and staunched his reservoir dam, and constructed a flume from the reservoir to the delta. Patiently he labored, day after day, for more than a year, until he had washed out the delta, and gathered from the naked bed-rock a mixture of gold dust and cassiterite sufficient to fill his water pail; and when time hung heavily on his hands, he labored around the margin of the garden, sifted and re-washed the soil at a lower level; but having exhausted the "pocket" at the delta, his labors were subsequently fruitless. During ten years of patient prospecting, he never was rewarded by another ounce of gulch gold.

As a matter of curiosity, rather than the hope of gain, he prospected for tin and found it. Starting above the dam, he traced particles of the cassiterite to the outlet of a very deep and narrow fissure. Entering at the base of this fissure, he dislodged a portion of the rock, and was satisfied, from the appearance of the broken edge, that he had discovered tin. In due time he sent this rock to San Francisco to be tested, and was gratified with the information that his rock contained some six per cent of tin. Following his discovery wherever deep gorges afforded him an opportunity of reaching a low level without sinking a shaft, he found the same indications at many places upon his homestead, and concluded his labors with the gratifying assurance that he was the owner of a tin mine. This discovery he resolved to keep secret until he had perfected title to the land,

and this he did at the close of the five years that must intervene between the entry and the final proof.

He had at last completed ten long years in solitude. He had neither written nor received a personal letter in all these weary years. Two presidential elections had been fought and won, but he did not know even the names of the Presidents elected, for he held no communication with white men, and he did not read the newspapers. His library consisted of a prayer book, a bible, a pocket dictionary, a copy of Shakespeare, Victor Hugo's "*Les Misérables*" in French, and the "Irish Melodies" of Moore. These books he delighted to read, and he read them until they were thumb-worm.

Many a time and often he exclaimed: "Oh, what blessed things are books!" Far from civilization and from friends, debarred from contact with living minds and speaking tongues, he could retire into his cabin at night, and by the light of a pine-knot or a tallow candle he could enter into communication with the spirits of many of the greatest minds, from Moses to Moore—minds that appealed to the loftiest aspirations of his soul, and neither deceived him, betrayed him, nor belied him.

One day he went to buy provisions at the store on Warner's ranch, three miles from Agua Caliente. A post-office had been there established. The thirst for intelligence overcame him, and he begged the postmaster for a newspaper. That courteous official was more than generous. He gave him as many as fifty newspapers—papers that had remained uncalled for in the office, belonging to various persons, and covering a period of several years. He bundled them into a gunny-sack, and on his return home sat down for a feast of news. Among the hundreds of items and articles that surprised, displeased or delighted him, three or four especially filled him with astonishment.

He learned with joy that the unhappy period of reconstruction had been passed, that the Southern people were in full control of their State governments; and his soul was filled with gratitude, for he would not make an Ireland of the South.

He also read that Horace Greeley had been the Democratic candidate for President. *Mirabile dictu.*

And he learned that an alien church establishment, which had fattened on the blood and sweat of Catholic Ireland for two hundred years, had been disestablished by an English act of Parliament, and that William Ewart Gladstone, a former persecutor of Ireland, was the emancipator.

And he learned that the old green land, which he had left apparently lifeless as "a corpse on a dissecting table," was up again battling in a land war against the hereditary lords of the soil in Ireland.

And he discovered that a great political leader by the name of Cleveland, a person of whom he had never hitherto heard, had arisen as the champion of English manufacture and commerce in America.

And he also learned that the Cobden Club, an English organization, had been naturalized in New York, and had commenced an active propaganda for the purpose of deciding national and congressional elections in the United States in the interest of England.

And another item set his blood in motion. It was to the effect that the dry bones of his *Erin Mor* were assuming flesh and blood, and that at San Francisco and Chicago, and other cities, Irish-Americans were actually organizing in the interest of America to do battle for American industry against the free-trade policy of England!

And he knelt upon the granite rock in the shadow of the mountain pines, and his heart and soul and eyes were turned in thankfulness to God, that some

Irishmen at last had seen their duty, and had the moral courage to do it; and there was at last a breach in that solid Irish vote which for thirty years had been the Northern garrison of the slave power and the chattel property of brutality and blackguardism in the cities of the North.

"And man," he said, "was made to move as well as 'to mourn'; there is a free fight ahead. The conflict will be long and bitter. England will make a desperate effort to control the commerce of this continent, especially the markets of the United States. By every sacred impulse that animates the heart of man; by every consideration of enlightened selfishness; by the memories of the past and the hopes of the future, the enlightened manhood of the Irish in America must stand by America in the battle for industrial independence."

He gathered up his scanty baggage and his sack of gold dust, and descended the mountain, bound for San Francisco.

Before his departure he had, as he believed, one duty to perform. Little Marcellina was now a girl of thirteen. He desired that she should have a proper secular and religious education, and with the consent of her grandparents, and of the good *padre* at San Diego, she was sent to a convent school at Los Angeles.

Dillon took his departure for the North on one of those splendid steamers that ply along the coast between San Diego and San Francisco.

CHAPTER XXXVI.

ATTEMPTED CONQUEST OF AMERICA.

IN the summer of 1879, Mr. Thomas Bayley Potter, Secretary of the Cobden Club, visited the United States officially. The Cobden Club, which he represented, has its headquarters in London, England. At the time of Mr. Potter's visit, the club numbered among its members eleven of the fourteen cabinet members of the British government, and two hundred of the six hundred members of the British House of Commons. Its avowed object was the extension of English commerce, and the special object of Mr. Bayley Potter's visit was to inaugurate an active propaganda for the breaking down of the American tariff system in the interest of free trade with England. Mr. Bayley Potter was

"The mildest mannered man
That ever scuttled ship or cut a throat."

He was willing to compromise with America. "We don't object, you know, to a five or ten per cent tariff, you know; but this beastly forty per cent—this barbarous prohibitive tariff is at war with civilization, you know," was a favorite expression of Mr. Potter.

Immediately after his arrival in New York, he made close connection with two distinguished Anglo-Irishmen, one of whom was Mr. Lawrence Bodkin, of Wicklow, the principal editorial writer on a so-called Republican daily newspaper of New York City, and the other a certain Richard Boaker, a leading spirit in the Tammany organization. Mr. Boaker was by birth Irish, as several generations of his ancestors were. He was of a family distinguished for its undying hostility to their Celtic fellow-countrymen; but all this was forgotten by the exiles in their contemplation of Mr. Boaker's burning zeal in the cause of Democracy. Mr. Boaker himself, speaking of this singular forgetfulness in Irish character, always became enthusiastic over what he termed their liberality; and when Mr. Potter observed that it seemed unnatural that a man with a family record like Mr. Boaker's should be voluntarily accepted as a leader in New York politics, Mr. Boaker explained:

"The Irishman," he said, "is the only citizen in America who never makes religious distinctions in politics, and who never inquires into the religion of a candidate for whom he votes at the polls."

Through Messrs. Bodkin and Boaker a conference was called at the office of Mr. Bodkin's paper. The persons present were Mr. Thomas Bayley Potter, Secretary of the Cobden Club; Mr. Bodkin, Mr. Boaker, a United States Senator from the State of Maryland, and a distinguished Democratic leader from the State of Connecticut, whom the members of the conference addressed familiarly as "Mules."

Mr. Potter said that England desired closer commercial relations with their American cousins. They did not object to a five or ten per cent tariff, such as the cheaper labor of England could bear, "but we do decidedly object to your beastly, barbarous protective tariff, you know."

Mr. Bodkin was of the opinion that an appeal for lower duties would secure the support of the dudes and the tories.

"Might I inquire in confidence," said Mr. Potter, "who the dudes are?"

"Certainly," said Mr. Bodkin. "The dude is a creature somewhat resembling a man, narrow of intellect and narrower of pantaloons, who affects the manners of the English, and wishes to be considered an Englishman; but 'tween you and me, Mr. Potter, he bears about the same relation to an Englishman that a sickly spaniel does to an African lion. He is not always of English descent. He may be German, or he may be Irish, but his consuming desire is to counterfeit the English manners. He is a curious creature, but he votes."

"And who," said Mr. Potter, "are the tories?"

"The tories," said Mr. Bodkin, "are Americans who are more English than the English, who always speak of the people of this nation as 'Anglo-Saxons,' and who curse God for the surrender at Yorktown. They are our friends, and I speak unreservedly respecting them, so that there may be a clear understanding of the situation."

"Are our friends, the tories and dudes, quite numerous in America?" said Mr. Potter.

"On the Atlantic coast," replied his informant. "They are not numerous in the West. It is said that there is something in the climate west of the Alleghenies that kills the dude, just as there is a mysterious something fatal to snakes in your sister kingdom of Ireland."

"Let me inquire," said the agent of the Cobden Club, "how an active fight for freer trade in the interest of England would be met by your numerous Irish-American population?"

"There are very many of the Irish," said Mr. Boaker, "who have no love for your free-trade."

"But," said Mr. Potter, "we are not asking for free trade. We only ask for freer trade."

"I understand," said Mr. Boaker. "But these enlightened Irish—the Nationalists, so called—don't want your trade free, freer or freest—either in the positive, comparative or superlative."

"That is not my understanding," said the Senator from Maryland. "My observation leads me to feel certain that you couldn't kick an Irishman out of the Democratic party. They are great talkers. They sing "The Wearing of the Green." They may love Ireland and hate England; but give me a brass band and a Democratic banner, and I don't give a d——n about the issues. Pardon my emotion, Mr. Potter."

Mr. Bodkin and "Mules" gave the judgment of the Maryland Senator unqualified indorsement.

"That is our understanding at 'ome," said the secretary. "You notice that we are always willing that our Irish fellow-subjects should find homes in America. They sometimes give us trouble in Ireland, you know, but in America they are our best friends; it is a Cobden Club maxim, you know, that 'the highest use England can make of an Irishman is to send him to America to vote for free-trade.'"

"In my judgment," said the Maryland Senator, "the Irish are O. K."

"But what," inquired Mr. Potter, "will you do with the educated, the independent, Ireland-loving, English-hating, Americanized Irish — with those blawsted Nationalists, who are so ungrateful as to desire the exclusion of English goods from the American market?"

"Oh, just damn their characters," said "Mules;" "call them turn-coats, traitors, bribe-takers, and the like; and in the heat of an election, a sufficient volume of blackguardism is irresistible."

"That is my understanding as to politics in America," said Mr. Potter. "Now, then," he continued, "in what quarter shall we look for recruits? We are all right in the South, Mr. G——, are we not?"

"The South is solid," said the Senator. "The word 'issue' does not appear in our lexicon. We are Democrats down there. To the West, especially to the Northwest, we must look for new allies on the issue of tariff reform. There we must inaugurate a campaign of education. We must teach the Western farmer to 'sell in the world's dearest market, and buy where he can buy the cheapest'; in other words, buy from England, Mr. Potter, you know."

"Capital point!" said the secretary.

The conference then proceeded to discuss the question of finances. Mr. Potter promised that tariff-reform literature would be abundantly supplied. The club would also supply the sinews of war. How much, if stated at the time, was never published; but the outcome of the conference was boldly avowed in the next issue of the New York *Evening Post* (July, 1879). That paper stated in plain terms (and this is not fiction, but fact) that "the Cobden Club was now fairly naturalized in America; that it was intended to turn its attention to the congressional elections; that it was established on a sound financial basis, with assured working capital for several years to come." From that hour to this the New York *Post* has been an English organ, not less loyal than the London *Times*.

The promise of the *Post* was fulfilled. In the presidential and congressional elections of 1880 (the Garfield-Hancock campaign) the American people were called upon once again to meet and conquer England in the effort of the "tight little island" to accomplish by corruption and intrigue what she had failed to achieve in war—the conquest of America.

And Greater Ireland (?), as usual, voted with England and for England. Numerous daring Irishmen, risking character, fortune and fellowship, took sides, for the first time, with America for protection, and broke the hitherto undisputed claim to perpetual and unquestioned allegiance to the Democratic party. The heart of Greater Ireland feebly but perceptibly throbbed.

CHAPTER XXXVII.

DAY DAWNS ON ERIN MOR.

EN route for San Francisco, Dillon committed little Marcellina to the care of the good sisters at Los Angeles. She was still a child, only thirteen years of age; a child whom he had treated as his own; but when the time for parting came at San Pedro (the seaport of Los Angeles), there was a scene. The child clung to him passionately, kissing him again and again; and her dark eyes flashed with a peculiar flame that was something more than childish. It was the sacred light of a girl's first love; but he neither anticipated nor appreciated it. To him she was still a child, and if the thought of her loving him once entered his head, the thought was but a theory to be lightly rejected. But the dark eyes of Marcellina were like the ghost of Banquo—they "would not down"; and when he retired to his stateroom and sought to sleep, the wavy golden locks of the girl, shining like the wheat fields in autumn when mellowed by California suns, and the dark face and the flashing eyes and the holy light would pass before his mental vision, and for the first time in ten long years he gave a serious thought to living womankind. The thought was born but to be set aside, and whenever the vision recurred he endeavored to withhold his will. She was but a child, an Indian, a barbarian. She would form new acquaintances in a broader, brighter civilization, and would forget him as he endeavored to forget her.

After weary years of solitude he arrived in San Francisco. When he had sold his gold dust, and had stored a comfortable fortune at the Hibernia Bank, his peculiar weakness again beset him. He set out in quest of his *Erin Mor*, his Greater Ireland, which he ardently hoped to find among the Irish of San Francisco. Here, surely, in the chief city on the Golden Coast; here in this new land of great opportunities, where hearts were young and fresh and pure, he would find his countrymen powerful, prosperous and politically independent. His investigation satisfied him that they had succeeded admirably in material things. They bore an active part in commerce, finance, education and religion. They were potent, too, in controlling local politics; but in the higher, broader, grander meaning of politics—in the moulding of public policies, in the shaping of the destinies of State and Nation—they were practically ignored.

He sauntered into a densely populated district of the city known as "Tar Flat," among the dwellings of the poor and the unfortunate. It was a district of cheap lodging houses and poor tenements, and of the inevitable accompaniment of poverty and cheapness—the cheap saloon. He desired to travel in this quarter without entering any of those establishments, but he yielded to his spirit of curiosity when he came to the "Kilmaroo." This center of civilization occupied a corner. The name of the proprietor was not apparent. The gilded letters upon the plate-glass window bore only the simple legend, "The Kilmaroo," and a large rosewood box inside, resembling in size and outline an ice-chest, also displayed in gilded letters the name of "The Kilmaroo."

A policeman came out of the side door, evidently suffering from some acute affection of the stomach. Dillon, witnessing his agony, first inquired as to the cause of his suffering. The guardian of the law bent himself in the shape of a quarter-moon, as if he had eaten too freely of unripe cucumbers.

"Bad luck to that green bartender!" he said. "I asked him for water and he gev it to me. It's the first I've drank since I jined the force, and it nearly killed me."

A powerful organization called "The Kilmaroos" made headquarters at this establishment.

"What is the fellow with the shovel doing?" inquired Dillon of the policeman.

"*Och*, he's jist feedin' some snakes to the craythur."

"But I don't see any snakes," said Dillon.

"Naythur do I," said the officer. "But the boys on the bench see a whole field full of snakes. These gentlemen are members of the gang, and whenever any of the gang is troubled wid the traymens, and sees the snakes, ould Tim has the snakes fed to the Kilmaroo, and it aises the feelings of the boys."

"But the snakes are purely imaginary?"

"Yis, me boy," said the officer, "and so is the Kilmaroo. If ye'll keep the saycret, and don't give me away, I'll give ye the whole snap. It's ould Tim himself that's in the rosewood box."

"And who, pray, might ould Tim be?"

"Oh, come off wid ye," said the officer. "What are you givin' us? You must be a foreigner—(bad luck to the foreigners! it's immigration that's killin' San Francisco)—Don't know Tim Devereux, the chief of the Kilmaroos?"

"Tim Devereux!" said Dillon. "This must be "Slippery Tim," my old friend of the San Diego Mountains." And it was.

"And who are the Kilmaroos?" inquired Dillon.

"They are an organization for upholding Democratic principles," said the officer.

"Organized to defend free speech and the sanctity of the ballot, I suppose?"

"It's right you are as far as you go, my friend," said the officer. "They never break up a meetin' unless it's again' the Democrats it is, and they never knock anybody down who votes the Democratic ticket. If you'll come up to Horticultural Hall tomorrow night, you'll see the Kilmaroos smash an Irish-Republican meetin' into smithereens. I'll give you the hailin' sign of the order;" and the officer passed the forefinger of his right hand diagonally across his nose.

"Now," he added, "yer fixed. The devil a sowl will dare to touch you when you have the sign. You're an Irishman, and a Dimocrat, av coorse."

San Francisco, at that time, had a great many Irish societies, varying in shades of intensity from the blood-red of advanced nationalism to the pale green of landleagueism. The tinseled emerald regalia and the green-dyed ostrich plumes of Irish processions were frequent sights in San Francisco; and if English cruelty and rapacity could be curbed by burning resolutions and green ribbons, it was a clear case of *Delenda est Britannia*.

The presidential campaign was in progress, and a number of Irishmen, with sense enough to understand that England was proof against Patrick's-day parades, but quite vulnerable to the assaults of protective tariffs, and believing that these Irish societies were honest in their professions of hostility to England, actually resolved to put their professions to test by calling a meeting of Irish-Americans to assemble at Horticultural Hall, in support of the Republican policy of protection and against the British policy of free-trade.

This call aroused the wrath of the Kilmaroos, and it was resolved to smash the protectionist meeting. These pioneer Irish Republicans found it necessary to call a militia company, "The Garfield Invincibles," to protect them against a probable attack. Tim Devereux was then notified that any attempt to break up the meeting would result in several funerals. The warning was almost completely effective. The main body of the Kilmaroos remained at their headquarters, and the few stragglers who came were unceremoniously kicked down stairs and corded on the sidewalk. The citizens present were not all of the Republican faith, but they were all Irish-Americans, and were unanimous in adopting the following resolutions:

"*Resolved*, That a time and an occasion have come in American public affairs, when Irish Americans, in the maintenance of their self-respect, if from no other motive, must assert the right hitherto denied to them—a right freely and fully exercised by all other races of men in this country—the right to vote with some regard to the persons to be voted for, and the issues and the questions to be determined.

"*Resolved*, That in American politics there should be no green flag. We are, first of all things, Americans. This Nation is our home. We are a laboring people, whose best interests are inseparable from the industrial prosperity of America, and we will be faithful to America against every foe, native or foreign."

These resolutions were adopted with a cheer, and without a dissenting vote. Several brief rousing speeches were made, and the right of Irish-Americans in San Francisco to free discussion and a free ballot was vindicated.

Dillon, who was a silent spectator, was overjoyed at the proceedings. This was the first time during his fifteen years residence in America that he had ever seen a public meeting of Irish-Americans daring to differ with the Democratic party, or daring in any manner to express any political opinion except such as the Democratic conventions dictated.

"This," said he, "is the beginning of the end—day dawning on my *Erin Mor.*"

"Amen, amen," said the president of the meeting;

and then it was that Dillon recognized in the speaker the same Charles Henry Scanlan who, with revolver in hand, protected the freedom of the ballot at New Limerick a dozen years before.

Dillon laughed heartily as he drew a carving knife from his pocket.

"What in the world were you doing with that?" said Scanlan.

"Well," said Dillon, "I feel a trifle ashamed for carrying a weapon like that; but the clerk at the hotel advised me that the surest way to secure peace with the Kilmaroos was to be prepared for war; that if I went unarmed, and the Kilmaroos made an attack, I might need to defend myself, but that a display of my carving knife would make its use unnecessary."

"That's correct," said a stranger who stood listening to the conversation. "Next to a blackthorn stick, a long-bladed knife is the boss among hoodlums. They are so often shot at that they succeed in dodging a pistol bullet. But they quail before cold steel every time. Your ruffian and bully of the slums is generally a coward, unmanned by his vices. Show him a courageous front and your means of defence, and he will hardly ever show fight."

"Might I ask your name, sir?" said Dillon curiously.

"Certainly, sir," said the stranger. "My name is Peter McIntyre."

"Peter McIntyre? Peter McIntyre?" exclaimed Scanlan and Dillon in chorus. "Great God!" added Scanlan, "can this be 'Peter the Pagan,' the lover of Maggie Sullivan, the victim of Isaac Marx and the Devoys?"

"The same," replied McIntyre; "but, boys, how changed! This hair of mine, black as a raven when I left New Limerick, became white as snow within a few months after."

"No use crying over spilled milk, Peter," said Scanlan. "Let us go."

And they went to a comfortable San Francisco home, and they talked of old times and old friends, and the bright hopes for *Erin Mor* in the future of America.

The Irish-Americans in considerable numbers supported General Garfield; and though he would, without doubt, have been elected without their support, still the courageous fight they made in many cities that year was a noteworthy historical and political fact. It was the first general movement of Irish-Americans to dispute the absolute ownership of their suffrages by the Democratic party; the first noticeable manifestation of Irish-American resentment at the alliance between England and the Democratic party. It was the commencement of a revolution which has been fruitful of credit and honor to the Irish race, and a valuable aid to the cause of a sound American nationality.

CHAPTER XXXVIII.

ENGLISH CIVILIZATION SOCIETY.

"PETER the Pagan" had resided for years in one of the prosperous cities of the Missouri Valley. His blacksmithing business, under the fostering policy of protection, had expanded into a foundry and machine shop, and a carriage and wagon factory. Declining health compelled him to seek a more congenial clime; so, selling out to his partners, he took his departure for California.

"Come with me to God's country," said Dillon. "Come to Southern California, where 'the climate is as mild as a mother's smile, and the soil as fruitful as God's love.'"

"The United States of America is God's country," said the "Pagan."

"True enough," said Dillon, "but you have lived long enough in the frigid North. Come down to San Diego. If you seek a lovely country, there it is. There is not on the face of the earth, as far as I know, a more delightful climate than that of the bay region of San Diego. It is a land of eternal sunshine—never hot and never cold. If you desire to live to a ripe o'd age, come down. It is there that the pulse of youth goes bounding in the bending forms of the aged; a land that literally flows with milk and honey; where 'you tickle the earth and it laughs potatoes'; the land of the lemon, the orange, and the olive, where you can indeed sit in peace under your own vine and fig tree. Come with me, *ma bouchal*, and we'll give you a *cacd millé failthe.* We are both unmarried. We can keep bachelor's hall, and live a life of freedom on the sea-shore or in the mountains."

"I have often questioned," said McIntyre, "whether a man born and reared in a cold climate, and who has lived for half a life-time amid the snows, the forests, and the rushing rivers of the North, would ever be contented under your eternal sunshine, with perpetual summer."

"But it is not perpetual summer," responded Dillon. "There is no sudden change from the suns that burn to the storms that chill. But we have a seed-time and a harvest. You feel all the delightful sensations of the spring-time when the rains of December coax forth the young vegetation; and you feel all the glory of summer in the month of March, when you stand in one of our southern valleys amid grasses and flowers knee high. In June, July and August you witness the ripening of the grape, the peach and other fruits, and the mellowing of the golden ear in the grain fields. There is no such word as winter on the sea-shore of Southern California; but if you must have a breath of frosty air or a little diversion at snow-balling, we can run up into the mountains fifty miles or so for a change."

"Very well," said the "Pagan," "I'll go you. I am a free commoner. If the San Diego country is all that you say it is, I will be satisfied."

And on Sunday afternoon they found themselves on board of one of the splendid coast steamers, passing out of the Golden Gate, and into the broad Pacific. Three days later they were at Fern Hill, in San Diego County. They located timber culture entry claims side by side. Neither then nor subsequently was their chosen habitation known to fame. It is not named upon the maps, nor designated by the name of Fern Hill upon the assessment rolls. They gave it its name from the great variety and beauty of the ferns. It was a wilderness within easy reach of civilization—behind the ocean valley and the *mesa*, amid the rolling hills that border the great valley of El Cajon. The hand of man has greatly altered its conditions. There are groves of eucalyptus and sycamores and cottonwoods, and hedge rows of cypress, and long lines of magnolias that shed their fragrance all around them; and there are hedge-rows of marguerite, with their wealth of snow-white blossoms, and roses in abundance scattered upon their isolated bushes, or trailing along the roof and walls of the cottages. The traveler may climb upon one of the highest hills and see the white-sailed ocean ships sailing around Point Loma into the Bay of San Diego; or turning the eye in another direction, he will observe the Sweetwater River flashing back the sunlight, and beyond the river the little wooded parks that nestle at the foot of the San Miguel Mountain, and beyond those pretty patches the mountain itself rising majestically, almost perpendicularly, from the valley to the clouds. Looking eastward, through some opening between two hills, he will see the orange groves and vineyards on the slopes of El Cajon; and far away to the east the circling mountains with their dark forests and snow-covered peaks.

There were quails and rabbits innumerable, and the wild bees stored their wealth of honey in hollow trees and rocks in all the surrounding country. After the first rains, in November and December, mushrooms of enormous size could be gathered everywhere upon the sheep pastures in the valleys and on the hillsides, and great water-melons grew in the shallow river beds from seeds scattered by accident or design upon the sands in the early summer. Cuttings of the grape-vine set in fertile crevices among the rocks grew into luxuriant vines with a vigor that taxed the industry of the husbandman to trim and control. Strawberries ripened during every month of the year, and in every regard Nature liberally rewarded the toiler for a little labor. The climate of the foot-hills was still more salubrious than the air upon the sea-side. The ocean moisture that came up in cloud or fog was dissipated by the sun before the breeze that bore it passed inland over Fern Hill; so that even in those days, long before the advent of railroads, many invalids from the north camped and wandered around the foot-hills to prolong their lives by breathing its balmy atmosphere. Here it was that the two old bachelors, political exiles, martyrs of circumstance, made their homes.

They had many transient visitors; but there was

one visitor who clung to them with wonderful tenacity. He was the aged Pridmore, whom they learned to call "Old Prid" for short. He was one of the most amiable men that ever lived. He had come from London to San Francisco as a free-trade missionary, but the unappreciative and ungrateful hoodlums of the Pacific metropolis never took kindly to his doctrines. It was impossible to doubt his sincerity. He was well satisfied that it was the mission and duty of England and the English to civilize all the nations of the earth, and to seize the earth by way of compensation for their missionary labors.

He was now acting as an agent for the "Anglo-California Civilization Society." The purposes of this corporation were ostensibly benevolent. They had seized many thousands of acres of the richest lands in the Mexican State of Lower California under some arrangement with the Mexican government, and they were now engaged prospecting San Diego County, with a view to seizing its water supply. Water is life in Southern California. The mountain lake at Cuyamaca and the Sweetwater and San Diego rivers are the great sources of supply for San Diego. Pridmore's mission was to examine and report upon the subject of water to the Civilization Society. Dillon and McIntyre saw the intent, and foresaw the consequences of the enterprise. They foresaw that in the event of war with England she would have a foot-hold in Northern Mexico and an outpost in San Diego County; that a time might come, and doubtless would come, when, taking advantage of Mexico's weakness or misfortune, England would seize Lower California, and establish her power on the southern border of the United States.

Dillon felicitated himself upon the fact that the English had fallen in love with San Diego County; "because," he would say, "its resources and its prospects are so great as to appeal to their rapacity, while of course this country will not permit them to seize the land."

McIntyre held a different view. "If they get a foothold here on any pretense," he said, "whether they come as miners, traders, benefactors or missionaries, they will plunder Southern California, just as surely as they ravaged the Valley of the Ganges, and converted Ireland into a wilderness and a plague spot. They have set their eyes upon its water supply, and they'll get it by purchase, or by corrupting influential citizens and public officials. They have seized and debauched the wine business of the State already, and they have made the name of beer in California a mockery and a delusion since they bought up the breweries."

Mr. Pridmore explained that the company was animated only by love for their English-speaking brethren in America, and desired to invest their English capital in supplying water to the natives, you know. There was a beautiful spring in the neighborhood of Fern Hill, near which bands of Indians occasionally camped for the night. One evening Mr. Pridmore rushed up to Fern Hill, breathless from exertion and excitement. He had visited the Indian camp, and on behalf of the society he sought to make a treaty with the red men, by the terms of which they would pay tribute to the Civilization Society for the use of the spring. They chased him out of the camp into the friendly shades of Fern Hill, and when he found himself safe with his Irish friends, he forgot for the moment his missionary morality, and "blowed and blawsted the bloody h'eyes of the blawsted American peasantry." "Ah, lads," he added, "h'it's little better than h'old h'Ireland if a British subject may be chased by the blawsted h'American peasantry."

Pridmore was a most plausible liar. They often laid schemes to induce him to tell the truth, but they never succeeded. Neither by chance, accident, inadvertence, or design, was he ever known to make a statement strictly true.

Yet they hailed him as a jolly good fellow, and a professed friend of Ireland and the Irish; but whenever they drove him to the wall in controversy, he ended the discussion by assuring them that "the trouble with the Irish, you know, is that the government is too easy with them, you know." And when he had bade them his good-byes, Dillon would remark what a good-natured soul he was. But Peter the Pagan had less faith in British benignity.

"If Old Pridmore," he said, "with all his benevolence, sat at the gate of heaven where St. Peter is supposed to be stationed, and my soul approached the gate, if I had to enter heaven by his permission, I would never enter it. It is impossible for him and his to love us and love their prey, our native island.

"Should the Saxon snake unfold
At thy feet his scales of gold,
Trust him not."

Days and seasons came and went at Fern Hill. Dillon and McIntyre employed the labor of men and teams to break the land for their groves, and occasionally an Indian assisted at their garden work, while they themselves labored assiduously to beautify their homes. McIntyre heartily sympathized with his friend Dillon in his bright hopes for *Erin Mor*, and it was mutually agreed that three years later they would visit the East to feel the pulse of Ireland in America during the presidential campaign.

At latest accounts the English Civilization Society held a mortgage on the city of San Diego to secure payment for its water supply. Their colonization in Lower California proved a failure; but colonization was not their purpose. When war between the United States and Chile seemed probable, the Civilization Society stood ready to seize an English coaling station at San Quentin, on the Lower California coast, and to build a railroad from San Quentin to the border of San Diego County, at Tia Juana.

CHAPTER XXXIX.

GREATER IRELAND IN COUNCIL.

THE people of Ireland, under the leadership of Charles Stewart Parnell, presented in the battle for Home Rule a practically united front in 1884, and the nation, that seemed bleeding to death in 1847, and lay "like a corpse upon a dissecting table" in 1848, had risen again, putting forth as best she could all the feeble strength in her possession, with the hot blood of national life bounding through her myriad veins. Her Spartan cry for help followed the exiles in the track of the emigrant ships across the waters of the Atlantic. *Erin Mor* responded with lavish generosity. But while the Irish in Ireland continued their gallant struggle for native government and industrial independence, the great mass of the Irish in America were the best friends of England's interest on this side of the Atlantic.

There appeared in the political firmament of the United States, in the northern part of New York, a bright particular star in the person of a man named Cleveland—variously called Stephen Grover, Stephen G., S. G., and finally Grover Cleveland. He had been Mayor of Buffalo, Sheriff of Erie County, New York, and Governor of the Empire State. He was a type of the phenomenal politician who occasionally comes to the surface in American politics; who dazzles by the splendor of his successes, while he puzzles the minds of the multitude who shout for him, as to why they are shouting. He was a young man during the war of the Rebellion, in the fullness of such manhood as he ever attained; but no one ever heard of him, except that, when drafted for service in the army, he hired a substitute, and was wounded for his country, by proxy, on the field of Gettysburg. Suddenly this man appeared in the arena of national politics as the champion of English free-trade for America. "Tariff Reform" was what he called it; and he rested his claim to the presidency on this idea of tariff reform, and the other idea, that no one ought to be elected President for a second term—*except him*. He became a fetich in American politics. The hat was passed in London for him, and vast sums were raised by the Cobden Club and other British organizations to advance this apostle of tariff reform. All England—from Gladstone in the cabinet to the beggar on London Bridge—shouted for him. The British press bepraised him to the skies, and the sons and kindred of the Irish famine exiles in America echoed the hosannas of the London *Times*. Pictures of him were hung in every bar-room from Maine to California, and virtuous Irish mothers had framed lithographs of him exposed to the gaze of their innocent daughters, in parlors and in drawing-rooms. He was compared by his idolators to George Washington, to Andrew Jackson, and to Thomas Jefferson, and in certain Irish circles St. Patrick and Robert Emmet took back seats when this new god Grover was "to the fore."

It was during this idolatrous rage that a great convention of the Irish National League met in the city of Chicago. It was probably the greatest assembly of representative Irishmen that ever convened in Ireland or America. Twelve hundred delegates represented the states and territories of the Union and the Dominion of Canada, and several Irish members of Parliament were present, as were at least a dozen members and ex-members of the American Congress, a score of judges of courts of record, and fifty priests of the Catholic church. An Episcopal clergyman presided, and a Methodist minister occupied a place beside him on the platform. The convention pledged to Ireland two hundred and fifty thousand dollars for the advancement of the Home Rule cause, and the pledge was sacredly fulfilled. The sensational feature of the proceedings was the introduction of a resolution by an awkward-looking delegate from California.

"Mr. Chairman!"

The chair: "The gentleman from California."

Delegate Andy Dillon: "I move you, sir, the adoption of the resolution which I read:

"*Resolved*, That this convention of the Irish National League is in favor of boycotting English merchandise in America; that we, the delegates, will buy no English goods, and that we will endeavor to induce the millions of Irish-Americans to cease buying English goods, and we pledge our sacred honor that we will never buy a blade of English hardware, nor an inch of her dry goods, until the relations now existing between England and Ireland are radically changed."

This resolution was greeted with mingled hisses and cheers. The delegates from New York City and Boston bitterly opposed it, but it received the earnest support of every delegate who sincerely loved America, and who intelligently hated England. After a lively and good-natured debate, a vote was taken, and to the surprise of Andy Dillon himself, and of the other real Nationalists present, the resolution was adopted.

Right hearty were the congratulations that greeted the Californian, and when a recess was taken, groups of old friends and of new ones gathered around him. Patrick Ford, of the *Irish World*, declared that the cloud which had darkened the mind of Greater Ireland had been rent, and that this resolution was the beginning of the end. There was astonishment and consternation among the ward politicians, and many of them who had voted for the resolution retired from the hall in deep dissatisfaction. Albert Michael Devoy and Perry Tonitis Devoy were outspoken in their denunciations.

"They don't mane it," said Albert Michael. "Wait till the votes are counted in the fall, and ninety-five per cent of 'em will be cast for tariff reform."

"I don't give a ———," responded Dillon. "Majorities are powerless to destroy a principle. *Erin Mor* has spoken; has uttered God Almighty's truth; has declared for a principle that every honest Irishman believes in; and sooner or later the seed sown by this declaration will bear bitter fruit for England."

The seed sown by the resolution fructified much sooner than the sower anticipated. On the very night of its adoption a private meeting of selected delegates was held in one of the club-rooms of the Grand Pacific Hotel. The meeting numbered about fifty men. There were no "Irishmen by trade" present. The meeting was composed of those who, in various ways, had proven their devotion to Ireland and to America.

Captain James Sullivan, of the armless sleeve, was there, and so was Colonel Denny Burke, laden with lead fired from English muskets by brave Confederates during the war for the Union. And there was the veteran Methodist preacher from Ohio, Dr. William McNevin; and there were men who had been glorified by the death sentence in English courts of justice (?) in Ireland, and men who had been tortured in British prison hells for devotion to Ireland, and men who had been hunted down like wolves and driven into exile, and men whose grandfathers' blood had mingled with the waters of the Slaney in '98, and sons of the men of '48, and men who had taken to the hillsides in 1865, and descendants of those who had perished upon the scaffold and in the dungeon. But the children of those who died of hunger were not invited.

And there was a man up the chimney. An old newspaper reporter had been appointed inside guard, with instructions to seek for intruders. He lit a match, looked up the fire-place, made a haul, and at first dragged down the coat-tail and then the body of *Shemus Ruadh*—Red Jim McDermott, an active Democrat, and a spy in the service of England.

They kicked him out, and flung after him the contents of his pockets, consisting of a biography of Grover Cleveland and a copy of *Harper's Weekly*, containing a cartoon representing an Irishman with the face and tail of a baboon.

A genteel little man of keen blue eyes and fair complexion, a citizen of the State of Nebraska, presided. This man had held very responsible positions in Irish affairs, and though an exceedingly mild, refined and courteous gentleman, was regarded by the British government as a very dangerous person. He stated the purpose of the meeting to be some practical effort to counteract British influence in American national politics; especially to defeat, if possible, the conquest of America by the Cobden Club and its allies, and to arouse the intelligence, patriotism and conscience of the Irish in America to a sense of their duty as American citizens.

There was little discussion, and no formal resolutions, but an expressed and unanimous determination that for the love of America, for the honor and dignity of the Irish race, in vindication of their self-respect, they must break the bonds that made the Irish the body-guard of England in American politics.

There were no fiery speeches and no cheers; but in the hearts and eyes of those assembled there was desperate resolve, and it was agreed that each would take an active part upon the American side in the forthcoming presidential battle; and before the lights were extinguished these devoted exiles clasped each other's hands with a pressure that was more expressive than an oath.

To the soul of Andy Dillon this silent exhibition was like the sight of "sky and stars to prisoned men;" and he grasped the hand of the Methodist minister, and led him to a corner of the hall where Dr. Barry was standing, and these three men renewed the vow made fifteen years before in the foul tenement of the dying Murphy, at New York, that they "would make no peace with England."

The candidates nominated by the Republicans for President and Vice-president were James G. Blaine and John A. Logan, a brilliant statesman and a gallant soldier. Blaine was descended from Celtic stock, of revolutionary and Irish ancestry; and the gallant Logan, "the Marshal Ney of America," the idol of the volunteer army, was the son of an Irishman. The revenue plank of the Republican platform took issue squarely with Cleveland's Tariff Reform.

Surely, if there was a living soul in Greater Ireland, here was an inspiring appeal to all that was wise and generous and heroic in that soul. It was yet a problem if the time had come. Had penal laws, free-trade and famine, the emigrant ship and the stifling tenement, and the lash of the slave-holder, and the whip of the ward politician, and "the world, the flesh and the devil" rotted out the once heroic soul of the ancient race?

CHAPTER XL.

AFTER FIFTEEN YEARS.

ON a summer morning, in the year 1884, two travelers arrived at the Union depot in New Limerick—two brawny-looking middle-aged men, with bearded, sun-browned faces. They inquired for the home of Tom Sullivan, but the young people whom they addressed scratched their heads dubiously, and it was some time before they found anyone who could give them the desired information.

"Tom Sullivan—poor Tom, the stone-mason?" said an old man to whom the inquiry was addressed. "Dead for many years; buried in the cemetery beyant the creek. You will have no trouble, sir, in finding his grave, with its white marble monument; the purtiest tombstone in the graveyard, except that of Barney Devoy."

"And the Sullivan family—Tom's children—what of them?"

"Scattered, sir. Captain James Sullivan moved to one of the cities of Northern New York, and became great as a lawyer, and wealthy in the banking business. Little Jerry—surely you must have heard

of Little Jerry who was killed at Fredericksburg—
everyone has heard of little Jerry. And Mary, she
entered a convent and is doing God's work among
the hospitals of New York City."

"And Maggie—what of her?"

"Oh, *Dea*, poor Maggie! poor, broken-hearted
Maggie! Surely you must have heard of her misfortune. She fell in love wid a black Republican
called "Peter the Pagan." He first went back on
his party and his blessed religion, and then took a
wild-goose chase to the West—the dirty blackguard!—
fifteen years ago, and never was heard from since.
Mag Sullivan threw the pearl of her love away upon
that swine. She wept and waited year after year,
till the silver threads appeared in her nut-brown
hair, and she finally joined her brother Jim up on
the shore of Lake Champlain."

"Living still, is she not?"

"Oh, yes, *agra*, a sort o' livin'—livin' the life of a
widow—an unmarried widow, weepin' for a dirty,
black-hearted blackguard who went back on the
party."

"And the Devoy family—how are they?"

"You know, of course, that ould Barney is dead.
Albert Michael and Miss Birdelia and the ould lady
and Perry Tonitis are livin' here still, flourishin'
finely; but Frank, the religious boy, he left the
country, and went, it was said, on a sacred pilgrim-
age to the Holy Land."

"And who is Perry Tonitis, that you speak of?
There was none of the Devoys called Perry Tonitis."

"That's the little fellow that tended bar at the
Buchanan Exchange. He runs a wholesale drug
store now. All of the family but him had high-toned
names; and Miss Birdelia, who is a Frinch and Latin
scholar, would never be aisy till Tony had a high-

soundin' name. He took the name Perry from an English gentleman who was makin' love to Miss Birdelia, and the name Tonitis, they say, is the Latin for Anthony."

The first stranger quietly slipped a silver dollar into the hand of the old man who answered the inquiries—judging from his seedy appearance that it would mean no offence.

"And who, sir, may I take the liberty to ask, is the big-hearted gentleman who gives me the dollar?"

"The stranger who takes the liberty to do so, if it please you, sir, is 'Peter the Pagan.'"

"And this other gentleman, your companion?"

"A man by the name of Andy Dillon. Both of us all the way from Southern California. And your name, if you please?"

"Finneran, sir; Tim Finneran. It's many a rousin' time I had wid ould Barney in his day; but I got into financial difficulties—got in debt to Barney, borrowed money from Albert Michael. He saized my cattle and the ould blind mule, and I never recovered from that misfortune."

The strangers turned to go, but were subjected to a painful exhibition on the part of Finneran. He took off his old soft hat, thrust it under his left arm and commenced muttering a string of prayers for the eternal and temporal welfare of "his Honor Pagan Pete," and "his Honor Andy Dillon," and as he bent himself submissively, "Pagan Pete" found it hard to resist the impulse to kick him in the face.

"A curse upon you, you old hypocrite! lift up your head and put on your hat. Have you breathed in vain the free air of America for a quarter of a century?"

"They are not all dead yet," said Dillon. "There's a fair specimen of creatures whom England starved and brutalized; ignorant, superstitious, treacherous, hypocritical; 'free raw material' for Democracy. It will be a blessed day for Ireland and America when the last of them is in heaven."

And the strangers turned in the direction of the Catholic cemetery, and walked unrecognized within the precincts of God's acre.

"Pagan Pete" knelt in prayer beside the tomb of his departed friend, Tom Sullivan; and Dillon walked in the direction of the tombless grave of Nancy McHugh, under the old elms in the corner. He expected to find it neglected and weed-covered; but he was happily mistaken. The grave was tastily sodded, and the tender blue grass, moistened by the dripping of dews and rains from the trees above, wore its summer sheen; and there were roses blooming at the head of the grave, and a beautiful white lily at the foot; and above poor Nancy's breast there grew in beauty and fragrance a bunch of forget-me-nots. So, filled with the sweet and bitter memories of the past, and softened in the contemplation of the grass plot and the flowers, he knelt beside the grave, and wept and prayed; and as he thought of the loving hands that beautified the sacred spot, he modified his estimate of mankind, and admitted to himself that in this cold world there is much of sunshine amid the shadows, and of mercy, and of pity, and of charity and love.

A tasteful tomb now marks the spot where Nancy's ashes lie.

Turning from the grave-yard, the strangers wandered through New Limerick, to note its progress and to seek old friends. Among the arrivals were the family of Dalton, the Claddagh fisherman. The "king" himself was dead, but his sons had joined the colony of Claddagh fishermen, who had settled on the coast of Massachusetts; and the girls, Mary and Bridget, after working for a time in the factories, were now married to prosperous Irish-American mechanics.

Albert Michael Devoy had become immensely wealthy, had an influence in politics commensurate with his wealth, and was a regular member of the Cobden Club of New York City, and the trusted political co-laborer of Thomas Bayley Potter, for the advancement of English commercial interests in America. He inherited the charitable disposition of his father, and continued to contribute regularly at every Christmas two barrels of pigs' feet to the poor, at a cost of three dollars a barrel; and it was also remembered, to his eternal honor, that he came to the rescue of a young man who had become besotted at the Buchanan Exchange, by paying a fine of nine dollars for him at the police court. These charities had great weight in the election, which fulfilled the measure of his ambition by making him a member of the school board.

Perry Tonitis Devoy was in the wholesale drug business. Having risen above the business of dram-selling, he sold whisky now by the bottle and jugful, with a little quinine and a few pills at times; but he sold ten gallons of whisky for every box of pills, and at the same time maintained the dignity of the family. He was a member of the City Council, and secretary of the Tariff Reform Club.

Miss Birdelia Devoy very nearly became a countess. For many years the family insisted that she must marry a title, and when this fact became public, numerous suitors sought her hand. There was first an English lord (so called), said to be the younger son of Sir Charles Bilke, of Bilkey Hall. He appeared in New Limerick one morning, wearing an eye-glass and a cane, carrying several band-boxes, and accompanied by a bull-dog. He was received into the best society, and within a week from the date of his arrival, scores of the Irish-American dudes each wore an eye-glass and a cane, and each was accompanied by a dog.

Birdelia's mother, Mrs. Barney Devoy, inadvertently spoiled this love affair. Albert Michael had led Sir Arthur Bilke, the suitor, to believe that the Devoys were of Huguenot French extraction; "partly," as he explained with an apology, "partly born in Ireland;" but when Mrs. Devoy, in her working dress, came from the kitchen to the drawing-room, and calling the family to supper, shouted at her banker son: "Albert Michael, you devil, come in te yer tay!" it was too much for the prejudices of Sir Arthur, and he left the town next morning, accompanied by his faithful bull-dog. Her next suitor was the Italian Count Bassiano. This count temporarily displayed plenty of money and a patent of nobility; and to crown his efforts he was assisted in his suit by Mr. Isaac Marx, the venerable and powerful New York political leader. Mr. Marx and the count made frequent visits to the Devoy mansion, and were royally entertained on such occasions. It so happened that as these two worthies were riding in an open carriage from the mansion to the depot, Andy Dillon and "Pagan Pete" observed them, and the "Pagan" remarked to his companion that he had seen the count before. It seemed to Dillon as if the "Pagan" for an instant became deathly pale, and anon his face turned red in passion, and his eyes flashed with a strangely malignant light.

"Do you know the count?" inquired Dillon.

"Yes," responded the "Pagan;" "that is the scoundrel who fractured my skull at the Clifton House, fifteen years ago; who caused my insanity, and drove me out into the world. He it was who robbed me of Maggie Sullivan's love and made me a guiltless outcast on the face of the earth. Take care of yourself for a day, Andy," he added. He then hurried to the depot, and rode in the same car with Isaac and the count from New Limerick to New York.

Between the social extremes, ranging from the penniless Finneran up to the aristocratic Devoys, there was now at New Limerick a numerous, powerful and prosperous Irish-American element. The "old timers" were dying off. The Buchanan Exchange was in the hands of strangers. There were some of the younger generation who were no improvement upon their fathers; but there was also a later generation, the men who came over after 1865, bearing in their heads a common school education, and in their hearts fraternal love for their fellow-countrymen, and a decent regard for the institutions and the feelings of the American people. There was a still younger generation, born on American soil, educated in American schools, and nurtured upon the milk of America's generous bosom. They had eaten the bread grown upon her soil, and in their pockets jingled the liberal earnings paid to American labor. New England boys by birth, they were not wholly indifferent to the glorious history and traditions of New England. These young men had opinions in politics, and many of them were in hearty sympathy with American industry and American ideas. Windfalls dropped and kept dropping, it was true. Nature exercised her prerogative in the survival of the fittest. Irish mothers transmitted to their daughters the legacy of virtue and fecundity. The church and the school were cheerfully maintained, and, all things considered, Dillon was proud of the rising generation, and hopeful for his *Erin Mor*.

CHAPTER XLI.

CLEVELAND AND THE IRISH.

THE presidential campaign of '84 opened during the month of August. A meeting of Irish-Americans was held at Chickering Hall, in the city of New York, under the direction of the *Irish World*. That great newspaper, always remarkable for its radical independence, exerted its tremendous power battling against the free-trade conquest of America. Three thousand Irish-Americans were crowded within the hall, and five thousand more clamored around the building, in vain, for admittance. Andy Dillon and "Pagan Pete" occupied seats upon the platform, and listened with deep interest and enthusiasm to the eloquent speeches that were made. One of the orators was the Rev. Dr. William McNevin; another was a descendant of the famous patriot and political economist, Henry Carey, of Philadelphia. John Roach, the great Irish-American ship builder, was represented by his son. The meeting was thoroughly American in tone and sentiment. The remarkable speech of the evening, the speech that sounded the key-note for Irish-Americans, and that woke a responsive chord in every heart, was made by an uncouth, pale-faced, gloomy-looking Celt from Western Iowa; a man who has passed out of public life, and who recently died, it is said, somewhere in the State of California. Great meetings were subsequently held at the Brooklyn Opera House, at Faneuil Hall in Boston, at Newark, Baltimore, and other great cities all over the country; and Greater Ireland was aroused for a great principle, and everywhere evinced an enlightened patriotism and fervid enthusiasm never hitherto manifested by the race in American politics. This activity aroused a counter feeling among the enemies of American industrial independence, inaugurating an era of political iconoclasm. New York City became the battle-ground.

The Irish-American protectionists were the apostles of a new sect, preaching a new heresy among the faithful of the Democratic fold. Dillon and "Pagan Pete" traveled in pairs, and spoke from a truck whenever opportunity offered. A short time before the election it seemed certain that Blaine and Logan would be elected, despite the united efforts of Democracy, mugwumpery, toryism and English money. Greater Ireland was apparently acting a gallant part, and earning the gratitude of its American friends and neighbors in the Northern States.

Suddenly Burchard spoke. At a meeting of Christian ministers assembled at one of the great hotels of New York City, for the purpose of receiving and honoring James G. Blaine, one of these ministers uttered his famous alliteration, "Rum, Romanism and Rebellion." Mr. Blaine, who was engaged in conversation at a point remote from Rev. Burchard, did not hear the odious remark, and of course did not sympathize with it; but these three words undoubtedly decided a presidential election.

On the Sunday morning succeeding this event, Mr. Isaac Marx was distributing hand-bills in front of St. Andrew's Church, on Chambers street. Albert Michael and Perry Tonitis were similarly engaged at the Church of St. Loyola at New Limerick, and zealous Democrats rendered like service at all the principal Catholic churches in America. These handbills bore the ominous heading—

| RUM, ROMANISM AND REBELLION |

Followed by an argument holding Blaine responsible for the senseless ebullition of bigotry. Bigotry won.

The Irish had been unaccustomed to reason on American political subjects, and thousands of them who were theretofore active supporters of Blaine, were repelled by the Burchard incident. Thus Blaine was defeated, and thus was retarded for four years more the triumph of freedom and independence in American politics of the Irish-American citizen.

Albert Michael Devoy was appointed postmaster at New Limerick. This appointment was presumed to be highly gratifying to the Irish. How, now, could any Irishman scratch a Democratic ticket after this recognition of the race?

The Irish in California, too, were reported to the reform President as clamorous for recognition; and to appease this alleged clamor, Francis Xavier Devoy was appointed postmaster of a California city; but it was somewhat inconvenient for him to perform the duties of the position, because he was just then "doing time" in the San Quentin penitentiary for robbing the identical post-office to which he had been appointed. A retired horse-thief subsequently obtained the appointment. Thus was exemplified the glorious doctrine of civil service reform; and instances of this kind were quite common under the administration of the reform President.

One day, as Albert Michael was smoking his after-dinner cigar, Senator Barnum, accompanied by two strangers, walked into Albert Michael's private office. One of these two was a deputy marshal of the United States, and the other a gentleman from Scotland Yard, London, England—a secret-service agent of the English government. Senator Barnum introduced the strangers, and briefly stated their business. The British government, with the sanction or connivance of Mr. Cleveland's deputy marshals, was taking a census of "dangerous Irishmen" in the United States, and collecting information as to Irish-American affairs. When requested to name the dangerous Irish of New Limerick—that is, those considered damaging to England—Postmaster Devoy suggested certain organizations.

"Do you mean the Knights of Saint Patrick, gentlemen?"

"What is their object?" inquired the secret-service man?"

"They eat and drink, and sing and toast on Patrick's nights and other festive occasions. They get their mutton for the feasts from Limerick and their whisky from Cork. They are rale patriots," said Albert Michael.

"Perfectly harmless," said the Englishman. "Let them sing; the more they sing and shout and feast and drink, the more harmless and contented they are. Their custom is a convenient safety-valve for their patriotism. Let them shout."

"Then," said Albert Michael, "you mean the Ancient Order of Hibernians?"

"What is their object?" said the Englishman.

"Friendship, love and true Christian charity. They wear lovely regalia and look fine in processions. They are purty much all good Democrats."

"England is perfectly satisfied," said the secret agent. "Let them be friendly, loveable and charitable; let them wear out their shoes parading, and wear the green until doomsday. They are perfectly innocent to English government at home and English interest in America."

"Then the Fenians, United Irishmen or *Clan-na-gaels?*" suggested Albert Michael.

"There are dangerous men among them," said the deputy marshal; "but Mr. Jenkins (the Englishman) doesn't mean them."

"Not as members of these organizations," said

Jenkins. "We can anticipate and baffle them. Through the courtesy of Mr. Cleveland's postmasters we are enabled to reach the correspondence of these societies. And, by the way," he inquired, "have you any letters here addressed to one Patrick W. Crowe?"

Albert Michael reached into the "C" pigeonhole and brought forth, among other letters, one for P. W. Crowe. The English agent took it; then drew from his pocket a tiny spirit lamp, with a miniature water boiler attached. Applying a lighted match to the lamp, the task of producing steam only occupied a few moments. He then adroitly held the sealed portion of the envelope over the jet of steam, and—*presto!*—the letter was opened. It was signed by the head chief of the dynamiters, and related to a scheme whereby Mr. Crowe would blow up the city of London by igniting the gas in the main gas pipes.

"Perfectly harmless," said the Scotland Yard man; and as he re-sealed the letter and restored it to the "C" pigeonhole, he looked impatiently at Senator Barnum.

"By dangerous Irishmen," said the Senator, "Mr. Jenkins means two classes: those who would commit political offenses in Great Britain or Ireland, and those who support the policy of protection in American elections, and defeat the cherished purposes of England and the Democratic party."

"Oh, I see," said the postmaster; and he hastily wrote the names of the fifteen or twenty "dangerous Irishmen" of New Limerick.

"The purpose of the inquiry," Senator Barnum explained, "is to enable our British friends to find any particlar Irishmen in this country that they may desire to extradite under the treaty prepared by Mr. Bayard, our Secretary of State, which will place

Irish political exiles who escape to this country completely within the power of the British government. Any of the 'dangerous Irishmen' may go back to Ireland any day, you know."

"Precisely so," said Jenkins.

The famous treaty never became operative. A Republican Senate killed it; and Secretary Blaine subsequently negotiated with the British government a substitute for the Bayard treaty, which (it is needless to say) was not framed in the interests of the English government.

CHAPTER XLII.

"ERIN MOR'S" AGE OF REASON.

IT was late in the month of October, 1888, amid the excitement of another Presidential campaign. Madison Square Garden was thronged with Irish-Americans. Ten thousand Celts were assembled within the walls of the vast inclosure, and quite as many more had to content themselves by listening to speakers at the overflow meetings outside. Within the building the principal speaker was James G. Blaine. Close beside him stood two very modest looking men, each answering to the name of Patrick. One was the editor of the *Irish World;* the other was the sober, timid little gentleman who, on the night of the great Land League meeting at Chicago, presided over a private meeting of Irish-Americans; a man who, in after years, was destined to play a conspicuous and honorable part in the diplomacy of the American Republic. This man was Patrick Egan of Nebraska.

The word "desperate" will best describe the appearance of Blaine on that memorable night. His ample lips, protruding from his closely-trimmed beard, appeared to be of blood-red color, in strong contrast with his gray hair and beard, and the ashen color of his face. His eyes shone with a peculiar light. It was not the fire of rage, nor the flash of malignity. It was more probably the light that shone out of a soul animated by the hope that a day of reckoning had come. The subject of his speech was the Murchison letter, and the reply of Lord Sackville West.

"Gentlemen," he said, " I speak to you to-night, not as Irishmen, not in your relation to the British Empire, but as Americans, in your relation to this great Republic, of which you and I are citizens." He then read the correspondence between Murchison and Lord Sackville West, and the subsequent utterances of the British Minister, as a last convincing, undeniable proof of the affirmative action and active sympathy of England with Cleveland and the Democratic party. At the conclusion of his speech, "Greater Ireland," as there represented, arose from their seats and cheered him until the roof of the massive building trembled. That meeting settled in advance the fate of English free-trade and its champion, the Democratic presidential candidate. The State of New York voted for Mr. Harrison; though in the same election David Bennett Hill, the Democratic candidate for Governor, was elected by some seventeen thousand plurality.

In the succeeding month of March, the Republicans entered upon the work of government, with a Republican President and a working majority in both houses of Congress—complete control in all branches of the government, for the first time in many years.

Congress passed the McKinley bill—famous or infamous, according to your sympathies, gentle reader.

This law, with its reciprocity provisions, became temporarily unpopular in America, and gave the whole British public a bad taste in the mouth, and has never been popular in England. It was not enacted for the benefit of England, but for America and Americans; and time has vindicated the wisdom and patriotism of its supporters. Among its effects were the vast increase of American exports and imports, and a commensurate decline in the manufactures and commerce of England. But it has caused immeasurable unhappiness to the press and people of England. Another act of the Administration, that was very distasteful to the British press and public, was the appointment of Patrick Egan as Minister to the Republic of Chile. This unhappiness has steadily increased. Egan—just think of it—Pat Egan! Not only was this man an Irishman, but his name was Pat, and he was guilty of the atrocious crimes of being a faithful Irishman in Ireland, and a patriotic and devoted American in America. Every Britisher, from Gladstone down to the beggar on London Bridge, howled with pain at the appointment of Egan. But his appointment cemented the alliance between Greater Ireland and American nationality, while it demonstrated to the Irish at home and abroad, and to England and all mankind, that America had for once an administration whose distinguishing characteristics were devotion to America and an undisguised disregard for English interest and English opinion.

At the dawn of the year 1892, it seemed as if the people of the United States would be compelled to chastise the South American Republic of Chile. In the Chilean city of Valparaiso several sailors of the navy of the United States had been brutally assaulted, and two of their number had been killed. It was reasonably certain that these men were assailed because they were Americans, and because they wore the uniform of the United States. They were attacked at various and widely separated points in the Chilean city, and the soldiers and police of Chile were among the assailants. The national administration of the United States, with the patience that is characteristic of merciful strength, waited in vain during three long months for apology and offer of reparation, but the Chilean government assumed an attitude of contemptuous indifference, as much as to say: "What are you going to do about it?" With the President and Secretary of State patience was ceasing to be a virtue, and every effort of the government was put forth to prepare the navy and coast defences for an anticipated war. Meanwhile the President was preparing the ultimatum of the American government to Chile.

Under these circumstances, a number of the surviving officers of Meagher's Irish brigade in the war for the Union, convened a meeting at Military Hall, New York, for the purpose of organizing a regiment to sustain the government in the event of war. The hall was crowded to its utmost capacity. Some historic characters were present, among them Colonel Denny Burke, smiling through the torture of his old wounds. Colonel James Cavanaugh, of the Sixty-ninth, made a hasty call to signify his sympathy and co-operation. Captain James Sullivan came down from Northern New York; Captain O'Grady, up from the "Commissary Department" down stairs; and private Patsy Bradley was there, minus the lower half of the right cheek bone, that he dedicated to the Union on the field of Gettysburg. Captain George Spearman put in an appearance, at the head of three score of his "Tall Tipperary Boys."

Just as Colonel O'Kelly called the meeting to order, Albert Michael Devoy entered the hall and approached the platform.

He came, he said, as a delegate from the "Reform Club" to give the meeting a "quiet tip." "Ye may spare yerselves the trouble," he said; "there will be no war. I've got it straight, and I'll give ye a pinter."

"How do you know?" inquired the chairman.

"Because," said Albert Michael, "Don Juan Castro, the financial agent of the Chilean government in London, has cabled Mr. Larry Bodkin, of the Cobden Club, that he couldn't make the riffle. Naythur Gladstone nor Salisbury nor Chamberlain nor the Bank of England would put up the stuff for Chile in a war wid the United States. Naythur would our Reform Club, nor the English bankers of New York. They all a kind o' figured that America would kick the lining out of Chile, and they didn't want to play agin' a sure thing, d'ye mind?"

"All right, Mr. Devoy," said Colonel O'Kelly. "Many thanks. We'll proceed with the business of the meeting just the same. We Irish-Americans are looking carefully for tips from London, studying carefully what London would have us do, to the end that we may do the other thing. Gentlemen, what is your pleasure?"

Again all eyes were turned toward the door. Mr. Isaac Marx entered, followed by a dozen of his lieutenants, from the vicinity of Chatham Square. Mr. Marx had a bundle under his arm, and a two-gallon jug in his right hand. The bundle contained a cotton rag about four feet square, with a figure resembling a grid-iron in faded gilt upon its field.

Everybody was anxious to know what relation this foul rag might bear to a meeting of American patriots. Mr. Marx relieved their inquisitiveness.

"This, mine *freunds*," he said, "is an Irish flag. I used it for seventeen yaar in the Patrick's day processions ouf mine boys. I come to present it to the meeting, und I got a leedle old goot bourbon in this jug for the boys of the new brigade."

There was a storm of hisses from the five hundred respectable Irish-American workingmen in the hall, and a scowl on the faces of the officers.

Patsy Bradley seized the fire tongs, and doubling up the green rag, grasped it in the tongs, and threw it out of the window.

"Now, Isaac," he said, "get out with your jug, purty quick, or I'll fling you and the jug after the dry goods. Out you go, d——n you! out you go!"

And he seized Isaac by the collar, and by the bosom of his pantaloons, when Colonel Burke stepped in and begged him to be patient.

"Let up, Bradley," he said; "don't be rash. Marx is all right. He means to be complimentary. He lives in the lower part of New York City; that is his conception of an Irish flag, and this is the estimate which our countrymen there have taught the bigot and the blackguard to place upon Irish patriotism and Irish character."

Then turning to Isaac, he added: "Get out, Mr. Marx. Take your jug. You will find your flag in the yard. Now get! These are not your kind of Irishmen."

And Marx and his lieutenants departed.

The business of the meeting then proceeded. Colonel Burke called for volunteers, and demanded a show of hands. Five hundred rugged hands were lifted, and five hundred fine young fellows, most of them in their working clothes, and many of them with the soot and grime of the forges, foundries and factories upon them, stepped forward to enroll their names. Many of them, when taking up the pen, uttered a patriotic sentiment; and when the enrollment was finished, Colonel Burke's face flushed with enthusiasm and admiration.

There was another interruption. Ex-Alderman J. P. Burns rose to make an inquiry. He desired to know, he said, whether a war with Chile would not disturb the title of the Democracy to the Irish vote; whether shipping Irishmen out of New York in defence of the government would not be a crime in the nature of "disposing of or removing chattel property?"

The chairman assured him that the suffrages of Irishmen were chattel property no longer.

"One word more," said the Alderman. "What about Pat Egan? Isn't his conduct in Chile offensive to England and the Democratic party?"

"I guess so," said Colonel O'Kelly; "but the President, the Secretary of State, the civilized world, and the Irish on both sides of the Atlantic, have approved his fidelity to duty, his patriotism, his moral and physical courage, and above all, his humanity in saving the lives of refugees."

Some one called for cheers for Harrison, Blaine and Egan, and old Military Hall echoed with hearty cheers from hundreds of Irish throats.

Captain O'Grady was appointed to tender to the government the services of the legion in case of war with Chile, and the meeting adjourned for two weeks.

* * *

When the meeting re-assembled in the closing days of January, the war cloud had passed away. The enemies of the great Republic shrank from a contest which meant the annihilation of Chile and the humiliation of England. Chile, in response to President Harrison's ultimatum, had tendered its abject apology, had withdrawn its offensive utterances and its demand for the recall of Egan.

But the tory and the dude, the mugwump and the doughface, the copperhead and the anglomaniac, were unhappy. They had tempted Chile to the verge of destruction, in their hatred of American nationality. But the Irish-American volunteers adjourned their meeting in a spirit of gratification; and the giant Bradley grasped the staff of the bright new American flag, and kissing the hem of the banner itself, led the procession out into the street, while the stars of the winter night looked down as with a benediction upon the stars of the flag that symbolizes the power of a nation strong in justice and mercy, and merciful in its strength.

* * *

On the same night the municipal council of the Irish National League of New York City adopted a resolution, thanking President Harrison for sustaining and vindicating Minister Patrick Egan, "a representative Irishman whom the President had been pleased to honor by appointment to that office." In this they voiced the opinions and feelings of Irish-Americans generally, and of their kindred in Ireland. In the remotest corner of the Republic, Andy Dillon read the resolution in a San Diego newspaper.

"Pagan," said he to Peter McIntyre, "what d'ye think of that?"

"Of what? of the conduct of the President or of the action of the municipal council?"

"Of both," said Dillon.

"There is nothing surprising in the President's action. The Republican party has always loyally upheld the rights of foreign-born citizens sojourning in other lands. That party repudiated and overthrew the English claim of perpetual allegiance, and rescued our imprisoned kindred from the hulks and prison hells of England in vindication of their rights and liberties as American citizens. Harrison has simply emphasized the Republican doctrine, and expanded it. He has given public notice that an American citizen of Irish birth, serving this government in a diplomatic capacity, so long as he does his duty, will neither be removed nor molested on any demand coming from Chile or from England. Harrison doesn't take instructions from the *London Times*, nor the Democratic press."

"But there was a time, Peter," said Andy, "when no body of Irishmen in America would offend the Democratic bosses by adopting such a resolution."

"True enough, *brathair*," responded the Pagan; "but the world moves. Your dream of *Erin Mor* is realized. Henceforth and forever, please God, the Irish in America will march shoulder to shoulder with the brain and soul and conscience of the American people, for the best good of humanity and the best ends in government. The older generation of Irishmen, now rapidly passing away, may continue to vote the Democratic ticket, with a sort of spent political force, as an engine goes down grade though its steam has become exhausted; but having once resolved upon the right to think, Irish-Americans will keep on thinking. The present generation are neither fools nor slaves nor bigots. If they are not fools they must certainly see the perfect unity of interest and purpose existing between England and the Democratic party. If they are not bigots, they will think about this until they arrive at just conclusions; and if they are not slaves, they will break every partisan tie that dictates to them the unnatural course of sustaining English interests in America, contrary to their own welfare and contrary to every sacred impulse that animates the heart of every true Irishman."

CHAPTER XLIII.

A RESURRECTION.

IT was during the Presidential campaign of 1884. The Opera House at Paterson was filled to overflowing. An Irish orator had been announced to speak. He was a man of national reputation, strongly built, gloomy and dark as night; with eyes that in repose were calm and inexpressive, but which fairly flashed fire when he endeavored to excite the gratitude that Irishmen owe to America. In the audience sat fifty men and women, natives of the same Irish village from which this man had been exiled in 1865. They all knew him well. He was neither an aristocrat nor a peasant. He was the son of a prosperous business man. He had been guilty of the crime of loving Ireland, and hunted down like a wild beast for the crime (?) The knowledge of these facts was his passport to the hearts of old neighbors. His crime was his patent of nobility. Andy Dillon loved him with a brother's love, followed him from city to city, and occupied a seat beside him in the Opera House. Irishmen thronged the hall. Front seats had been reserved for ladies, and girls from the factories took advantage of the special privilege. Dillon fixed his eyes upon the main aisle, philosophically studying the faces of the audience. Among the young ladies came a face and form that seemed to him familiar; a gentle face with hazel eyes and long dark lashes, that lent to the eyes the semblance of perpetual smile. There was the marble brow beneath a bank of coal, the rosebud lips, the swan-like neck, the dress of dark maroon, and the white lamb's-wool hood. It was, and it could not be—yet it certainly was! a trifle more robust, taller perhaps, a little less divine looking. He gasped, his brain reeled; he rose from his seat, staggered back into the dressing room, and fell insensible to the floor.

He had seen in the audience the ghost of Nancy McHugh!

Restoratives were administered to him without disturbing the speaker or the audience, and he slowly revived. He endeavored to explain the cause of his sudden illness, and his friends pronounced it a delusion —"the baseless fabric of a vision." They induced him to return to the stage. His eyes wandered to the front seat in which he had beheld the apparition, and still there, sure enough, sat the shade of Nancy McHugh. Did his eyes deceive him? Was there an empty seat personated only in his imagination?

"Do you," said he to a friend beside him, "do you see in the front bench to the right of the center aisle, a young woman with coal-black hair, dressed in maroon, with a pure white hood?"

"I do," said his friend. "The face is familiar to me, though I do not know her name. She comes from the vicinity of Orange. I have seen her often in the streets of Paterson, but unfortunately I cannot identify her."

The orator concluded his remarks; the audience rose to depart. There was a rush to the rear, and the occupants of the front benches were quietly adjusting their cloaks and coats, waiting for the exit of the throng behind. Dillon walked down the steps from the platform to the floor, and approached the apparition.

"Beg your pardon," he said; "your face is familiar. 'Tis the face of one long dead—of one who has reposed in death in the old cemetery at New Limerick for many and many a year, and in whose grave lies the heart of an unworthy lover, who loved her with a love that was more than love—

"Not wisely, but too well."

He mechanically extended his hand. The young lady hastily removed her glove, and placed her soft white fingers in the rugged palm of the Californian; and the touch of these fingers sent over his frame at first a thrill, and then a feeling of calmness and assurance. The soft white hand was no spirit hand, but a thing of flesh and blood.

"Great God, girl!" he said, "who are you? what's your name, and where d'ye come from?"

She looked at him inquiringly, with a look of calmness that was feigned rather than felt. She doubted his sanity, but gave him the benefit of the doubt.

"My name, sir, may it please you, is Mary McHugh."

"Was there of your family," he inquired, "a girl called Nancy?"

The wondering girl burst into tears. "There was," she replied; "the purest soul that ever dwelt on earth, or ever went to meet its God. But she has been dead these many years—died at New Limerick, near the Connecticut line, of consumption—and a broken heart. She was my sister Nancy. My name is Mary McHugh."

"I trust," he said, "I may see you again?"

"You can," she replied. "I am a teacher in the district school between North and South Orange, at the foot of Orange Mountain. There are no streets in the vicinity, but you can inquire near the Orange Valley depot. Everybody knows my name."

"And your name?" he repeated.

"My name, sir, is Mary McHugh."

He bade her good-night, and she felt greatly relieved as he removed the ample sun-browned hand from her little white fingers.

He hurriedly passed out of the hall, but he did not, as usual, join the politicians in the clubroom of the hotel. He retired to his room, extinguished the lights, lay down in bed and vainly tried to sleep. He closed his eyes, but the eyes of his soul remained wide open.

The events of his life passed before the spiritual vision like a panorama. There was the hawthorn hedgerow, with the twining woodbine, that sent their fragrance over the Irish fields. There was Nancy, dressed in her maroon, with the hawthorn spray upon her bosom, and the noneen and cowslips in her hair. A spirit voice repeated the plighted vows. There was the parting kiss and the tearful farewell. There passed the peelers and the red-coated soldiers upon his track. He saw the dim light in the window of Nancy's home, and the smoke curling in its ascent from his father's cabin; he saw the emigrant ship with its horrors. His heart throbbed once again, as it did upon the blessed morning when his weary eyes beheld the Jersey hills and the outlines of New York harbor. And he saw dear Nancy once more in her exile at New Limerick; and he saw the bloom fade from her cheek, and the love-light vanish from her eyes, and the hectic flush that followed, and the death scene upon the fatal night. And he felt the tragic touch of her poor pale fingers on his neck, and the death damp of her dying breath upon his bosom, and he felt upon his ear the merciless fall of the clods upon her coffin; and once again there seemed to move a heart from out his breast, and above that heart there lay the weight of earth that covered the mouldering remains of Nancy McHugh.

And he traveled in imagination across the continent to the mountain foot at Agua Caliente; and the glorious flashing dark eyes of Marcellina looked into his soul and appealed in vain to the spirit that was dead—to the spirit of love which lives but once, and is never re-animated.

And all these vivid figures disappeared.

And he slept and dreamt, and in his dream the form of Nancy re-appeared. They were husband and wife ; and in her arms she held a child, a son— a child with Nancy's face, with the same gentle forehead, the same calm sweet eyes, the laughing lashes, and the swan-like neck ; and the mother kissed him and blessed him, and the child leaped with joy. And the wagons rushing over the stony streets of Paterson woke him from his dream, and the sun climbing over the Passaic Falls beamed calmly through the lattice of his window.

He awoke with a fixed resolution. He would marry Mary McHugh. What! and abandon Marcellina ? Yea, abandon Marcellina ! Surely, if he loved the California girl, he would not exchange that love for the hand of another whom he had only seen but once, in a public meeting at Paterson? Yea, would he forsake the girl of the flashing eyes. It was not a question of love. He reasoned that he did not love, could not love. No man ever loves but once; and when the heart of the lover is buried in the grave of the beloved, there is no resurrection, and the feeling that animated him now was neither love nor passion, but a sentiment, a resolution to resurrect the dead, to perpetuate himself, so that before he died he might see the reflection of his own soul, and in the windows of the soul the eyes of Nancy McHugh.

He was rich, perhaps, if a tin mine were riches. He was at least possessed of worldly goods sufficient to keep him out of the poor-house. Marcellina was young and beautiful, and she would not suffer from dearth of adorers under the sunny skies of Southern California. She would wed a younger and a handsomer man, and be happier than she could ever be with him. Perhaps even now, during his temporary absence, her heart had wandered elsewhere. Surely she could absolve him from his tacit promise, without serious sacrifice; but come what may, he would marry Mary McHugh. She was neither wife nor widow, but a maiden still. Had she not said that her name was Mary McHugh? and his dream of last night was repeated in a waking dream; and he pictured Mary as his wife—not Nancy, but the form and face of Nancy. And the child, not Nancy's child, but Nancy's image, and the innocent eyes and the gentle brow and the raven hair, and the perpetuation of himself in flesh and blood, with the eyes of Nancy McHugh. Yes, he would marry Mary McHugh.

CHAPTER XLIV.

WEDDING BELLS.

THE wedding cards were issued, announcing the marriage of the Count Bassiano and Miss Birdelia Devoy, and the many dear friends of the high contracting parties were accordingly elated. Miss Birdelia's *trousseau* had been imported from Paris. Hundreds of guests were invited, and the local newspapers not only bepraised the intended bride, but paid high tributes to her "noble father" and her "distinguished brothers." The church of St. Loyola was profusely decorated with evergreens and flowers; the choir had been practicing for weeks. A rich Brussels carpet was laid from the sidewalk to the vestibule. The tones of the great organ arose within the church and captivated the senses of the throng out in the street. Heavy rain had fallen on the preceding night, and the public authorities of New Limerick, never over-scrupulous in the matter of street cleaning, had permitted quite a quantity of refuse matter to thicken the stagnant water outside the curbstone. The carriage drove up in front of the church, and Count Bassiano stepped from his seat and extended his delicate hand to lead forth the intended bride, when a powerfully built middle-aged man, with hair almost snowy in its whiteness, stepped up to the carriage and dealt the count a blow from the shoulder, with clenched fist, fairly between the eyes. The would-be bridegroom fell heavily on the sidewalk. The assailant kicked him into the gutter, and proceeded to dance a jig upon his prostrate body. Several citizens and one or two policemen came to the rescue of the count, and his assailant was violently dragged away.

"Poor 'Peter the Pagan' mad again," was echoed from mouth to mouth.

"Not much," interposed Andy Dillon; and addressing Albert Michael and Perry Tonitis, he added, "Don't you believe that the 'Pagan' is mad. He has saved your sister from an awful fate. Your count is no count. Postpone the marriage and be assured."

The intended bride was driven back to the mansion, and the would-be bridegroom to a bath-room and thence to the office of a surgeon, who dressed the wounds upon his face. The injuries to his body were not considered dangerous. Meanwhile "Pagan Pete" was hurried before the commissioners of insanity. Before proceeding to take testimony they gave the "Pagan" the privilege of making a statement.

"Gentlemen," he said, "I have no statement to make, except to give you the assurance that I am not mad, or, at least, that there is some little method in my madness. This 'Count Bassiano' is no count and no Italian. But let a more reliable witness speak for me. I will call Detective Burke of New York."

The detective stepped forward, was sworn, and produced his credentials.

"You are a member of the regular detective force of New York City?"

"I am."

"Do you know Count Bassiano? and if so, how long have you known him?"

"If you mean the individual calling himself Count Bassiano, the affianced of Miss Devoy, I know him. I have known him for fifteen years."

"State if you know his residence and occupation, and any other general facts in relation to him that you know?"

"He is nominally, occasionally, a musician, who sometimes plays at the fashionable haunts of vice on Sixth Avenue, New York City; but his character and occupation is that of a confidence man and blackmailer. He is a compatriot and factotum of his friend Mr. Isaac Marx, who accompanies him to-day. He passes under several *aliases*."

The commissioners, after brief consultation, ordered the release of "Pagan Peter," and the count and Mr. Isaac Marx returned to New York upon the evening train. The whole police force and several deputy sheriffs were required to protect them from the infuriated friends of Miss Devoy on their way to the depot.

On the morning succeeding these exciting events, "Pagan Pete" set out for the home of Maggie Sullivan, on the shore of Lake Champlain, and Andy Dillon took his departure for the foot of Orange Mountain. Dillon had already completed his courtship, and at evening, when the sun had set behind the Orange Mountain, he stood at the side of Mary McHugh, upon a shaded road at the mountain foot. The bright moon shining through the trees faintly revealed the blush upon her charming cheek, and the diamond ring which he had placed upon her hand in token of their engagement.

Meanwhile, "Pagan Pete" rekindled the smouldering fire of love in the breast of Maggie Sullivan. For the first time he plainly told her the story of the cruel outrage to which his enemies had subjected him.

"Don't mention it, Peter," she replied. "I never doubted you. Evil to those that think evil. Perhaps 'tis as well;" and her graceful arm stole softly around his rugged neck, and she kissed him fervently upon the cheek and brow.

"Maggie," said the "Pagan," "if you don't behave yourself I'll call your brother Jim."

"With a heart and a half, let him come," said the blushing Maggie.

In response to Peter's call, the Captain entered. "Well, what can I do for you now, Pete?"

"*Och*, merely give us your consent and blessing."

Captain Sullivan extended his single arm with open up-turned palm.

"Give me your hand, Maggie. And now your hand, Peter;" and Peter cheerfully obeyed the command. And the Captain, pressing both hands as well as he was able with his single hand, gave his consent and a benediction.

* * *

It was late in the month of November next succeeding these events of the fall, that two married couples stepped from an open carriage in front of the Hotel Arlington, at the sea-side city of Santa Barbara, in Southern California.

One of these couples consisted of a gray-haired, fresh-faced man of fifty-five, whose bride was his junior by perhaps ten years. She was the perfection of womanhood physically, with light brown hair and calm dark blue eyes.

The second couple consisted of a vigorous middle-aged man, whose beard was iron-gray, but the mass of dark hair that crowned his head still retained its original color. The bride was under thirty years of age, with coal-black hair and hazel eyes, with a face exceedingly fair, and a neck that, in the purity of its whiteness, showed in charming contrast with the ample braids of the raven hair. The couples were accompanied by a little party of friends, and by a middle-aged black man, a servant, to whom extraordinary kindness and deference were shown. Need it be hinted that the couples were "Pagan Pete" and Andy Dillon and their wives? that the man of color was Tony Sexton? The accompanying friends were three in number, consisting of Dr. Barry and his wife, who came upon Dillon's invitation to enjoy a winter in the balmy air of Southern California, and a young lady, whose dark complexion and sparkling black eyes, beneath a head of soft, wavy auburn hair, indicated that in her veins were mingled the blood of the Indian and of some fair race of Northern Europe. This lady was Marcellina, the child of the Indian woman, whom Dillon had rescued at sea near Ensenada when she was a child. She had been at school for three years at Los Angeles, and had recently completed her education at a St. Louis convent. If, as we may reasonably believe, she had once loved Andy Dillon, her thoughts were turned from earth and directed toward things more serious and sacred. She was soon to renounce the world and devote herself to the service of God among his suffering creatures at the leper colony in the Sandwich Islands.

Some days were devoted to yachting upon the ocean among the islands of the Santa Barbara Channel. There were excursions into the mountains, and a hasty journey into Lower California, picnics at Pacific Beach, and a season of rest at Fern Hill.

The faithful Tony Sexton continues in Dillon's service, the man of all work, the guardian and friend.

And now, that his Eastern friends have left him, Andy Dillon occasionally relapses into day dreams of his *Erin Mor*—of brighter days and greater things in store for the Irish in America.

He firmly believes that one of the two great "English speaking nations" must decline, and he dimly discerns the beginning of that decline. He sees the manufacture and commerce of America expand, while there is a commensurate shrinkage in the industries of Britain. He believes that protection and reciprocity will ultimately give the United States control of the American continent's commerce; and he sees in the brightening vista a dismembered British Empire and an independent and united Ireland.

And beside him, as he thus indulges in speculations as to the future of nations and of men, there are two objects that are very dear to him—that day by day make the world seem brighter to him, and that stimulate his soul and body to greater effort and loftier aims. His wife sits snugly in her rocking-chair, and on her lap there is a child, his infant son, reflecting, as in a looking-glass, his own rude Celtic facial outlines, and the gentle soulful hazel eyes of his unforgotten Nancy McHugh.

On Dillon's homestead at Fern Hill there is a forty-acre tract reserved for friends. It occupies a commanding site upon a hill-side, and slopes to the east and south. Far up the hill there is a bubbling spring, which forms a silvery rivulet, and this tiny stream is so conducted as to water the cypress hedge and the row of marguerites and the line of fragrant magnolias that separate the tract from the avenue that leads down to the public road. Within the inclosure the land is so divided as to make home-sites for a score of friends, giving to each a comfortable frontage upon the avenue. The hill-top is crowned with forest trees—with eucalyptus and sycamores and live oaks; and nestling near the base are miniature groves of orange, lemon, fig and olive. Luxuriant grape-vines climbing over trellis-work form numerous arbors and alleys, and amid the lilies and the roses, the tulips, violets and forget-me-nots, the honey-bees linger on their journey from the delicate white sage upon the mountain-side to the wild flowers in the ocean valley.

Two especially beautiful cottage sites have been set apart for Dr. Barry and Rev. William McNevin. The medical man looks forward hopefully to the time when his labors in New York City shall cease, when he may crown an active and useful life with an age of ease amid the beauties of Fern Hill.

The Methodist minister, who is temporarily engaged in the diplomatic service of the United States in one of the beautiful venerable cities of Southern Europe, expects to return at an early day, to enjoy in the closing years of his earthly career, in the joys of Southern California, a foretaste of that eternal bliss to which, in the exercise of his sacred calling, he has guided many a weary soul.

CHAPTER XLV.

SOME PERSONAL HISTORY.

ONE Saturday night the Devoy family were disturbed at their prayers by a violent knocking at the hall door of the mansion. Old Mrs. Devoy went down to open the door, as it was a general understanding that, in case of visits from robbers, the old lady would be the most suitable person for the emergency; that if any person was to be murdered on such occasion, she was the best prepared to die. In response to her inquiry, "Who's there?" came the answer:

"Me—Frank."

"What Frank?"

"Me, Francis Xavier, mother; your son, Frank Devoy."

The mother, recognizing the voice, drew the bolts of the massive door, and the prodigal son staggered into the hall.

Francis Xavier had left California somewhat hastily. A reform grand jury had indicted him for bribing a few members of the legislature. In those days the State of California, by a polite political fiction, was said to be governed under a Republican form of government; and the existence of a legislative assembly, of courts and other appliances of government lent an air of plausibility to the fiction. But the State in truth was governed by a blind saloon-keeper. His power was superior to that of courts and legislatures. Popular elections merely ratified his will in the selection of public officials. The good people of San Francisco became virtuous spasmodically.

They witnessed with stoical fortitude a series of crimes against the lives and liberties of citizens for years at a time, and then suddenly their virtuous indignation is aroused; an elisor is appointed, a special grand jury is impaneled, and indictments fly like snow-flakes. One of these virtuous juries undertook to indict the blind saloon-keeper and a number of his lieutenants and accessories. The chieftain himself fled to Canada for protection under the British flag; and his lieutenant, Francis Xavier Devoy, chief of the Kilmaroos, *alias* Tim Devereux, rushed back to New Limerick. Learning of the outrage that had been committed upon the family by the bogus count and Isaac Marx, he vowed vengeance against them, and during one of his protracted sprees he pursued the count among the dens on Sixth avenue, and artistically carved him with a bowie-knife, which had seen service for years in the hands of San Francisco hoodlums. Though death did not result immediately, the titled villain never recovered from the effects of the carving. At last accounts Francis Xavier was "doing time" for this murderous offense at one of the penitentiaries in the Empire State.

The history of Albert Michael Devoy and his brother Tonitis, up to date, may be briefly told. Neither of them ever married. They lived the lives of old bachelors under the roof of the family mansion, with their aged but vigorous mother, at the time our record ceases. There is a reasonable prospect that Francis Xavier will die in prison, and ground for hope that the male line of the Devoy family may terminate with the present generation.

Birdelia Devoy became Bridget O'Neill, the happy and honored wife of a very worthy merchant at New Limerick. She was a child of fortune whom the fickle goddess sorely tempted and very nearly ruined. Born in abject poverty, cradled in ignorance, she became in early life surrounded by wealth, as if some fairy goddess showered gold and gems into her lap. As she became a young girl, she was feasted, flattered and petted by all the vulgar sycophants and hypocrites who feasted under the name of society in the family mansion; but she rose above these unfortunate surroundings — rose above pianos and French and imported *trousseaux*. On the Sunday morning succeeding the unfortunate fiasco with the count, she appeared at the family breakfast table clothed in a plain grey suit, such as her female servant wore; and when she set out for mass, she put upon her shoulders a ten-dollar woolen cloak, and a four-dollar hat, which, though genteel and becoming to her sex, was exceedingly plain, with its dark trimmings and destitution of ornament. Albert Michael, in helping her to the omelet, addressed her as "Sister Birdelia."

"Michael," she said, "my name is Bridget. I want this privately and publicly understood and declared."

And from that hour forward, Bridget it was. She was no longer young. She was "fat, fair and forty." She was vigorous, vivacious and entertaining, with the freshness of appearance and frankness of manner which generally characterize the woman who is pure and clean of heart; and such was Bridget Devoy. Need it be wondered that Edward O'Neill, the genial and chivalrous dry-goods man, was among the most ardent of her admirers, and soon won his way to her heart? They were married at the church of St. Loyola. There was a glorious old-time wedding. The mansion was brilliantly lighted from garret to basement. The parlor, drawing-room and library were cleared of furniture and of carpets for the dance, and when the banquet was ended, young and old wheeled and circled in jigs and reels and hornpipes until the gray hours of morning. The basement was set apart for the convivial ones. The Irish of New Limerick never so heartily enjoyed themselves before; and when the night's festivities were ended, and guests circled around the happy couple to say good-bye and wish them joy, the honest heart of the bride was filled with earnest pride and thankfulness to Heaven as she gazed upon the intelligent manhood and the womanly beauty surrounding her, that she was one of them, not only in name, but Irish to the heart's core—every fiber of her body, every pulse of her heart.

Bridget had one amiable weakness. The efforts of certain bishops of the Catholic church to christianize the negro excited her warmest enthusiasm. She was present at the congress of colored Catholics in Philadelphia, held during the close of the year 1891. She heard read the communications from

Cardinal Gibbons and from Bishop Ireland, breathing the spirit of true Christian charity and of human liberty. She would not dare to doubt the sincerity of a bishop speaking *ex cathedra;* but it puzzled and pained her sympathetic soul to think that her brothers and millions of their race in America, who were willing to admit the negro into their pews, were hostile to his rights and liberties as an American citizen. Her enthusiasm became very embarrassing to Father Ventura and to the leading members of St. Loyola's.

"Ah, Father," she would say, "if God would only send the spirit of the Holy Ghost into the hearts of our people in America, and that spirit would enlighten them as to the sacredness of human right under American law, what a harvest the church would reap among the negroes!"

"My dear child," the good Father replied, "our church makes no distinction on account of race or color, and we do not interfere in politics except where some political question is inseparably connected with some grave question of morals."

"But, Father, couldn't the church just hint to its membership that the outrages committed against the negro in the South are a violation of law and morals?"

"Dear Mrs. O'Neill, it is not our people who commit these outrages. There are comparatively few of our people in the old slave states of the South."

"Yes, Father, but they go the polls in the North and ratify those crimes by their votes."

"True enough, my child; but you will excuse me now. There is a delegation of the St. Vincent De Paul Society waiting in the parlor to see me."

Bridget vowed that she would "appeal to Cæsar;" that she would petition Cardinal Gibbons, and if he failed to respond, she would visit Rome and have some declaration from the Pope. She lives and labors in the hope and belief that if the Irish could ever be softened into a spirit of charity toward the

colored race, and obedience to the law relating to
him, that the church might carry the cross of Christ in
triumph from the Ohio River to the Gulf of Mexico.

Writers of romance and of poetry would sacrifice
the truth in the interest of poetic justice in relation
to Isaac Marx. They would charge their pens with a
million volts of lightning and kill Isaac by electrocution, and consign him to a quick-lime grave, consistent with poetic justice; but in a truthful narrative we
may not tell a lie and at the same time usurp the power
which the Almighty reserves for himself. Mr. Isaac
Marx still lives, and exerts his growing power in the
politics of New York City. It was his Irish customers who died. They fed from a different dish and
drank an inferior stimulant. Most of the famine
exiles laid their weary bones at rest in Cavalry Cemetery. They died slowly in the foul atmosphere of
the miserable tenements in which necessity compelled
them to live. To the day of their death Mr. Marx
manipulated their caucuses and herded a majority of
them at the polls; and when the older generation of
them died, he stoutly asserted his authority over the
suffrages of their sons upon the doctrine that being
Irish they were Democrats; that their blood was
tainted politically, and that the old masters were entitled to the allegiance of the new generation.

Mr. Marx is a regular attendant at the meetings
of the famous Reform Club (the Democratic auxiliary
in America of the Cobden Club of England). His
polished pate flashed back the light of its chandeliers
on the occasion of Mr. Ricardo Trumbull's reception,
and the portly form of Isaac shook like a barrel of
pigs' feet jelly as he listened to the renegade American, Richard Trumbull, delegate in the Chilean Congress, echo the brutal and insulting sentiments of
England and the English press in assailing America
and the American administration. He was overjoyed
when Trumbull abused Patrick Egan, the wise,

heroic and dutiful minister of our government to Chile; and some of his Irish constituents who accompanied him licked the feet that kicked them, by echoing the gee-haws of Mr. Marx.

Bill Percival, the venerable Knownothing, stands high in the councils of the Democratic party in New Limerick. He is a particular friend of the Devoys. He is a leading member of the "A. P. A.," and an ardent supporter in caucus of the Irish-American candidates, whom he earnestly labors to defeat at the polls; and among the ignorant and depraved of his constituents his popularity increases, while he repeats the venerable falsehood that Knownothingism sprang from the Republican party.

But Percival finds very few believers of this atrocious falsehood among the present generation of Irish-Americans, because they read history, and reason for themselves. Doing this, they must realize that Knownothingism was utterly incompatible with the doctrines, purposes and *personnel* of the Republican party. They realize also that, if a mob were required to burn a church, you could not find the right material among Republicans.

CHAPTER XLVI.

CONCLUSION.

ON the night of the spring election in Rhode Island (April, 1892) blue lights appeared in the tall tower of the New York daily *World*. These lights were intended as the signal of distress to the friends of British free-trade. It was so preconcerted that, if the Democrats won in "Little Rhody," the *World* would display the scarlet signal of England in its tower; if the result was a victory for the American principle of protection, the blue lights would signal the calamity.

There was a notable gathering at the rooms of the Reform Club (Democratic auxiliary of the London Cobden Club). Grover Cleveland had just returned from Providence. Sir Julian Pauncefote, the British Minister at Washington, sent his private secretary. The British Consul at New York was represented by Mr. Jenkins, an English secret agent from Scotland Yard. Isaac Marx came up from Chatham Square, and Albert Michael Devoy came down from New Limerick. The Democracy had based its hope upon "the Irish vote" of Rhode Island. If those Irish who were enfranchised by the new Constitution voted for tariff reform, it meant a victory for England, and *vice versa*.

"The Irish have gone back on us," Mr. Cleveland observed.

"Looks that way," said Albert Michael. "We have lost our grip upon the Irish vote."

Albert Michael was right. "Greater Ireland" had "swelled beyond the measure of her chains." Slowly the children of the exiled Celts realized the preciousness of their heritage as citizens and co-heirs to the rights, liberties and dignities of Americans. They contemplated with joy the splendid spectacle of American nationality under the administration of Harrison. The Blaine extradition treaty with England had secured all Irish political exiles against the unfriendly touch of British power; the McKinley bill had increased the manufactures of the United States, and swelled its import and export trade beyond all anticipation and precedent. Chile had gracefully surrendered under the kindly, firm diplomacy of the administration; Italy rejoiced under the generous treatment extended to the families of the *Mafia* fiends killed at New Orleans; and the same power which in the consciousness of right and strength was patient with Chile and merciful with Italy, "brought England to her knees" in the Behring Sea controversy.

The year 1892 witnessed the consummation of Andy Dillon's hopes. The Irish exiles scraped away the parasites and barnacles that fed and fattened on the race in American politics while they befouled it in the eyes of the American people. As the Irish extended their hands in sympathy and fellowship with the soul, the brain, the manhood and conscience of American national life, the American hand was extended responsively. When Irish-Americans did anything to be proud of, other Americans traced the family record and claimed kindred with them. Republican orators were invited to voice their sentiments. Chauncey M. Depew delivered the eulogy on Parnell at the memorial services in New York; and the glorious eloquence of Jonathan P. Dolliver made the great hall of Cooper Union ring with a vindication of the character and motives of Emmet. The church and creed of the exiles also rose in popular estimation as *Erin Mor* flung aside the barbarism and bigotry which Democracy had so persistently inculcated; and the church of St. Loyola, at New Limerick, instead of being considered fit material for a bonfire to make a Knownothing holiday, was at last regarded in its proper light — a sacred edifice sheltering a congregation not less loyal to America than other Americans.